Christianity in Iraq

Christianity in Iraq

Its Origins and Development
to the Present Day

Suha Rassam

GRACEWING

First published in 2005
by

Gracewing
2 Southern Avenue,
Leominster
Herefordshire HR6 0QF

UK ISBN 0 85244 633 0

Typeset by Action Publishing Technology Ltd,
Gloucester GL1 5SR

To all those who opened my eyes and
helped me have a glimpse of the Beyond

Contents

Prologue

Suha Rassam's book, *Christianity in Iraq*, comes to fill a large vaccum in the knowledge of those in the West, many of whom are still not aware of the fact that from ancient times Christianity was firmly rooted in Iraq and the rest of the territory now seen as the 'Arab Middle East'. A Christianity that has inspired this East with the aroma of its spirituality and enriched it with the breeze of its theology, enabling the region to ascend to the forefront of civilization through what it has given in spiritual activity and intellectual depth, through its monasteries and schools, and through its monks, and saintly priests. This book should also be a reminder to those Iraqi Christians who have been in Europe for a long time and who have nearly forgotten their country of origin and its importance both in terms of the development of civilization in general and Christianity in particular.

Dr Rassam moves elegantly among the various corridors of ancient history and unravels the important events that marked all stages of Christianity in Iraq, whether in the secular or ecclesiastical spheres, and from the times of the Apostles. Passing through the period under Muslim rule, she shows the cultural interaction that occurred between members of the two religions, and how the Church in Iraq took an active role in the creation of Abbasid civilization through its schools, translators, physicians and teachers. This Church remained active in spite of Mongol and Ottoman rule, and continues to be alive, even to the present hour, in a process of exchange and dialogue in daily life, and contributing to intellectual, spiritual, civil and political development.

The author has not neglected the modern history of the Church in Iraq after the fall of the Ottoman Empire and the emergence of independent Arab states. She concentrates on the political evolution of the country since the time of the British Mandate until the fall of Ba'thist rule and the emergence of new political horizons in which the citizens of Iraq today, looking forward, perceive the unfolding of a new model of life with more freedom.

I would like to congratulate Suha Rassam for the efforts she has taken in order to light a candle and take the hands of Western individuals, roaming with them through the corridors of the ancient Church of Iraq, so that they may come to know the civilization of Mesopotamia with its great nation and Church; remembering that history began in this land, and that God created the first man from the sand of its earth, and that the Magi came from Babylon to greet Jesus and adore him, becoming the first heralds of the Gospel in the land of Iraq, and that Christianity took root here from the first Christian century.

Mikhael Al Jamil
Patriarchal Vicar of the Syrian Catholic Church of Antioch to the Holy See
Visitor Apostolic for Europe

Commendations

The presence of Christians in Iraq since the beginning of the first millennium, is an essential part of Iraq's identity. In this book Dr Suha Rassam draws a clear and vivid picture of the Christians' ceaseless contribution in building and enriching the culture, heritage and civilisation of Iraq. As I recommend the book, *Christianity in Iraq*, we testify that it stands as an important source of knowledge about Christianity, its denominations, its long witness and coexistence within the rich diversity of Iraq and the Mesopotamian tapestry of faiths, traditions and cultures.

Mor Gregorios Yohanna Ibrahim
Metropolitan of Aleppo for the Syrian Orthodox Church

Dr Suha Rassam has done a great service in writing about Christianity in the homeland of our Father Abraham in Mesopotamia, and how Christianity has continued to be a significant religious and cultural presence in Iraq up to the present time.

Suha Rassam has shown her true love of her Church by writing this remarkable book. It is a book that ought to be widely read.

I would like to congratulate Suha for her successful work.

Andrawis Abouna
Auxilary Bishop for the Chaldean Patriarch

Foreword

Most people are unaware that Christianity was already present in Iraq well before it reached Britain, and that it has continued to be a significant cultural and religious presence in that country right up to the present day. In the aftermath of the recent invasion and war, the indigenous Christian Churches in Iraq face a threat perhaps even more serious than any of those which they have so frequently had to face in the past. This makes Dr Suha Rassam's book all the more timely and important: not only does it very successfully provide a clear and well-balanced outline of the long history of Christianity in Iraq, as represented by the two main Syriac ecclesiastical traditions, that of the Church of the East and that of the Syrian Orthodox Church, each with its Eastern Rite Catholic counterpart, the Chaldean Catholic Church and the Syrian Catholic Church, but also, above all, her book sheds much-needed light on the present dire situation for Christians in Iraq, this being something of which all too few people in the West are aware. Being an Iraqi herself, she is in a position to write on the contemporary situation with an insight that is based on her own experience, this making her book all the more vivid and valuable. It is a book that ought to be widely read.

Dr Sebastian Brock
The Oriental Institute
Oxford University

Preface

Recent events have brought Iraq to the forefront of our daily news. Despite television, radio and newspaper reports focusing every day on the current political and military situation in 'the land between the two rivers', there is surprisingly little information about the social, religious and cultural make-up of modern-day Iraq; consequently many misunderstandings and misconceptions have arisen. Over the years, during talks with people in the 'West', i.e. in Europe, the United States of America, and Australia, I have frequently noticed that they have been astonished to learn that the population of Iraq includes a sizeable Christian minority. They are even more amazed to realize that the introduction of Christianity in Iraq was not the result of European missionaries proselytizing in the eighteenth and nineteenth centuries, but is far older, its presence spanning almost two thousand years.

The origins of Christianity in Iraq are ancient, and hark back to the apostolic age. Despite the vicissitudes of history, it has celebrated an unbroken existence spanning almost two millennia. It comes as no surprise therefore that a variety of churches have emerged in Iraq. The Church of the East (previously known as the Nestorians) and the Syrian Orthodox Churches resulted from the doctrinal decisions that were realized at the Councils of Ephesus and Chalcedon in AD 431 and AD 451 respectively. Despite an inherent rivalry between them, these two churches remained the major entities in Iraq for more than twelve hundred years. It was only after the sixteenth century, with the advent of Roman Catholic missionaries, that divisions in the ancient churches culminated in the formation of the Uniate churches: the Chaldaean Church and the Syrian Catholic Church.

Today both the Chaldaean Church and the Syrian Catholic Church have sizeable communities in Iraq. They represent new dimensions of an ancient heritage, linking Christianity in Iraq with Rome. In doing so, they have not only surmounted barriers that were previously untenable, but also have taken advantage of new opportunities and perspectives. The stimulus of the Catholic institutions in Iraq was particularly evident in its educational activities, which were only supplanted when strictures of the previous Ba'athist government placed all primary and secondary education under the aegis of the state. In response to these measures, all churches in Iraq have mounted vigorous social and educational programmes in the evenings and at weekends to instil in their young members pride in their Christian faith and their rich heritage.

Along with being an expression of faith, Christianity in Iraq is very much a badge of identity. This is perhaps its greatest difference from Christianity in western countries, where nationality surpasses religious affiliation. In Iraq today, the various denominations reflect a complexity of cultural and social nuances. Adherents of the Uniate churches, i.e. the Chaldaeans and Syrian Catholics, are now predominantly Arabic-speaking, and reserve Syriac as a liturgical language. The Assyrians – the epithet now adopted by adherents of the Church of the East – as well as the Syrian Orthodox, speak modern dialects of Syriac as their mother tongue and use the classical language in their churches, although accent and script differ and mark the division between east and west. Since the declaration of the free zone in northern Iraq in the 1990s, neo-Syriac has become revitalized; many publications have been written in this language, and it is also used in schools and for media broadcasts by all of the Christian Communities. The

Assyrians have also embraced a vigorous national identity, whereas the other denominations tend to view themselves as a denomination within Iraq.

These exciting new horizons are the product of changes that have occurred in Iraq since the 1990s, but they are also counteracted by upheaval and social disturbance. In particular, an overall breakdown of law and order in Iraq has ushered in an increasing instability for Christians of all denominations who are being targeted by Islamic extremists. Demands have been made for women to wear the hijab or suffer the consequences (death or mutilation); Christians have been kidnapped, clergy have been ritually murdered and churches have been bombed. Yet it is important to realize that despite these alarming trends, Christians and Muslims have lived together in mutual concord and respect for many centuries, and, with the emergence of the modern state of Iraq in the twentieth century, Christians had been able to assume a social profile that is otherwise unavailable in many parts of the Middle East. But hopefully, drawing on their long experience, the communities will be able to weather the storm.

Today, all Christian denominations in Iraq have sizeable diaspora communities, spread throughout the world. The exodus from Iraq largely began not as a result of religious differences but largely in response to the economic sanctions that were imposed during the 1990s, impoverishing much of the population. Paradoxically, the emergence of the diaspora has revived the international perspective of Christianity in Iraq, which disappeared after the ravages of Timur-Lang in the fourteenth century reduced the Church of the East and the Syrian Orthodox to enclaves in northern Iraq. Prior to this catastrophic era, for five hundred years between the ninth and thirteenth centuries, the dioceses of the Church of the East had rivalled the scope of the Latin Church, earning it the title of the 'Third Branch of Christianity'. This legacy is still felt today: the Mongolian script is derived from Syriac, which was the liturgical language of the Syriac-speaking churches, uniting its disparate dioceses that stretched across Iran, Afghanistan and Central Asia to China, as well as to India, Arabia and the Gulf.

As the Church of the East and the Syrian Orthodox Church responded over the centuries to the linguistic and ethnic complexities of their vast communities, Christians of all denominations from Iraq, who are now settled in various European countries, the United States of America, Canada, Britain and Australia, are rising to the challenges of their new surroundings. Inevitably, these communities will undergo many changes, and new dimensions will emerge. Indicative of their well-honed ability 'to adapt and adopt' is the spate of publications, magazines and, embracing the newest technology, web sites and electronic journals that have emerged amongst the various communities. Strenuous efforts are being made to preserve the ancient heritage, language and culture, but inevitably there has been a shift from the traditional languages of Arabic and Syriac to English, to meet the needs of younger generations. The by-product of opening these new horizons is to make accessible a Christianity that has lain outside the mainstream of Western interest.

This book is a direct product of these new horizons in Syriac Christianity. Its author, Suha Rassam, who was born in Mosul in northern Iraq, arrived in England in the early 1990s. With a growing circle of English-speaking friends, she realized that, despite the vigorous interest of Iraqi Christians in their faith and heritage, little information was available other than in Arabic. Although many interesting books and articles had appeared since the seventeenth century, when European scholars first began to write about the various Christian communities in the Middle East, these tended to be pitched to scholars and above all to specialists in Syriac, the language of the various Christian denominations. Moreover, there was almost no specialist treatment of Christianity in Iraq. To redress these shortcomings, Suha undertook the challenging task of writing a book that would give to the general interested public a comprehensive and informed insight into two thousand years of Christianity in Iraq. It gives me much pleasure to say that this long-awaited book has finally come about which releases the rich and precious heritage of these ancient Christian communities.

Erica C. D. Hunter

Teaching Fellow in Eastern Christianity,
Dept. for the Study of Religions,
School of Oriental and African Studies,
University of London.

Affiliated Lecturer in Aramaic and Syriac,
Faculty of Oriental Studies,
University of Cambridge.

Acknowledgements

I was in Rome in January 2003 attending the ordination of Father Andrawis Aboona, the chaplain to the Chaldean community in the United Kingdom since 1991. He was ordained bishop by the Holy Father on the Feast of the Epiphany and was going to Iraq after that to serve as auxiliary to the Patriarch of the Chaldean Church in Baghdad. During a dinner party given in his honour, he introduced me to the journalist Gregg Watts who was there to report on that event. He had read an article written by me in the parish newsletter, and had asked Bishop Andrawis if it was possible to introduce me to him. At dinner we talked about Christianity in Iraq and what made me interested in the subject. He asked me about the sources and as I was talking of the paucity of references on the subject, especially for the non-specialist, the idea of writing a book for such readers emerged. That evening marked the birth of this book. It was also through Gregg's initiative that I was invited to give a talk on 'Christianity in Iraq' at Westminster Cathedral Hall, during the festival of Catholic culture 'Towards Advent' in November 2003, and that was where I met Tom Longford who showed interest in publishing such a book for me. I am grateful to all three for their initiatives and support.

It is also my pleasure to acknowledge Dr Erica Hunter for her help in the preparation of this book. Her lectures on Eastern Christianity at the school of Oriental and African studies, where I did my Masters Degree in this subject provided me with a stimulus for further exploration of Christianity in Iraq. She read the text at its early stages and advised on many aspects, especially on the early history of the Church, and contributed by writing the Preface. I am also grateful to Amir Harrak and Sebastian Brock for the interest they showed when I told them that I was writing this book. Amir Harrak read the last two chapters and his comments on Christianity in modern Iraq were very helpful, while Sebastian Brock read the whole book and his expert comments were really invaluable.

My thanks go to many of my friends who showed interest in this work and advised on technical aspects that make the book more appealing to a person with little or no knowledge of the subject. Father Patrick Shanahan, Eileen Elube and Elain Cousins read some chapters of this book and their suggestion in this respect encouraged me to include more stories, which I hope will make the reading more enjoyable. Thanks also to friends who lent me some of the photographs displayed in this book: Iqbal Zebouni, Aziz Abdul-Nour, Amir Harraq, and Erica Hunter.

Special thanks to Aziz Abdul-Nour and Father Giwargis Khoshaba for their help in literature and comments on matters related to the Syrian Orthodox Church and the Church of the East respectively; both read the first proofs and their comments are greatly appreciated. Thanks also to Bishop Mikhael Al Jamil whose support and prologue for the book are greatly appreciated.

I would also like to thank the Iraqi priests who act as chaplains to the Iraqi Christian communities in this country and who provided some information about the corresponding churches: Father Habib al-Nawfali from the Chaldean Church; Father Safa' Habash from the Syrian Catholic Church; and Father Toma Da'wd from the Syrian Orthodox Church.

I am indebted to my husband Faiz whose unfailing support and advice were invaluable, and to my daughter Nada for her help in preparing many of the photographs in this book.

Chronology of Important Events

BC

745–727	Tiglathpileser III – The first exile of the Jews by the Assyrians.
597–582	Nebuchadnezzar – The second exile of the Jews by the Babylonians.
539	The Elamite king Cyrus captures Babylon.
538	King Cyrus'decree to return the Jews to their homeland.
323	Alexander the Great dies near Baghdad, after which Iraq was ruled by his general Seleucus.
129	Iraq under Parthian rule.

AD

224	The Sassanids replace the Parthians as rulers of Iraq.
312	The Emperor Constantine wins a battle in the name of the Christian God and decides to make Christianity the official religion of his empire.
313	The edict of toleration of Milan.
325	The first ecumenical council at Nicea.
381	The second ecumenical council at Constantinople.
431	The third ecumenical council at Ephesus.
451	The fourth ecumenical council at Chalcedon.
637	The Arabs conquer the Sassanids at the battle of Qadisiya.

750	The Abbasids establish their rule in Iraq.
1258	The Mongol Khan Hulago conquers Baghdad. End of Abbasid rule.
1295	The Mongol Khan Ghazan converts to Islam.
1393	Timur Lang conquest of Baghdad
1534	Baghdad and northern Iraq comes under Ottoman rule.
1546	All of Iraq comes under Ottoman rule.
1914	British forces land in Basra.
1918	1 November: Armistice between the Allies and Turkey is announced. 8 November: British army enters Mosul.
1920	The League of Nations establishes a British mandate over Iraq. Rebellion in southern Iraq against the British.
1921	Faysal bin al-Husain enthroned first King of Iraq.
1932	Formal independence of Iraq under the monarchy.
1958	A revolution led by General Qasim and the Free Officers overthrows the monarchy.
1963	Abd al-Karim Qasim is killed and Abd al-Salam Arif becomes president.
1968	The Ba'ath party seizes sole control of government.
1979	Saddam Husayn becomes president of Iraq.
1980–88	The Iraqi–Iranian War.
1990	Invasion and annexation of Kuwait.
1991	American–led coalition forces evict Iraqi troops from Kuwait.
2003	19 March: The start of the war on Iraq by American and coalition forces. 9 April: US forces enter Baghdad. Iraq under American and British occupation. 28 June: The Coalition Provisional Authorities (CPA) established a Provisional Governing Council headed by L. Paul Bremer III.

2004	3 March: An interim constitution signed.
	1 June: An interim government formed with Ghazi-al-Yawar as president and Ayad Allawi as Prime Minister.
2005	30 Jan: First Iraqi general elections.
	16 March: First National Assembly convened (six Christians out of 270 members).
	6 April: Jalal-al-Talabani appointed as first Kurdish president of Iraq with two vice-presidents, Ghazi-al-Yawar (Sunni) and Adil Abd al-Mahdi (Shi'ite).
	10 April: Ibrahim al-Ja'fari appointed Prime Minister who formed the cabinet in which there are seventeen Shi'ite members (one of whom is female), eight Kurdish members (three of whom are female), five Sunni Arabs (one of whom is female), and one female Christian.

Important dates for the Church of Iraq

AD	
339–79	The forty years' persecution by Shapur II.
410	The Synod of Isaac.
424	The Synod of Dadisho.
486	The Synod of Seleucia–Ctesiphon.
544	The Synod of Mar Aba I.
585	The Synod of Ishu'yab.
612	Babai the Great formulated the official theology of the Church of the East.
629	The Syrian Orthodox community is recognised as an independent community by the Sassanids.
	Tikrit becomes the centre of the Syrian Orthodox Church with its first bishop, Marutha, called the maphrian of the East.
775	The seat of the patriarchate of the Church of the East moves to Baghdad.

1553   The first union of the Church of the East with the Roman Catholic Church.

1662   The first union of the Syrian Orthodox Church with the Roman Catholic Church.

1790   A bishop was ordained for the Syrian Catholic community in Mosul. The birth of the Syrian Catholic Church in Iraq.

Table 1

The First Four Ecumenical Councils

AD325   **The first ecumenical council at Nicea**
Discussed the Arian controversy: the relation of the Father to the Son
The formulation of the Nicene Creed

AD381   **The second ecumenical council at Constantinople**
Finalized the Nicene Creed
Statement about the Holy Spirit added

AD431   **The third ecumenical council at Ephesus**
Discussion about the nature of Christ
Convened in haste by Cyril of Alexandria before the arrival of all parties
The Church of the East was not represented
No special formulation of faith documented
Nestorius deposed

AD451   **The fourth ecumenical council at Chalcedon**
Discussion about the nature of Christ
Decision: Christ in two natures, human and divine, in one Hypostasis
The Church of the East and the Armenian Church were not represented
Led to division of the Church into
1. The Chalcedonians (part of East and all West)
2. Non Chalcedonians (some Eastern, now called 'Oriental Orthodox')

Table 2

The Churches after the Council of Chalcedon

I. The Chalcedonians

The Churches that followed the two nature–Chalcedonian Christology:

'Two natures in the incarnate Jesus, and one hypostasis'

1. The Roman Catholic Church
2. The Eastern Orthodox Churches:
   The Orthodox Churches of Greece, Russia, Bulgaria, Romania, Georgia, Czech republic, Cyprus and Slovakia.
3. The Eastern Churches that united with the Roman Catholic Church. They include:
   The Chaldean Church
   The Syrian Catholic Church
   The Maronite Church
   The Greek Catholic Church
   The Coptic Catholic Church
   The Armenian Catholic Church

II. The Oriental Orthodox Churches
(have also been called the non-Chalcedonians)

The Churches that followed the 'Miaphysite' theology:

'One nature of the incarnate Word of God after the union and one Hypostasis'

1. The Coptic Church

2. The Syrian Orthodox Church
3. The Ethiopian Orthodox Church
4. The Armenian Orthodox Church
5. The Indian Syrian Orthodox Church
6. The Eritrean Orthodox Church

III. The Church of the East

was not involved in the Council of Chalcedon.
It developed its own theology based on that of Theodore
of Mopsuestia:
**'Two natures in the incarnate Jesus with their two
Qnomi and one Parsopa'**
Joint common Christological declaration with the Roman
Catholic Church on 11 November 1994.

Table 3

Important Synods of the Church of the East

AD410   The Synod of Mar Isaac.
The Church of the East accepted by Persian authorities as an independent community.
Officially adopted the Nicene Creed and that of Constantinople.
There was a representative from the West (Bishop Marutha).
Convened in the capital Seleucia–Ctesiphon.

AD424   The Synod of Dadisho.
The Church of the East announced its auton omy.
Convened at al-Hira.

AD486   The Synod of Seleucia–Ctesiphon.
The first preserved Christological creed of the Church of the East.

AD544   The Synod of Mar Aba I.
The unity of the Church of the East under the Patriarchal See restored.

AD585   The Synod of Ishu'yab.
The authority of the theology of Theodore of Mopsuestia confirmed.

Table 4

Other names given to the Church of the East

1. *The Nestorian Church*
   A term given to it erroneously by the Byzantines since it followed the theology promulgated by Nestorius.

2. *The Persian Church*
   Since it flourished within the realms of the Persian empire.

3. *The East Syrian Church*
   As it uses the Eastern dialect of Syriac (generally located east of the Euphrates).

4. *The Diophysites*
   Since they were accused of following the two nature Christology.

5. *The Ancient Church of the East*
   The community that did not accept the reforms of Mar Shimon in 1964.

6. *The Assyrian Church of the East*
   The community that accepted the reforms of Mar Shimon.

Table 5

Other names given to the Syrian Orthodox Church

1. *The Jacobite Church*
    A term erroneously given to it by the Byzantines after one of its prominent bishops, Jacob Baradeus.

2. *The West Syrian Church*
    As it uses the Western dialect of Syriac (generally located west of the Euphrates).

3. *The Monophysites*
    Since members of this church were erroneously accused of following the one nature Christology.

4. *Non-Chalcedonians*
    Since they did not agree with the decisions of the Council of Chalcedon.

5. *Ephesusians or Pre-Chalcedonians*

Abbreviations

BC	Before Christ
AD	Anno Domini or In the Year of Our Lord
SOC	Syrian Orthodox Church
CMS	Church Missionary Society
SPCK	Society for Promoting Christian Knowledge
SPG	Society for the Propagation of the Gospel
ABCFM	American Board of Commissioners for Foreign Missions
WCC	World Council of Churches
MECC	Middle East Council of Churches

Murat

Melitine

Samosata

Firat

OSRHOENE

Amida
(Diyar Bakir)

Sirt

Tigris

Tarsus

Mopsuestia

Edessa
(Urhay/Urfa)

Nisibis

Nineveh

Antiochia

Qinnisrene

Haran

Cyprus

MEDITERRANEAN SEA

Orontes

Aleppo

SYRIA

Apamea

Emesa
(Hemesa)

Dura-
Europus

Euphrates

Berytus

Palmyra

Heliopolis
(Baalbek)

Jordan

Damascus

Capernaum

Pella

Jerusalem

Gaza

ARABIAN

DESERT

N

0   100   200 miles

0   100   200   300 km.

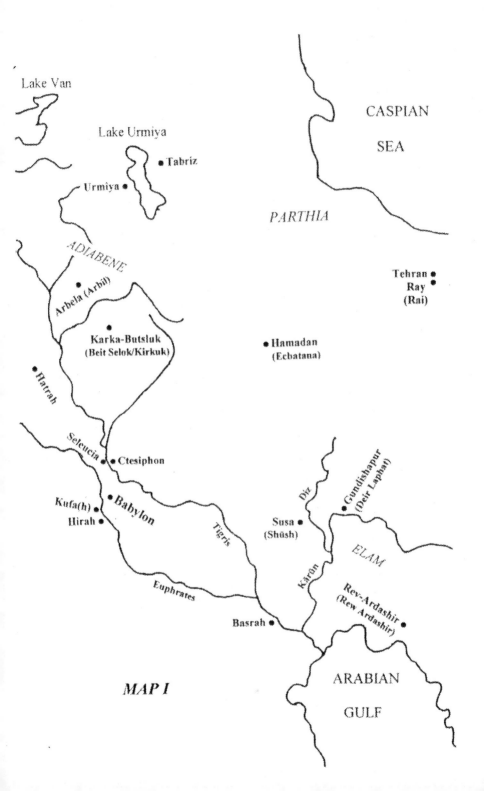

Lake Van

Lake Urmiya

Tabriz

Urmiya

CASPIAN

SEA

PARTHIA

Tehran ●

Ray ●

(Rai)

ADIABENE

Arbela (Arbil) ●

Karka-Butsluk
(Beit Selok/Kirkuk) ●

Hamadan ●
(Ecbatana)

Hatrah ●

Seleucia

Ctesiphon ●

Diz

Gundishapur
(Deir Laphat) ●

Kufa(h) ●

● **Babylon**

Hirah ●

Tigris

Susa ●
(Shūsh)

ELAM

Kārōn

Rev-Ardashir
(Rew Ardashir) ●

Euphrates

Basrah ●

MAP I

ARABIAN

GULF

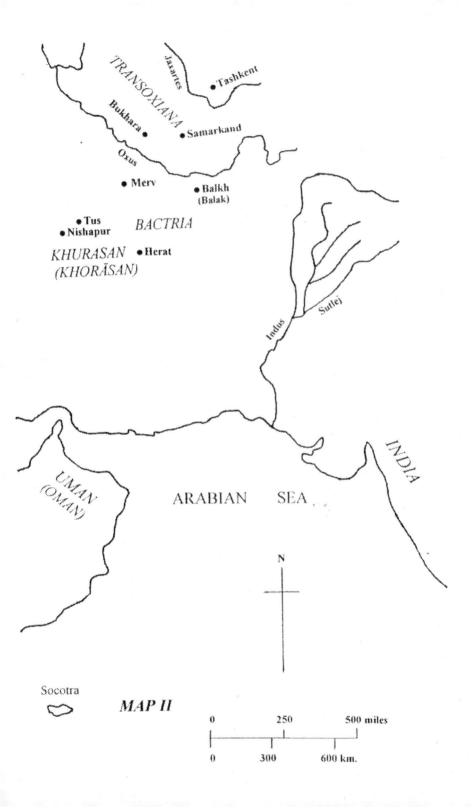

TRANSOXIANA

Jaxartes

●Tashkent

Bukhara

●Samarkand

Oxus

●Merv

●Balkh
(Balak)

●Tus
●Nishapur

BACTRIA

KHURASAN
(KHORĀSAN)

●Herat

Indus

Sutlej

INDIA

UMAN
(OMAN)

ARABIAN   SEA

N

Socotra

MAP II

0   250   500 miles

0   300   600 km.

TURKEY

Hakkari

Diyarbakir
(Amida)

Tigris

Julamerg

Zakhō

JEZIRA

Mardin(e)

Nisibis

Fayshkhābūr

Derabun
Semmel
(Summel)

Aleppo

Hasaka
(Haseke)

Sinjār

SYRIA

Euphrates

Khabur

IRAQ

MAP III

N

0   100   200 miles

0   100   200   300 km.

Introduction

To hear of a Christian from Iraq was news to most British people whom I met when I arrived in London in 1966 for my medical postgraduate studies. It was even bigger news for them to hear that the Christians of Iraq belong to one of the most ancient and glorious churches of the world. Christianity probably reached Iraq at the eve of the first Christian century and had emerged as a well-organized church by the end of the second century. It grew in spite of resistance and persecution from the occupying Persians and became independent of other churches at the beginning of the fifth century. It then spread its wings eastwards and southwards so that by the seventh century it had a large Christian congregation belonging to it in places as far as China, Central Asia and India.

It took me some time to discover the origins of this great church, its relation to the other churches and its most important characteristics. One of the hallmarks of the indigenous church of Iraq, as is the case of most of the Middle Eastern churches, is its association with the Syriac language. There was always the question of why the Christians from the urban areas where I grew up spoke no Syriac, except for the clergy, while those from the rural areas of northern Iraq spoke no language other than Syriac. The fact that there were more Syriac-speaking Christians in Iraq than Arabic-speaking Christians posed the question of whether my ancestors were originally Syriac speakers who lost their language at some stage in their history after the coming of Islam and the subsequent dominance of the Arabic language. However, the fact that there were a large number of Arabs who became Christians before the advent of Islam, not only in Iraq but also in Syria and the Arabian peninsula, very early in the history of Christianity, poses the question as to whether some of the Christians in the cities were these original Arab Christians who had maintained their faith and Arabic language. It is impossible to give an exact answer to this question, but since the Bible and the liturgy were not translated into Arabic before the coming of Islam, it seems more likely that the Arab Christians who did not convert to Islam became Syrianized. In fact, the Arab Christians used to call themselves the 'Syrian Arabs', the educated among them learnt the Syriac language and all listened to the Mass in Syriac. However this does not exclude the possibility that some of the Arab Christians who lived in or moved to the cities of north Mesopotamia maintained their Arabic language.

As I grew up in the city of Mosul in northern Iraq, it was inevitable to realize that we were a vulnerable community amongst the larger Muslim population, and it was understandable that our families were over-protective. Our house was in a central part of Mosul where most of our neighbours were Christians, and within a five- minute walk there were three churches which we attended: the oldest, Miskenta, named after a female martyr of the fifth century, in which Mass was said in the Eastern Syriac dialect; the second, Mar Toma, named after the apostle Thomas who is believed to have stopped to evangelize Mesopotamia on his way to India, in which Mass was said in the Western Syriac dialect; the third was a relatively modern church built by Dominican missionaries who came to Iraq in the middle of the eighteenth century, in which Mass was said in Latin. We found no difficulty in praying in any of the churches, partly because the readings were in Arabic, and partly because we had been instructed in the essential elements of the Mass, but mainly because that was the *status quo*. We prayed in Arabic with our parents, and grandmother told us different

Bible stories before going to bed. Our picnicking was in ancient monasteries where we were introduced to the stories of the martyrdom of their founders or patron saints.

My primary education was in a school run by Iraqi Dominican nuns whose convent stood between the Dominican church and the school, and where the majority of the teachers and students were Christians. Thus, until going to secondary school, the only Muslims I had met were those in the shops and those whom my grandparents met in business, although we knew of three students at school whose mother had married a Muslim. Officially they were Muslims, but their mother wanted to give them a Christian education. It was even rumoured that they had been baptized. The nuns took great care of them, but our parents were cautious, because inter-faith marriages were taboo among the Christian community in Mosul as the whole family in which it happened became stigmatized. They certainly didn't want it to happen to any of their children.

Secondary education was in state schools, where we received equal opportunities for secular education. Religious education was confined to Muslims, and we were only too happy to have a free hour to hang around in the school or to go home early if it happened to be the last lesson. Relations with Muslim girls and teachers were very good, although our parents had to approve as to whom we socialized with.

College education was in Baghdad, and since my parents still lived in Mosul, they had to make sure that I stayed with the nuns. The Presentation Sisters, who were French, had a large secondary school in central Baghdad and the headmistress, Jeanne Madeleine, was a cousin of my father. The school accepted both Christian and Muslim students from all over the country and those from outside Baghdad were accommodated in special boarding facilities. I spent three years as a 'pensioner' with the Presentation Sisters, while studying medicine, until my family moved to Baghdad. That was a very special experience. Not only was I free to make friends with Christians and

Muslims alike, but I also met foreigners, learned French and was introduced to Western culture. I felt at ease with the French nuns, amongst whom many were Iraqis. The nun responsible for my dormitory had just arrived, and spoke no language other than French, so the two of us had great fun teaching each other our corresponding languages. I met two Carmelite priests who had established a Christian cultural club for college students in Baghdad, in which I enjoyed the intellectual and cultural activities. Through these people new vistas were opened to me, and life was never the same again.

The question of Arab and Christian emerged when we started to hear about the Arab Ba'ath Socialist Party whose founder was a Christian from Syria. At the same time there were many belonging to the Communist Party who considered Arab nationalism irrelevant, and some belonging to Islamic movements who considered both Ba'ath socialism and communism to be anathema.

During those years the Second Vatican Council changed the liturgy of the Church, so we were no longer required to hear Mass in Latin or Syriac. The Carmelites who served us in the Christian cultural club were the first to say Mass in Arabic, and that boosted our faith as we started to understand the Mass better and follow it step by step.

My Iraqi identity came as an automatic result of growing up within the modern state which had just been formed. However, I needed to gain a personal knowledge of the ancient history of Iraq and its rich heritage from prehistory to present times before realizing a special affinity to it. Although we were taught some of the ancient history of Mesopotamia in school, the emphasis was on Arab history and Muslim achievements. There was no mention of the presence of Christians on Iraqi soil before Islam, nor was their role in the emergence of the Arab Abbasid civilization that was established in Iraq ever raised. This created in me and in many other Christians a reaction against the Islamic history and culture which were taught more than once during our intermediary and secondary education. It caused in us Christians a feeling of tension regarding our identity as Iraqis.

During my second visit to England in 1990, searching for my roots became an obsession, and I started to investigate the history of Iraq and my Christian background. I was astounded at the paucity of material available on our churches, whether in English or in Arabic. This led me to serious research on the subject, which took me to scholarly books and to undertake an MA in Eastern Christianity at the School of Oriental and African Studies in London.

As Iraq has come to the forefront of world news, it is important not to forget the great contributions it has given to the world throughout its long history, and the many great civilizations that flourished on its soil. In southern Iraq flourished the great civilized city- states of the Sumerians where writing and canal irrigation were first developed; in Babylon innumerable astrological and arithmetic discoveries were made; in Ur of the Chaldeans, the father of the three great monotheistic religions, Abraham, was born.

Thoughts about the origin of humankind, the relationship to a creator god, the quest for eternity and knowledge of good and evil can all be found within the many legends and epics discovered in the libraries of the ancient Mesopotamians. The impact of Mesopotamian thought on many neighbouring peoples is now well recognized. Of special importance, especially in relationship to our subject, is its influence on the Hebrew people, who were exiled to Iraq and who stayed there for a considerable period of time. Its indirect influence on subsequent European thought is also widely acknowledged. That a thriving Christian community existed in Iraq, however, and that its indigenous church had a role to play in the formation of the twentieth-century State of Iraq, is hardly known.

At the dawn of Islam the church in Iraq had its centre at the capital of the Persian empire, Seleucia–Ctesiphon, where the patriarch lived. The patriarchate moved to Baghdad in 775 after the latter became the new capital of the Arab Abbasid empire. Several Christian centres of learning had flourished before the coming of the Arabs. The learning and knowledge of the Christians of Iraq contributed to the development of the Arab Abbasid civilization which flourished on its soil. They played a major role especially in the field of medicine, and in translations from Greek to Arabic. These Greek writings found their way to Europe through the Arabs of Spain and played a significant role in the development of European civilization. Some Greek works were preserved only in Arabic.

Although the Church of Iraq has suffered many onslaughts over the years, and many of its members have emigrated in recent years to various Western countries, Christians continue to have a significant presence in a predominantly modern Muslim state. They proved to be of special value in the emergence of modern Iraq at the turn of the twentieth century.

It is my intention in this brief work to present the history of Christianity in Iraq in a form accessible to the English speaker.

In the first chapter I will briefly survey the regional changes in the Middle East with special emphasis on Mesopotamia and the historical, cultural, and religious background of the territory around the time of Jesus. In addition, I will review very briefly the situation of Christianity in the Middle East, especially in relation to the ecumenical councils which led to schism and the separation of Christian communities, and how in Mesopotamia two main churches emerged, the Church of the east and the Syrian Orthodox Church.

The subsequent five chapters follow the birth, development and transformation of the Christian communities that had been implanted in Mesopotamia over the centuries until this area became the modern State of Iraq. Because present-day Iraq includes most of what was called Mesopotamia, I have often used the term, the Church of Iraq to indicate the church that developed in Mesopotamia.

Finally, I will briefly outline the present situation of the Christian community in Iraq. This has proved to be very difficult because of the paucity of statistics, especially in relation to numbers of the different communities. Some of the figures are, at best, rough estimates given by the priests looking after the various communities in the United Kingdom, while others are obtained from a variety of sources as indicated.

During the writing of this book, I have avoided the use of names given to some of the Churches which these communities disapprove of, such as 'Nestorian' or 'Dyophysite' for the Church of the East, and 'Jacobite' or 'Monophysite' for the Syrian Orthodox Church (see tables 4 and 5). The reasons for the use of these terms and the sensitivities that ensue regarding them will be explained in the text. However, on the occasions when I have used these names, it is because they were used by the writer in the particular text or document which I was quoting and I have put it between small brackets. Although these terms have been commonly used by scholars and by members of these churches themselves until recently, they are better avoided. I have also used the terms 'East Syrian' for the Church of the East and 'West Syrian' for the Syrian Ortho-dox Church. These terms are legitimate and are used by both communities in reference to their churches. The difference between East and West Syriac is that of dialect. The Church of the East uses the East Syriac dialect, while the Syrian Orthodox Church uses the West Syriac dialect. After union with the Roman Catholic Church the corre-sponding Uniate Churches continued to use their own dialect in liturgy, the Chaldean, being an offshoot of the Church of the East, continued to use the East Syrian dialect, while the Syrian Catholic, being an offshoot of the Syrian Orthodox Church, continued to use the West Syriac dialect.

1

The matrix of Christianity in the Middle East

Iraq and Mesopotamia

The name of present-day Iraq was first used officially only in 1921, when it was declared an independent state after World War I. The land included in this territory had always been called in Arabic 'the land of Iraq', meaning the fertile land.

Iraq today is part of an area that in ancient times was called Mesopotamia, a Greek word which means the 'land between two rivers', the Tigris and the Euphrates. Both originate in present-day Turkey, the Tigris flowing directly to Iraq, while the Euphrates flows through Syria before entering Iraq. In antiquity, Mesopotamia included all of what is now Iraq, as well as a small part of north-east Syria, southern Turkey and of north-west Iran. Mesopotamia covers a triangular area limited by arbitrary lines drawn between Aleppo, Lake Urmia in the north and Shatt al-Arab in the south.

Within Mesopotamia at the time of Christ was a small vassal or buffer state called Osrhoene, which occupied a small area of north-west Iraq near its border with Syria and Turkey as well as part of north-east Syria and a similar area of southern Turkey. Its population was largely Aramaean although there was a significant presence of Arabs and Armenians. Its capital Edessa[1] was a cosmopolitan city, standing at the crossroads between East and West. This small state was the melting pot of

Greek, Aramaic and Persian cultures, and as will be seen later, was of great importance for the spread and development of Christianity in the Middle East.

Historical background

The geographical area of Mesopotamia was matched in pre-Christian times by a striking cultural unity. Within this area flourished the great civilizations of the Sumerians, Akkadians, Babylonians and Assyrians. From roots set deep in prehistory these civilizations blossomed in the dawning light of history and lasted for nearly three thousand years. The centres which they generated such as Ur, Uruk, Nippur, Babylon, Assur and Nineveh were all situated on or near the Tigris and the Euphrates, in an area which is covered by present day Iraq. They nourished the entire Middle East for thousands of years until they eventually came under attack from both East and West. Babylon fell to the Persian/Elamite king Cyrus[2] in 539 BC. The Persians were in turn defeated by Alexander the Great, who swept through the whole Middle East and Iran, reaching as far as Bactria[3] and Punjab, in the early fourth century BC. He died of fever in 323 BC, on his way to Babylon, in a place near Baghdad , a small town, which is named after him and is called al-Iskandariyya. His general Seleucus, as well as a whole dynasty after him, ruled the entire Mesopotamian region as well as Syria, Palestine, Lebanon and parts of Turkey, while his general Ptolemy ruled Egypt. The Seleucids ruled until Iraq fell again under Persian rule in 129 BC, when the Parthian[4] dynasty assumed control. The latter were replaced by the Sassanids, yet another Persian dynasty, in AD 224, until they were overthrown by the Arabs in AD 637. In Syria, Palestine and present-day Turkey, the Seleucids were replaced by the Romans in 63 BC.

Edessa, the capital of Osrhoene, was originally a Seleucid foundation but came under Persian/Parthian rule in the winter of 130–129 BC, after which it seems to have become independent for a short period of time. Being a vassal state, its kings oscillated in their allegiance between the Persians and the Romans until it became a Roman Colonia in AD 213.

Osrhoene was situated at the crossroads between the Roman/Byzantine empire in the west and the Persian empire in the east. Consequently it became the meeting point of numerous cultures, namely Greek, Syriac, Armenian and Persian. Although its inhabitants were mainly Aramaeans, many of its kings had Arab names (Abdu, Abgar, Bakru and Ma'nu), some were Persians, and still others were Armenians.

Although not completely independent except for a short period of time, it had relative freedom even when it was under Persian or Roman rule. Its kings managed internal affairs fairly competently and were open-minded and receptive to new ideas and religions.

This small state was very important for the development of Christianity in the East. Legend has it that its king heard of Jesus while He was alive and wrote Him a letter asking Him to come and live in his country, since he had heard that He was persecuted by the Jews. Jesus had replied, telling him that He could not come but that He would send him His apostle Addai, who arrived soon after Jesus' death and cured the king of an incurable illness. The king became a Christian, and his kingdom followed him.

Legend apart, it is very likely that Christianity had reached Edessa through Jewish converts during the first Christian century. Its king Abgar VIII, 'The Great', may have converted to the Chistian Faith during the second half of the second century. Christianity subsequently flourished in this small state, and Osrhoene became the first kingdom to adopt it as an official religion. The relative freedom which people enjoyed in this state, together with its multicultural atmosphere, were of paramount importance in the propagation of Christian learning and the emergence of Edessa as one of the earliest Christian centres of learning.

When Christianity began to be established in Mesopotamia, most of the area was under Persian/Parthian rule; that was followed by the Persian/Sassanid rule in AD 224. By contrast, Syria, Turkey and Palestine were under Roman rule. The Persian rulers of Mesopotamia were tolerant of other religions, though when Zoroastrianism[5] was adopted as the official religion of the state in AD 286, apostasy from Zoroastrianism became punishable by death. The majority of the general population were pagans who worshipped the ancient gods of the Sumerians, Akkadians, Babylonians and Assyrians. In addition there were Arabs, particularly in Hatra, Sinjar and Mesene, who worshipped their own gods; there was also a sizeable Jewish community.

The presence of Jewish ancestry in Mesopotamia is traced back to the time of Abraham, as he was a citizen of the Babylonian city of Ur (Genesis 11:31). Historically, however, the presence of the Jewish community in Mesopotamia is related to the exile of Jews from Palestine during the Assyrian and Babylonian wars. The first exile occurred in the eighth century BC under the Assyrian king Tiglathpileser III (745–727 BC) who initiated a policy of mass deportations in the areas he conquered. The second exile occurred in the sixth century BC after the Babylonian king Nebuchadnezzar conquered Judea in 604 BC (three waves of deportations followed in 597, 587 and 582). The Assyrian exiles were dispersed among the population in the region of Adiabene[6] and the Kurdistan mountains, while the Babylonian exiles were placed in settlements of their own near the city of Babylon. They were allowed to build their own houses and to earn a living in any way they could.

Cyrus, the Persian king, took over Babylon in 539 BC; he allowed the Jews to return to their homeland in 538 BC. Many of them, however, did not return as they had by then developed a community, become affluent, and enjoyed comfortable living. The number of Jews in Mesopotamia increased in the late first century AD following the Roman conquest of Palestine. Some of the Jews had started an armed resistance against the Romans in the year AD 63 with the aim of establishing an independent Jewish state. The Jewish Christians did not take part in this movement and fled to Pella, a town east of the river Jordan. In AD 70, the Jews lost the war to the Romans, who destroyed the third Temple, and the majority of them fled Palestine to various countries. In AD 132 Bar Cochba claimed to be Messiah and led another uprising against the Romans, resulting in the Emperor Hadrian's destruction of Jerusalem. All remaining Jews were expelled from the city, which was renamed 'Aelia Capitolina'.

The diaspora that followed both wars increased the number of Jews in Mesopotamia, as those who fled their country during these wars joined friends and relatives, many of whom were already there. The arrival of Jewish Christians who had not taken part in the Jewish war must have played a major role in the spread of the Christian message in both directions, east and west.

Christianity was spreading within the realms of the Roman empire in spite of the active persecution by various Roman emperors. From its Palestinian origin, Christianity became embedded within Roman society, attracting followers from various classes. The first Christian centre to emerge after Jerusalem was Antioch, the capital of the province of Syria in Roman times,[7] to be followed by Alexandria and Rome.

When the Emperor Constantine fought a battle invoking the help of the Christian God in AD 311 and won, he began to champion the Christians. Together with his counterpart in the eastern Roman territories, Licinius, he issued an edict of toleration of the Christians in 312 (called the Edict of Milan). This edict announced religious freedom for all individuals within the realms of the Roman Empire. Although Constantine was only baptized upon his death bed in 337, he had promoted Christianity soon after he became sole emperor in 324, and began to use it as a force in unifying his empire. He provided church leaders with land and money, and became interested in the new religion which he saw as the salvation of his empire. These developments had a tremendous influence on the political and social situation of the area, as well as on the status of the Church which began to assume an imperial character. After a short period of persecution under Julian the Apostate (361–3), Christianity was declared the official religion of the Roman empire in 392.

Cultural context

In the Middle East, the Aramaic language had assumed a special importance by the time of Jesus – who is known to have spoken in Aramaic. The Aramaic people who inhabited present-day Syria and adjacent areas, followed the Phoenicians in using the alphabet in around 1000 BC. Both the Phoenicians and the Aramaeans were good traders and took their language with them: the Phoenicians westwards by sea, the Aramaeans eastwards as they travelled by land. Since the alphabet was simpler than the complex cuneiform script, all the peoples of the area, whether Persian, Assyrian or Hebrew, began to use it in their intellectual activities and commercial dealings as well as in their daily life. Around that time, Aramaic culture and language became dominant in the Middle East and remained so for the next fifteen hundred years, until the coming of Islam. Following that, a major decline occurred in the use of Aramaic as it was superseded by the Arabic language.

The Jewish people were familiar with Aramaic, and it is closely related to the Hebrew language. Moreover, there is an ethnic relationship between the Aramaeans and the Hebrew people. Jacob is described in the Bible as a 'wandering Aramaean' (Deut. 26:5), and many Jews, including Jesus, spoke the Aramaic language. It is interesting to note that Jesus' final words on the cross are recorded in the Gospels of Mark and Matthew in Aramaic:

> *'Eli, Eli lemana sabachthani'* which means 'My God, My God, why have you forsaken me?' (Matt 27:46; Mark 15:34.)

Both the Hebrew people and the Aramaeans came under the influence of Hellenism, the cultural legacy of the Greeks. Alexander the Great had a great vision of unifying East and West by Hellenizing the areas he conquered in the first half of the fourth century BC. His generals continued to propagate Hellenism after him, and so did the Romans who replaced the Greeks in 63 BC. They set out to introduce the Greek style of life by building complexes that contained gymnasiums, stadiums and amphitheatres. The Greek language and philosophy soon became of utmost importance to all the educated people of the region, in spite of initial resistance from both Aramaeans and Jews.

When Christianity first took root in the Middle East it was only natural that it should be communicated to the people in the Aramaic language which the apostles and the Jews spoke. The Aramaic dialect of Edessa, 'Syriac', became especially used in Christian circles, mainly because Christian learning had flourished very early in the small state of Osrhoene. It was a cosmopolitan place where intellectuals and traders met and in which we find one of the earliest intellectuals who had converted to Christianity, a man of noble birth called Bardaisan. The latter was a friend of the king of Osrhoene, Abgar VIII, who seems to have become a Christian under his influence at the end of the second century (as did a large proportion of the population). Thus the Syriac dialect became dominant in Christian circles, and gradually the word Syriac replaced Aramaean. The link between this dialect of Aramaic and Christianity became so strong that in time Syriac became synonymous with Christian. This shift had a practical significance for the Christians since it distinguished them from the non-Christian, pagan, Aramaeans. Christian theology and dogma developed in the first five centuries in areas under Roman rule, (modern Syria, Egypt and southern Turkey). These areas had come under the influence of Hellenism very early even though their original cultures were strongly rooted. In Syria and Palestine the Aramaean inhabitants were proud of their language and cultural heritage and showed some resistance to Hellenization. Moreover the use of the Syriac language was strengthened by non-Aramaic people who converted to Christianity, such as the Persians and the Arabs. They needed to learn the Syriac language when they converted to Christianity, and many of them in time became Syrianized. Syriac had become the sacred religious language of Eastern Christians just as Latin was to become the sacred language of the Roman Church.

The use of Greek philosophy in formulating Christian theological ideas caused tension between the Greek-speaking and Syriac-speaking Christians. This cultural clash was most prominent under Roman rule in Syria, Palestine and Osrhoene, while it was less acute in Persian-ruled Iraq. In time, though, all intellectual Christians including the Syriac-speakers had to become acquainted with Greek language and philosophy, because Greek philosophical terminology was used by almost all Christian theologians in expressing their faith. Greek theological works were then translated into the Syriac language. In spite of the Hellenization of theology, the Christians of the Middle East continued to use Syriac as the main language of communication amongst the people, whether in Syria, Iraq or southern Turkey. Intellectuals and religious leaders continued to use Syriac in their writing and in the liturgy in spite of the influence of other languages.

The theological dimension – the Ecumenical Councils of the first five centuries

The early Christians were faced with the problem of explaining the relationship between Jesus whom they acknowledged as the Son of God, the Father from whom He came and to whom He returns, and the Holy Spirit who they continually invoked for guidance. This relationship had to be expressed in human language in such a way that the fundamental oneness of God was maintained. Moreover, the revelation they received from Jesus, and which was consolidated after the resurrection, that He is God and man at the same time, had to be put in such terms that neither His humanity nor His divinity was compromised.

The dogmas of the Christian faith that came to be known as the Trinity and the Incarnation took some time to emerge and, needless to say, did so after much controversy and misunderstanding. To express these dogmas and the relationship between the humanity and divinity of Jesus, Greek philosophical terms were used.

The first major controversy to arise among intellectual Christians was the Arian controversy. This was promulgated by an Alexandrian priest called Arius against his bishop, Athanasius of Alexandria, about the relationship of the person of Jesus to the Godhead. Arius said that the Son could not be equal to the Father, because there was a time when He was not. Thus, according to this theology, Christ was to be numbered among the creation of God the Father, though the first-born of all creation. This caused a major outrage amongst many theologians and strife between different Christian communities, the news of which reached the Emperor Constantine soon after he came to power. Constantine was concerned about divisions amongst the Christians because he was attempting to use Christianity as a unifying power within his empire. In order to solve the problem, he called on all the Christian communities to meet in a council. The first Ecumenical Council was convened in Nicea in 325, over which Constantine presided. Representatives from most parts of Christendom attended, including two from Mesopotamia. In this Council it was decided that the Son is consubstantial with the Father and the canon of faith was formulated. Another Council followed in Constantinople in 381, which included the role of the Holy Spirit. The formula of the Nicene Creed testifies that the Son is of one substance with the Father: 'God of God, Light of Light, true God of true God, begotten not made, consubstantial with the Father …' According to this creed the full divinity of Jesus is asserted.

Further disputes over the person of Christ and the relationship between His humanity and His divinity led to the Councils of Ephesus in 431 and that of Chalcedon in 451. The key concern in all disputes concerning the person of Christ was to ensure his redeeming work. In order to redeem humanity and be Saviour, all theologians agreed that Jesus had to be fully human as well as fully divine. Any theology that diminished his humanity would jeopardize His redeeming work as much as any diminution in His divinity.

When these realities were put in theological formulations, many problems arose that led to misunderstanding between different parties. The first problem was that of the linguistic terms used by different parties and their meanings. When examined carefully, the pivotal terms used to express the different aspects of the human/divine Jesus: *Nature/Physis/kyana, Person/Hypostasis/Qnōma*[8] were found to mean different things by the different parties concerned. For example the Chalcedonians used the word nature to express the reality of being, while the non-Chalcedonians used it to mean the state of being[9] (see *Glossary of theological terms* and Table 2).

The second problem was the difference in approach, philosophical backgrounds and methods. For example, the Antiochene school followed Aristotelian historical and exegetical methods, while the Alexandrian school followed Platonic philosophical and theological methods. Antiochene thought started from the conception of the Incarnation as a union of the Word of God with a man, while the Alexandrian approach spoke of the union of the Word and flesh. On this basis it was more natural that Antiochene theology emphasised a duality of natures, the divine and the human in Christ, whilst the Alexandrian school centred on the unity of Christ's person.

The third and not the least of the problems was a clash of personalities. Rivalries between the different centres and schools had much to do with the unfortunate results that followed. Each of the theologians concerned was following his own methods, reaching his own conclusion, and unfortunately could not see that there could be different ways of putting the same fact (that Christ is perfect God and perfect man) into different formulations.

Representing the theology of the Antiochene school, Theodore of Mopsuestia[10] made a clear distinction between the humanity and divinity of Jesus and maintained that there are two hypostases and two natures in Jesus. The distinction made between the human Jesus and the divine Jesus led some to conclude an unacceptable division in his personality. For example, Theodore explained that when Jesus said 'O Lord why have you forsaken me', it was the human Jesus talking, while when He performed miracles it was the divine Jesus talking. This is why he explained that Mary should be called 'bearer of Jesus' (*Christotokos*) and not 'bearer of God' (*Theotokos*), a term which was in common use by then and which had come to be cherished by the majority of Christians. His concern in making this distinction was to ensure that the humanity of Jesus was preserved, because it seemed to him that the Alexandrian school by stressing the divine Jesus had threatened His humanity.

Nestorius, the Bishop of Constantinople, had promoted the theology of Theodore of Mopsuestia and started to attack the term *Theotokos* publicly, causing an intense counter-attack from Cyril, Bishop of Alexandria. This controversy led to the convocation of the Council of Ephesus in 431. The council was convened in haste by Cyril before the arrival of all parties concerned, and Nestorius, Bishop of Constantinople, was deposed from his position. The party from Antioch, under the leadership of John of Antioch, arrived four days later and convened its own synod. The two synods anathematized each other. There was no document of faith from the Council of Ephesus, only two synods cursing each other. However, there was later a meeting between Cyril of Alexandria and John of Antioch, and a compromise formula was produced in 433:

'Christ is perfect God and perfect man consisting of

rational soul and body, of one substance with the Father in His Godhead, of one substance with us in His Manhood, so that there is a union of two natures; on which ground we confess Christ to be one and Mary mother of God'.[11]

The two-nature Christology continued to be disputed by the Alexandrian school who argued that it is against logic to have two natures in one subject. The concern of the Alexandrian school was to maintain the unity of the person of Jesus. They argued that the presence of two natures meant the presence of two subjects: thus although Jesus Christ pre-existed in two natures, in Incarnation He could have only one nature. The union of the two natures occur without confusion, change, division or separation. The term 'Miaphysite' is now used for this formulation, which gives a sense of composite nature after the union.

These issues were debated at the Council of Chalcedon. Although Pope Leo I did not attend this council himself, he sent representatives who read his *Tome* in which the two-nature Christology was affirmed. It was read in front of all, and a decision was taken against the one-nature Christology. The Chalcedonian formulary stated that Christ is perfect God and perfect man, consubstantial with the father in His Godhead and with us human beings in His manhood. He is made known in two natures without confusion, change, division or separation. The properties of the two natures are preserved and intact and come together to form one person and one hypostasis.

In retrospect it is easier to see why all these misunderstandings arose. To the Antiochene school, the Alexandrian tradition was paying too much attention to the divinity of Christ, thus compromising His humanity. To the Alexandrian school, the Antiochenes were insisting so much on the differences between the two aspects of Christ, the human and the divine, that they were compromising the unity of the person of Jesus.

The Church of the East was not represented in either of the two Councils and its formulation of Christology will be discussed later. However it is noteworthy to mention here that its members started to be called 'Nestorians' by the Byzantines, because they were seen as following the same theology used by Nestorius. They were also called 'Dyophysite' because they were erroneously seen to conceive Christ in two different persons. The Church of the East clarified its position at a later stage, and in its definition of Christology introduced the term *Qnōma* to denote the quality of the nature, and the term *Parsopa* for person. The Church of the East defined Jesus 'In two natures with their two Qnōmē and one Parsopa'.

Notes

1 Edessa was so named by the Greeks after its namesake in Macedonia as it was established by Seleucus, who after the death of Alexander the Great governed Mesopotamia. It was also called Urhay in Aramaic and survives in modern Turkey under the name Urfa. The word Osrhoene may have originated from the Aramaic Urhay. See map no. 2.

2 In ancient times, the modern state of Iran was home to two powerful national groups, the Medes in the north and the Elamites in the south. The Medes allied themselves with Babylon and overthrew the Assyrians in in 609 BC. They were in turn overthrown by Cyrus, king of Elam, in 550 BC.

3 The area named Bactria by the Greeks is present day North Afghanistan, see map no. 2.

4 The Parthians were the inhabitants of the ancient kingdom of Parthia which lay south-east of the Caspian Sea in present-day Iran. See map no. 1.

5 The Zoroastrian religion was founded by Zarathustra, a prophetic figure who lived some time before 600 BC. Zoroaster is a Greek corruption of his name, from which the name of the religion originates. His dates have been widely disputed, ranging from the middle of the sixth century BC to some time in the middle of the second millennium BC. Scholars are also divided about Zoroaster's original teaching. Some regard him as a monotheist and see later dualistic Zoroastrianism as a corruption of his original teaching. Zoroaster's teaching maintains that the world was made by one 'Wise Lord', Ahuramazda, who created the world with

the help of his holy spirit and six other spirits. He was, however, not all-powerful but was opposed by an uncreated evil spirit, Ahriman, supported by other evil spirits. The created world was the arena for a combat between good and evil. Human beings, having free will, have the duty to choose good. At death, each individual is judged according to his deeds. All human striving is to be directed towards the salvation of the world. In the last days of the world, the 'World Saviour', Saoshyyant, will come in glory, and there will be a battle in which good will triumph over evil.

6 Adiabene was a province in northern Mesopotamia which stretched from the river Tigris to the border of modern Iran. Its capital was Arbela, a city which in modern Iraq is called Arbil. It was also called the land of the Assyrians.

7 Antioch is a city close to the Mediterranean Sea and situated in the north-west area of Greater Syria and Lebanon. Presently in southern Turkey, it is the city where the Christians were first called by this name. (Acts 11:26).

8 The word 'nature' in theological perspective has a descriptive functional content meaning 'essence or substance', and is not related to our present use of the word as in 'the world of nature'. Theologians preferred to use the Greek word *physis* instead of 'nature' in theological definitions, as this word has a descriptive functional content. Thus the term 'Mono-physis' means one nature and 'Dyophysis' two natures. The Syriac Christians used the word *Kyana* for physis. *Hypostasis* is the Greek word used to express the quality of being a person. It is a philosophical term that expresses self-existence and was used in Trinitarian theology 'One God in three hypostases'. It was used in theological formulation instead of *prosopon* because the latter had theatrical connotations and expressed the role being played rather than the quality of the person. *'Qnōma'* is the Syriac equivalent for Hypostasis as used in Trinitarian theology. It was used in Christological definitions to express the quality of individuated natures. Thus it had a different meaning from what the Alexandrians understood by Hypostasis (see glossary for theological terms).

9 See *Christianity Through its History in the East*, p. 214.

10 Theodore of Mopsuestia (350–428), an Antiochene theologian and Biblical exegete. He entered the school of Diodore in a monastery in Antioch where he remained for nearly ten

years. In AD 392, he became Bishop of Mopsuestia, where he spent the rest of his life and developed a wide reputation for learning and orthodoxy. The Antiochene school, which Theodore represented, followed literary, literal and historical interpretations, with precise differentiation between the divine and the human natures. The integrity of Christ's humanity had to be preserved as well as his divinity. This was specifically important in opposition to the teaching of Apollinaris of Laodicea who de-emphasized the humanity of Christ because he believed that the '*Logos*' or the divine had occupied the place of the human reason.

11 *The Early Church* by Henry Chadwick, p. 199.

2

The first four centuries

The earliest times

The very first beginnings of Christianity are shrouded in mystery. The early Christians were Jews who worshipped in the synagogues and read the Hebrew Bible as their Holy Book. They differed from their fellow Jews only by their faith in Jesus of Nazareth as Messiah, whom they believed was the fulfilment of the promises God had made to their ancestors. They met in their homes to celebrate the death and resurrection of Jesus, which was symbolized in the breaking of the bread. Their earliest preaching was: 'This man Jesus who was crucified, God has raised him from the dead and we are witness to that ... Repent and be baptised in the name of Jesus Christ and you will receive the gift of the Holy Spirit' (from Peter's address to the crowds in Acts 2:22–41).

In spite of constant friction between mainstream Jews and Jewish Christians, the latter remained a sect within Judaism until the year AD 70 when the war against the Romans was lost and the Temple destroyed. The Pharisees met in Jamnia in order to decide the future of Judaism, and one of their decisions was to expel the Jewish Christians from the synagogues.

This exclusion of the Christians from the Jewish community forced them to organize themselves. Although they continued to read the Old Testament, a written document about the life and teaching of Jesus became essential.

The four evangelists wrote the four Gospels and the Acts of the Apostles in the second half of the first century. The letters of St Paul were written earlier and provide some historical details of the early church.[1] All New Testament writings were set down so that people might believe in Jesus; they are coloured by the theology of their authors and were not meant to be historical recording of all the events in Jesus' life. In spite of this we receive glimpses of the operations of the early Church especially from the Acts of the Apostles and the letters of St Paul. Although these writings deal mainly with what happened in Jerusalem, Syria, Asia Minor and westwards to Rome, Mesopotamia is mentioned. When Peter preached to the Jewish community gathered on Pentecost day, there were people from all over the Diaspora, and Mesopotamia is one of the countries mentioned:

> Now there were devout men living in Jerusalem from every nation under heaven, and at this sound all assembled, and each one was bewildered to hear them speaking in his own language. They were amazed and astonished. 'Surely' they said, 'all these speaking are Galileans? How does it happen that each of us hears them speaking in his own language? Parthians, Medes and Elamites; people from Mesopotamia, Judea and Cappadocia, Pontus and Asia, Phrygia and Pamphylia, Egypt and parts of Libya around Cyrene; residents of Rome, Jews and proselytes alike; Cretans and Arabs; we hear them speaking in our own language about the marvels of God. (Acts 2:5–11).

The Acts of the Apostles also tells us that at Pentecost after the sermon of Peter three thousand individuals were baptized in the name of Jesus. One of those who came from Mesopotamia could have believed on that day, and gone back to his family and community with the new message.

Church tradition tells us that those who brought the good news to Mesopotamia were the Apostle Thomas,

Addai (Thaddaeus) and his pupils Aggai and Mari.[2] Thomas and Thaddaeus were of the Twelve Apostles, while Aggai and Mari were from the Seventy who accompanied Jesus. There is no reason to doubt this tradition but, to put events in their historical perspective, we can stipulate that what happened in Mesopotamia was similar to what happened in Palestine, Syria and other adjacent areas as narrated in the Acts of the Apostles, where the Christian message was first propagated among the Jews. It seems very likely that some of the Jews who lived in Mesopotamia and who travelled to Palestine, whether for pilgrimage or for trade, became acquainted with the Christian message and came back to their families and friends bringing the good news and establishing the earliest Christian communities. The large population of Jews in Mesopotamia makes this a more than likely possibility.

Some believe that Christianity entered Iraq from Edessa, while others maintain that it was in Arbela that the first Christian message reached Mesopotamia. Still others believe that the Faith arrived through southern Mesopotamia from the sea, reaching Babylon first, then Adiabene and Nisibis. It is more likely that Christianity entered Iraq via all these routes simultaneously, since there were Jews in all three places and people at the time travelled extensively by sea and by land.

The second century – the early presence of Christianity in Mesopotamia

Historical evidence of churches, Christian writers and martyrs, points to the fact that Christianity was fairly well established in Mesopotamia by the second Christian century. Below is some of the most important historical evidence which substantiates this fact.

Tatian

A Christian convert of noble descent born in the region of Adiabene, the land of the Assyrians, of pagan parents.

After his conversion, he went to Rome and became a disciple of the famous Christian apologist, Justin Martyr. He returned to his country, Adiabene, in the year 172. Tatian wrote many philosophical and theological works in both Greek and Syriac. His most important work however, is the Diatessaron, which is a conflation of the four canonical gospels into one, also called the Gospel Harmony. He began with the gospel of St Matthew to which he added material from the Gospels of Mark, Luke and John. To a lesser extent he included a few excerpts from other gospels circulating at the time, which were later considered non-canonical.

It is believed that he wrote the Diatessaron in Syriac, although it is possible that it was written in Greek and was later translated to Syriac. This gospel was in common use among the Syriac speaking people of the area for about three hundred years. Its replacement by the official canonical gospels in the fifth century was resisted strenuously.

Bardaisan (154–222)

A Christian intellectual whose name suggests that he was from Edessa (the river Daisan passed through it). He was of noble birth and a friend of the king of Osrhoene, Abgar VIII, also called Abgar the Great (177–212). The latter may have converted to Christianity through his ministry at the end of the second century. Bardaisan was well rooted in the Greek philosophical tradition and its influence on his works is clear. He wrote theology and philosophy, mostly in Syriac, and used poetry and teaching songs to convey his ideas. He established a school in Edessa where he had many disciples. In *The Book of the Laws of the Countries*, fate and free will are discussed. This book was probably written by his disciple Philip in a form of dialogue between the two, using the style of Plato's dialogue with Socrates. Writing at the end of the second century, he mentions a number of regions in both east and west where Christian communities were to be found, as far as Bactria, which is present-day northern Afghanistan.

The epitaph of Abercius

Abercius was the bishop of Hierapolis, a town in Asia Minor, during the later part of the second century: he had visited the communities of his co-religionists in the east. The inscription reads:

> I saw the Syrian plain and all the cities even Nisibis and crossed the Euphrates. Everywhere I found Christians with whom to speak.[3]

The history of Edessa

This document, which was written in the sixth century, begins its history with the year 200 and mentions that a church in Edessa was destroyed by the flood of the year 201. The occurrence of such a flood is documented in other sources.

The Council of Nicea

Reports from this Council, which was convened in the year 325, show that there were two bishop representatives from Mesopotamia as well as from other Eastern churches.

The controversy over the date of Easter

Eusebius of Caesarea in his *Ecclesiastical History* relates that when argument developed about the date of celebrating Easter between the churches of Africa and Rome and other Western churches, the church in Mesopotamia was consulted. He wrote that the bishops of Mesopotamia met in 189–90 and took a decision in favour of the Western churches: they sent a letter to the parties concerned in which they stated their decision.

Although Tatian and Bardaisan were later condemned as heretics, their importance from the historical point of view is tremendous. The conversion of an intellectual from a noble pagan family at Adiabene in the middle of the second century points to the presence of a fairly well-established community that had started to penetrate the higher echelons of society. This is also true in the case of

Bardaisan, converted in the second half of the second century. The presence of a bishop and a church building in Edessa at the end of the second century points to an established presence of Christianity in the area from an earlier date.

After discussing whether Christianity in Mesopotamia first developed in Arbela or Edessa, Gillman and Klimkeit conclude: 'there is firm evidence for the existence of Christians in the area by AD 170 and indeed as far afield as Bactria'.[4]

The emergence of the Church of Iraq

When Christianity began to infiltrate Iraq in the first two centuries, it was under the Parthians, who were open to the practice of different religions and seem to have tolerated the introduction of Christianity into their empire. The Sassanid dynasty that followed in 224 adopted Zoroastrianism as the official religion of the state under the influence of the high priest Kartir in 286. The Zoroastrians did not impose their religion on the population in an aggressive way, nor did they object to conversions of non-Zoroastrian subjects from their original pagan religions to Christianity. But conversion of Zoroastrians, especially from the upper echelons of their society, was punishable by death. Consequently large numbers of pagans, who formed the majority of the population, became Christians, as did many Jews among whom the Christian message had first spread. Christianity was also attractive for Zoroastrians, because it offered the concept of individual salvation, and soon began to infiltrate it, initially in the lower social classes.

By the third century, Christianity had permeated all walks of life within the Persian empire, and had begun to threaten the religion of the establishment, Zoroastrianism. The number of Christians increased markedly, not only due to local evangelization but also because many Christians fled from Roman to Persian territories because of persecution of Roman emperors. In addition, the wars between the Persians and the Romans led to prisoners of war being brought from the Roman empire to the Persian empire. The most famous example occurred after the sack of Antioch by Shapur I in AD 253, who brought a large number of Christians from Antioch, Cappadocia, Cilicia and Syria, and settled them in various Persian provinces. They worked as tradesmen and artisans in Mesopotamia and Persia, and must have contributed to spreading the Christian message. Among them was Bishop Demetrius of Antioch, who subsequently served as Bishop of Beth Lapat, also called Gundeshapur.

In Mesopotamia, Adiabene was the most likely possible refuge for those persecuted by the Romans. The size of the Christian community grew markedly, so that by the early third century the church in Mesopotamia had centres in Adiabene,[5] Karka Beth Slokh (Kirkuk), Nisibis, Bet Lapat, Ray Ardashir[6] and Seleucia–Ctesiphon.[7] At the beginning of the fourth century, Bishop Papa (310–329) of Seleucia–Ctesiphon, the capital of the Persian empire, claimed primacy over other bishops within the empire, just as Rome had primacy over other churches within the Roman empire. This incident points to the presence of a large and well-structured church within the Persian empire by the end of the third century.

The growth of the new religion was affected by the differing attitudes of various Persian kings. The initial Arsacid ruling dynasty had no specific policy towards the Christians, who were not yet a threat. However, when the Arsacid ruling dynasty was overthrown by the Sassanid dynasty in the year 224 by King Ardashir I, the latter was faced with the problem of dealing with the Christians. Although he did not recognize them officially as a minority, he respected them and included the church of Kokhe[8] within the new capital he built near Ctesiphon, the remains of which can still be found today near the city of Baghdad.

The fourth century – the great persecution

During the third century, sporadic persecution of the Christians within the Persian empire by different Sassanid rulers took place under the increasing influence of the Zoroastrian priesthood, usually provoked by apostasy from Zoroastrianism. However, the major persecution occurred under King Shapur II between the years 339 and 379 during which there are records of sixteen thousand martyrs. This followed the breakdown of negotiations between Constantine, the first Byzantine emperor who had become a Christian, and Shapur II of the Persians. During political negotiations, Constantine had asked Shapur to protect the Christians (whom he called his people), within the Persian empire. When these negotiations failed the situation became tense, and the loyalty of the Christians within the Persian empire began to be questioned. Christians were commonly accused of collaborating with the Romans; localized persecution occurred in 318, 327 and 339, and susequently became fierce. Shapur II summoned Bishop Shimon Bar Subba'e (Shimon I), and asked him to levy a double tax from the Christians. When the bishop refused, complaining that his people were poor and should not be subjected to such heavy taxes, the king called all the bishops and priests and killed them in front of the patriarch, who was later also executed. This persecution continued until the death of Shapur II in 379, and since it lasted about forty years, it is called 'the forty-year persecution'.

One of the stories of the martyrs of this period especially captures the attention, since there still exists in Iraq a monastery founded in his name. Mar Behnam was a son of an Assyrian King Sennacherib who ruled under Shapur II. While on a hunting expedition he lost his way, and was forced to spend a night in a cave in the mountains north of Mosul. There he met Mar Matta who lived in one of these caves and told him of the new religion. Behnam was greatly impressed by the saint and, having heard of his miraculous powers, he asked him whether he could cure his sister Sarah who was suffering from an incurable skin disease, presumably leprosy. When she was cured by the saint, both Behnam and his sister Sarah became Christians. On hearing the news, their father asked them to renounce their new religion, but they were adamant and continued to profess their new faith. Seeing them defiant, he ordered them to be murdered, and subsequently lost his mind. In an attempt to help him, his wife took him to the place of the execution of Behnam and Sarah, and the king was miraculously cured. The king and his wife then had Mar Matta baptize them, and ordered a monument to be built at the place where his son and daughter died. This place was to become the nucleus of the monastery of Mar Behnam. They also asked Mar Matta what he might want, and a monastery on the mountain where the saint lived was built: it came to be known as Der Mar Matta.

After the death of Shapur II, the situation of the Christians improved, although scattered persecution continued until Yazdgird I came to power in 399. The latter began to negotiate peace with the Byzantines, and diplomatic exchanges between the two empires were initiated. The Christian hierarchy played a major role in these negotiations, and Persian diplomatic missions led by bishops from Mesopotamia were sent to the Byzantine empire. Likewise the Byzantine empire was represented at the Persian court by members of the Byzantine Church. Under the influence of one of the Byzantine delegations, led by the Aramaic Bishop Marutha of Maipherqat, Yazdgird I permitted the release of Christians and the rebuilding of churches.

Notes

1 Paul's letters were written between AD 50 and AD 62 while the four canonical Gospels and the Acts of the Apostles were written between AD 70and AD 100.

2 Based principally on the *Ecclesiastical History* by Eusebius, bishop of Caesarea (AD 260–340), who is considered the father of church history. His account of the history of Christianity from the apostolic age to his own day is the main source for this period.

3 *Edessa the Blessed City*, p. 69.

4 Gillman and Klimkeit, p. 109.

5 Revd W.A. Wigram quotes Mshiha Zakha in the chronicle of Arbela, which gives the succession of the bishops of Arbela and mentions that by 225 Arbela had twenty bishops and eighteen dioceses. However, the authenticity of this source has been questioned by scholars.

6 Ray Ardashiris is near present day Tehran. See glossary and map no. 1.

7 Seleucia–Ctesiphon, the capital of the Persian empire was also called al-Mada'in by the Arabs (the word 'Mada'in' is the plural for 'madina' or city, so 'Mada 'in' means cities). Its remains can be found 30 kilometres south of Baghdad, near a town now called Salman Pak. Al-Mada'in was a complex of several cities (between five and seven according to different historians). The most ancient of these was Seleucia, which was probably an ancient site modernized by Seleucus, Alexander's general, and is situated on the western side of the river Tigris. The second city of this complex was Ctesiphon situated about three miles to the north of Seleucia, on the eastern side of the Tigris. It was most probably a Parthian foundation, becoming their capital when they conquered the Seleucids in 129 BC. The third city is Feh Ardashir which was established by the Sassanid King Ardashir I in the year AD 230. Its site was south of Ctesiphon, east of the river Tigris, in an area of Kokhe which originally contained huts for the servants of the kings: thus the name 'Kokhe' which means 'huts'. When Ardashir built the city there was already a church which he included in his city. At the end of the first century the river Tigris changed its course and caused the region of Kokhe to be west of the Tigris, thus next to Seleucia rather than next to the city of Ctesiphon. Thus the remains of Kokhe are now seen to the west of the river Tigris rather than to the east, as would be expected from its original site.

8 One of the early churches built in the capital of the Persians, Ctesiphon, the remains of which can be seen near the capital of Iraq, Baghdad. Tradition attributes the building of this church to the apostle Mari. The *Acts of Mari* tells that the apostle arrived in the capital of the Persian empire and started to establish a community there. After curing the sister of King Artaban he was given a small site in Kokhe, where

there was a pagan temple. A. Aboona speculates that from this original nucleus a church was built early in the third century.

3

The fifth and sixth centuries

I. The Church of the East

The establishment of the Church of the East as an independent church

When persecution ceased, Christians within the realms of the Persian empire began to organize their church. The first great event that took place in this respect was a call for all the bishops of Mesopotamia and Persia to meet in a synod. The synod was instigated by the the Byzantine ambassador, Bishop Marutha of Maipherqat, who had become a friend of Yazdgird I in view of the services he had rendered him as a skilled physician. With the permission of Yazdgird I, a synod was convened by Bishop Isaac in the year 410. This is the first East Syrian council, also known as the Synod of Isaac.[1] This synod was attended by forty bishops of the Church of the East together with Bishop Marutha. A letter from the Western fathers which Marutha had brought was read and the synod adopted the canons and the creed of Nicea.

The Persian ruler acknowledged the Christians under his rule as a community with some privileges of self-rule and responsibility for their protection. The leader of the church was to manage internal affairs of his community such as marriage, inheritance and personal disputes, and was responsible before the shah for the behaviour of his community and the collection of taxes. The privilege of ordination of the bishops within the Persian empire was given to the bishop of the capital Seleucia–Ctesiphon, while the appointment of the bishop of the capital had to be approved by the Shah. This made the bishop of the capital the definitive head of the church and led to the whole institution being linked to the Persian empire, and it was from that time often called 'The Persian Church'. At this synod six provinces, each with its own metropolitan, were recognized, ten of the bishops being in areas outside metropolitan jurisdiction as far away as Qatar and Ray.

Another synod followed in 424, when Dadisho was bishop, also called the Synod of Dadisho. It was convened in al-Hira, the capital of an Arab vassal state south-west of Baghdad. At this synod, the church in the Persian empire announced its independence from western influence. This was a political move to eliminate any accusations of association or collaboration with the Byzantines. Persecution had restarted at the end of the reign of Yazdgird I, and Bishop Dadisho was imprisoned under the accusation of being a Roman sympathizer. When peace was achieved between the successor of Yazdgird, Bahram V, and the Byzantine emperor Theodosius II, Bishop Dadisho was released and returned to his office. No representative from Antioch or other centres within the Roman empire attended the Synod of Dadisho. The issue of the primacy of the bishop of Seleucia–Ctesiphon was affirmed and it was made clear that no further reference to any other patriarchal throne was necessary, be that Rome or Antioch. This means that in case of controversy, the final judge is the head of Church of the East, the bishop of Seleucia–Ctesiphon. At this stage theologies were not fully defined, and the separation from the Western churches was mainly motivated by politics.

In 486 Bishop Akakios convened a synod in Seleucia–Ctesiphon in which the first definitive creed of the Church of the East was produced which clearly professed Dyophysite theology; it will be discussed later. Thus the official church within the Persian empire had not only become autonomous and autocephalous, but also professed a different theology from other churches in the West. This is not to exclude some of the Christian centres within Mesopotamia who did not agree with this theology, especially in Tikrit and within and around Der Mar Matta. This will be discussed under the second section of this chapter, 'The Syrian Orthodox Church'.

Several other synods of the Church of the East followed. The Synod of Mar Aba I in 544 was important in consolidating the unity of the Church of the East, while Ishoyab I convened a synod in which the doctrinal authority of Theodore of Mopsuestia was affirmed, and his memory blessed.

The patriarch of the Church of the East resided in the capital of the Persian empire, Seleucia–Ctesiphon, where one of the earliest churches of Mesopotamia was built, the church of Kokhe. All bishops were ordained in this church, even after the seat of the patriarch moved to Baghdad in the middle of the eighth century, when the latter became the capital of the newly-established Arab Abbasid dynasty. Other important centres in Mesopotamia were those of Adiabene, Nisibis, Hira and Basra.

Independence from the Western church meant complete separation from the Byzantine empire and closer links with the Sassanid shah. The Church of the East thus became a national church with greater freedom of movement within the Persian empire, and came to be called 'the Persian Church'.

Expansion of the Church of the East

Soon after gaining independence and autonomy, the Church of the East embarked on vigorous activity, sending missions eastwards to Iran, Central Asia and China, and southwards to regions of the Persian Gulf, Yemen, and other parts of the Arabian peninsula and as far as Socotra. Wherever they went they took books with them and established schools, hospitals and monasteries.

Iran

Christianity had reached Iran in the early centuries. Among the nations that responded to the Christian message on the day of Pentecost were 'Parthians and Medes and Elamites'(Acts 2:9).

Historically-documented Christian centres were established from the fourth century, especially in Elam (southwest Iran, also called Rew Ardashir), Ray (present-day Tehran) and Gundeshapur also called Beth Lapat. In the latter a monastery is known to have been built in 367, and a school was established in the sixth century. The school had two separate institutions, a theological and a medical school: both were under the jurisdiction of the metropolitan of the Church of the East.

In east Iran (Khurasan), the cities of Merv and Herat were the seats of bishoprics and were represented in the first synod of the Church of the East in 410. Both became seats of a metropolitan in the middle of the sixth century. From these early centres, missions were sent eastwards to Central Asia and China.

Central Asia

Central Asia and Bactria are wide expanses of land that link Iran and the rest of the Middle East with China. They contained a wide system of interlaced routes, well-known as the Silk Route, along which traders travelled to China looking mainly for silk. Missionaries and monks of the great world religions travelled along this route together with traders, political envoys, and soldiers. This is why it is not surprising that news of Christians might have travelled fast in these areas.

It has already been mentioned in chapter 2 that the presence of Christians in Bactria was noted by Bardaisan, who wrote at the end of the second century. In addition a document, whose author is unknown and which is dated to about 250 (*The Doctrine of the Apostles*), speaks of Christians among the Gilanians on the Caspian Sea and Turks on the Oxus river.[2]

However, definite evidence of an established Christian

presence in this area only occurs several centuries later. Recent archaeological evidence has revealed the presence of well established Christian communities in west Turkestan[3] by the sixth century AD.[4] Texts have been found which indicate that Sogdians, an east Iranian people, were active in translating Syriac Christian texts into their language. The patriarch of the Church of the East, Timothy I, who was of paramount importance for the spread of Christianity eastwards, tells of a Turkish king who had adopted the Christian religion of his church.[5] In one of his letters he tells of the king of the Turks who had become a Christian and had asked him to ordain a metropolitan for them: 'The king of the Turks, with nearly all his country, has left his ancient idolatry, and become a Christian, and he had requested us in his letters to create a Metropolitan for his country; and this we have done'.[6] He also wrote that after ordaining a bishop for the Turks he was going to ordain one for Tibet.

By the ninth century, Samarkand had become a metropolitanate of the Church of the East. From west Turkestan, Christianity made considerable advances and by the tenth century had reached east Turkestan.[7]

China

Christians may have been present in China as early as the sixth century. However, the main spread of Christianity in China occurred during the period of the Tang dynasty (AD 618–907), when China had political control over wide areas and came in contact with many cultures. The emperor T'ai-tsung (626–49) officially received the first Christian missionary A-lo-pen. The official decree he issued in 638 mentions the Persian monk A-lo-pen bringing scriptures and a new religion to China, speaks of its teaching as mysterious, wonderful and calm, fixes on the essentials of life and perfection and announces that it is right that it should spread within the empire.[8]

Our main source of information for the activities of the Church of the East in China comes from the famous monument of Xian, erected in 781 in the premises of a monastery that belonged to the Church of the East. It was discovered by a Jesuit priest during archaeological work in AD 1623.[9] The text is written in Chinese, giving a short history of the Christian religion which is called 'The Luminous Religion of Ta Ch'in' from the arrival of the Christian monk A-lo-pen to the time of the inscription. The monument narrates the grand reception of A-lo-pen by the Emperor T'ai-tsung in AD 635, and mentions the names of four subsequent Chinese emperors who supported this religion, as well as a man called Essu, a Nestorian priest and a general in the Chinese army, who was responsible for the erection of the monument. The tablet also mentions the translation of scriptures into Chinese, the establishment in the capital of the empire of the Ta Ch'in monastery with its twenty-one monks, and that the portrait of the emperor was painted on the wall of the monastery, pointing to the close relationship between the emperor and the new religion. The names of the monks and priests written in Syriac on the sides of the monument comprise one hundred and twenty-eight persons including the author of the text, a priest of the Church of the East called Adam, whose Chinese name is Ching-Ching.

In addition to this monument several manuscripts were found at the beginning of this century in walled grottoes in Tunhuang in Northern China which included several works translated into Chinese: a discovery which points to Christianity being well established in China by the eighth century. To quote Baum and Winkler: 'By the turn of the millennium, more than 500 writings including the entire New Testament and a few books of the Old Testament had been translated from Syriac to Chinese'.[10]

Christianity continued to flourish in China until the ninth century, growing to ten provinces with four metropolitanates by the end of the eighth century.

In the ninth century there are many pointers to a gradual decline, intensified when a general persecution of foreign religions began in 845. Thousands of monks and nuns, Buddhists as well as Christians, were forced to return to secular life, and massacres are reported. The decline of Christianity continued, and by the end of the tenth century the Church of the East was practically extinct in China.

There was a revival of Christianity during the thirteenth and fourteenth centuries in China after Kublai Khan established the Yu'an Mongol dynasty in 1271. Most Mongol kings displayed considerable tolerance of religion, especially of Christianity. Kublai Khan's mother, Sorghoqtani, was a Christian, but though he expressed interest in Christian learning and was open to Christian influences, he himself never converted.

The famous Venetian traveller Marco Polo[11] describes in his travel accounts how the khan celebrated the major Christian feasts at his court, and notes that many Christians of the Church of the East were active in his administration.

India

Tradition attributes the presence of Christians on the west coast of the Indian subcontinent to the apostle Thomas, one of the twelve disciples of Jesus. A story tells of the arrival of Thomas in India in order to build a palace for a 'King Gundaphar'. He was given a large sum of money by the king in order to begin building the royal palace, but Thomas felt indignant at the countless poor he saw, and could not bring himself to build a palace that would provide more luxury to the king. He went around distributing the money to the poor and performing miracles and cures. When the king asked him about the progress of the work, Thomas answered that the palace was finished. When the king asked to be shown the buildings, Thomas answered that the palace was not on earth but in heaven. After Thomas was put in prison, the king in a dream saw his deceased brother who told him about the palace which Thomas had built for him in heaven. Waking, the king sent for Thomas and asked him to preach to him his message of salvation, and then to baptize him. On his becoming a Christian, the whole population of his kingdom followed.[12] While the detail of the story may be legendary, recent excavations have unearthed coins with the name of King Gundaphar which have been dated to the first century. Moreover, travel by sea to the west coast of India was a fairly frequent occurrence in those days. These facts, together with the strength of the tradition of the associa- tion of Thomas with the evangelization of India, suggest that an early connection was indeed established.

Historical evidence is available for the presence of wel- established Christian communities in India by the middle of the third century, even possibly from the end of the second century. The Christian community in India had early connections with the Church of the East. David, the bishop of Basra, visited Kerala in 296–7. Subsequently John of Edessa was appointed as third bishop in India by the patriarch of the Church of the East in 354 . Timothy I is also known to have consecrated a bishop for India at the beginning of the ninth century, and by the end of the same century it had become a metropolitanate of the Church of the East. Its priests were sent to be educated in Mesopotamia, and patriarchal links between the metro- politanate of India and the Church of the East continued down to the sixteenth century.

The early presence of such Christians in India is substantiated by the fact that the Syriac tradition is still followed in their liturgy.

The Arabs

Arabs are mentioned amongst those who heard the Chris- tian message at Pentecost (Acts 2:11) and Paul states that he spent three years in Arabia after his conversion in Damascus (Gal. 1:17–18). The emperor Marcus Julius Philipus (244–49), known as Philip of the Arabs, was a Christian. He was contemporary with the first known Arab bishop of Jerusalem. Many other bishops were later ordained for Arab Christian communities in areas within both Sassanid and Roman empires as well as in the Arabian peninsula, so that by 451 there were eighteen metropolitans and bishops representing various Arab communities at the Council of Chalcedon.

In Mesopotamia, Arabs from the tribe of Tanukh settled in an area west of the Euphrates, a few miles south of Kufa, at the beginning of the third century. They lived first in tents, which in time developed to a permanent settlement called al-Hira.[13] This eventually became the capital of a small vassal Arab kingdom, the Lakhmids, that co-operated with the Sassanids.

Christianity was already well established amongst the Arabs of al-Hira by 380. Al-Hira was represented by a bishop in the Synod of Isaac that was convened in Seleucia–Ctesiphon in 410, while the Synod of Dadisho was convened in al-Hira itself (see table 3).

Although the Lakhmid kings did not officially convert to Christianity until much later, they were kindly disposed to it, which led to the conversion of a considerable number of its population to Christianity. Arab writers referred to the Arabs of al-Hira as 'Ibad', a word which means worshippers (of Christ).

Many Lakhmid kings had mothers and sisters who were Christians. The Lakhmid king al-Mundhir III was surnamed 'ibn Ma' al-Sama' after his Christian mother Mariyah whose sobriquet was 'Ma'al-Sama' meaning 'water from heaven'. His wife, Hind, was a Christian princess, and their son Amru was also given the sobriquet 'ibn Hind' after his mother. Hind is known to have established a monastery that was called *'Der Hind al-Kubra'*[14] which existed until the second century of Islam, in which there was an inscription in which Hind calls herself 'The maid of Christ and the mother of his slave and the daughter of his slaves'.[15] Another Christian princess, the daughter of Nu'man III, was patron of the building of Der al-Lajja, a monatery that was named after her. Recent excavations have shown remains of several churches and monasteries near the towns of Najaf and Karbala where the Lakhmid Arab kings ruled.[16]

Only the last king of the Lakhmids was baptized: al-Nu'man III (580–602). He was assassinated by Khosrau II, probably for disloyalty, after which the Lakhmids revolted against the Sassanids and constantly raided

Persian territory until the appearance of Islam in the seventh century.

Al-Hira became a very important centre for the Church of the East, from which missions were sent south to the Arabian peninsula. There is little information about the missions of the Church of the East to Arabia at early stages, but it is probable that it was from al-Hira that missions were sent to christianize Najran.[17]

In earliest times, the Christian message was probably carried to Arabia by hermits who found suitable solitude in desert areas. Traders too must have played a significant role as Arabs were important middlemen in the caravan trade between the Arabian peninsula, Mesopotamia and the Byzantine empire. West Syrian sources refer to a native trader called Hannan who was converted to Christianity during a visit to al-Hira, and took his faith back to Najran where he converted his family and many members of his tribe. Moreover, since there was a significant Jewish presence in southern Arabia, especially in Najran, Jewish converts to Christianity could have brought the Christian message to Arabia.

During the early sixth century , the Christians of Najran were persecuted by Dhu al Nuwas, the Himyarite king of Yemen who put many of them to death. The Christians sought help from the Byzantines and Abyssinia, who came to their help and established control over al-Yemen. Abraha, who was appointed governor of Yemen, built a great cathedral there. When Yemen became a Persian province in 597, the Church of the East started to send its missionaries there and established its form of Christianity within the Arabian peninsula proper.

There were also significant Arab Christian communities in Basra and many areas of the Gulf (Qatar, Bahrain and Kharj). A bishopric of the Church of the East is reported in Bet Qatraye (modern Qatar) in 225 and its bishop certainly attended the Synod of Isaac in 410. Excavations have revealed evidence of a monastery in Qatar that has been dated to the end of the third century, as well as in other areas along the western shore of the Persian Gulf in

Bahrain and Kharj, all belonging to the Church of the East.

Missionaries of the Church of the East also made their way to Yemen once it came under Persian control in 597. East Syrian Christianity flourished during this period in Yemen and Najran until the coming of Islam at the beginning of the seventh century. Although a large number of Christians became Muslims or had to leave the Arabian Peninsula during the Radda Wars,[18] there continued to be numerous Arab Christians in the Arabian peninsula, especially in Yemen. Patriarch Timothy I appointed a bishop for Yemen and San'a' as late as the end of the eighth century.

Socotra
Missionary expansion of the Church of the East to the island of Socotra dates back to the sixth century. The presence of Christians on the island was reported by Marco Polo in the thirteenth century, who wrote with surprise that a bishop there did not owe allegiance to the pope in Rome but to the patriarch in Baghdad.

Theology of the Church of the East

We have seen in the first chapter that discussion regarding the nature of the person of Jesus led to the councils of Ephesus and Chalcedon, and how after each of these councils, schism within the Church ensued. The council of Ephesus deposed Nestorius from his post as Bishop of Constantinople and confirmed the term 'Theotokos' or 'Bearer of God' in its definition of Mary. Those Christians who followed the theology of Theodore of Mopsuestia were called 'Nestorians', and were considered heretics.

The Church of the East was not represented in the council of Ephesus which deposed Nestorius, nor did they choose the name for themselves. In fact, members of the Church of the East had made their opposition known to the use of this name for their church from early times. The tenth century Arab writer al-Mas'udi mentions that adherents of the Church of the East reject the designation

'Nestorian' which had originated with the Byzantines, and that their patriarch had written that the name Nestorian for their church was incorrect, as Nestorius neither spoke the language of the Church of the East, nor was he its patriarch. The Church of the East did not follow Nestorius: rather, Nestorius followed it.

Most Christian centres in Mesopotamia had followed the theology of Theodore of Mopsuestia from an early time. His theology was officially taught in the 'school of the Persians' in Edessa, and his works were translated into the Syriac language by its Bishop Ibas (435–57).

The theology of the Church of the East was officially consolidated in a synod convened by Akakios in the capital Seleucia–Ctesiphon in 486. The profession of faith of this Synod is preserved and states:

> Let our faith in the dispensation of Christ be in the confession of two natures, of the divinity and the humanity, while none of us shall dare to introduce mixture, mingling or confusion into the differences of these two natures; rather, while the divinity remains preserved in what belongs to it, it is to a single Lordship and to a single object of worship that we gather together the exemplars of these two natures, because of the perfect and inseparable conjunction that has occurred for the divinity in respect to the humanity. And if someone considers, or teaches others, that suffering and change have attached to the divinity of our Lord, and if he does not preserve, with respect to the union of the *prosopon* of our Saviour, a confession of perfect God and perfect man, let such person be anathema.[19]

The final formulation of the theology of the Church of the East came at the beginning of the seventh century with Mar Babai the Great, who denied any doctrine which mixed human and divine qualities. A statement he made was incorporated in the liturgy:

> One is Christ the son of God, worshipped by all in two

natures. In His Godhead begotten of the Father without beginning before all time. In His manhood born of Mary, in the fullness of time in a united body. Neither His Godhead was of the nature of the mother, nor His manhood of the nature of the Father. The natures are preserved in their Qnōmē, in one person and one Sonship.[20]

Babai the Great was one of the most outstanding figures of the Church of the East, who led it during a period of vacancy of the patriarchate from 608–28. His literary legacy is enormous and his theological formulation was used during a debate that occurred between the Syrian Orthodox community and that of the Church of the East before the Sassanid Shah Khosroe II.[21] He clarified the position of the Church of the East regarding the nature of Christ as 'Christ in two Kyane (natures), with their two Qnōmē and one parsopa', the official repudiation of the term '*Yaldat Alaha*' (*Theotokos* or bearer of God), and confirmed the term '*Yaldat Mshiha*' (*Christotokos* or bearer of Christ).

In the formulation of Trinitarian theology, the Syriac term *Qnōma* was equated with the Greek term *hypostasis*. However in the Christology of Babai, *qnōma* did not denote a self-existing hypostasis but, as he described it in his book *The Book of Union*, each *Kyana* or *Physis*, or the abstract nature, in order to exist concretely needs a *Qnōma*. Here *Qnōma* points to concrete existence which the abstract nature needs in order to exist concretely. And that these two natures with their two *Qnōmē* unite in one *parsopa*. Thus the misconception regarding the theology of the Church of the East, that Christ exists in two natures and two persons, because Qnoma was initially used to denote 'person'. For the Church of the East, Christ exists in two natures with their two Qnōmē, but there is only one person.

The culture of the Church of the East

The Syriac language and culture were the mainstay of the Church of the East. As was described in chapter 1, all converts to Christianity, whether Persians, Arabs or Indians, learned Syriac, the Aramaic dialect of Edessa, and in time Syriac became synonymous with Christian. This was the case in Mesopotamia as much as it was in Syria, Palestine and southern Turkey. The liturgy was performed in the Syriac language in all churches wherever they happened to be established, regardless of the nationality or the language of their congregation. For example, it was common for the Arab Christians of the Church of the East to call themselves the Syrian Arabs. In their centres of learning, the main language was Syriac, although by the end of the fourth century Greek language, rhetoric and philosophy were taught in nearly all these places.

Syriac Christian literature flourished from the second Christian century. However, only a small number of these texts survive from early periods. The writings of Bardaisan and Tatian belong to the second and early third centuries; however, these writers were later considered heretical. It has already been mentioned that the Diatessaron of Tatian belongs to the second century and was used extensively in the area of the Middle East. The Acts of Thomas, the Odes of Solomon and the translation of the Old Testament from the Hebrew to the Syriac language also belong to this early period. The Odes of Solomon are of special interest: a set of poetic hymns on salvation, whose author is unknown, dated to the end of the first and the beginning of the second centuries. The Acts of Thomas, which relates the story of the Apostle Thomas preaching in India, belongs to the third century. Incorporated in the Acts of Thomas are two older poems, the Song of the Bride of Light and the Song of the Pearl. However, the most important work of second century Syriac literature is the Syriac translation of the Old Testament from the Hebrew original.

To the fourth century belong two great figures, Aphrahat and Ephrem Syrus. It has to be stressed here that these early Syriac writers are claimed by all Syriac-speaking Christians and are not exclusive to the Church of the East, since they wrote and taught before the separation of churches. Both Ephrem Syrus and Aphrahat are equally revered by the Syrian Orthodox Christians as well as members of the Church of the East.

The Persian sage Aphrahat (d.345)

Aphrahat is one of the earliest great East Syrian fathers; he is also called 'The Persian Sage'. He was born in northern Mesopotamia, and converted to Christianity as a young man. He became a 'Son of the Covenant', an ascetic group famous at the time (see the section on asceticism and mysticism), which he considered central to the life of the Church. He seems to have held an important ecclesiastical position, most probably as a bishop. Our knowledge of him comes from twenty-three 'Demonstrations' which have also been called homilies. He wrote only in the Syriac language, and was orthodox in his approach. His theology showed no awareness of Western Hellenistic Christianity current at the time, rather a strong influence from the Jewish tradition. Amongst the themes he discussed were the Passover and circumcision. He also witnessed and wrote about the forty-years persecution of Shapur II. Later tradition linked him with Mar Matta monastery.

Saint Ephrem the Syrian (c.306–73)

Born in Nisibis, most probably to Christian parents, he was ordained deacon by its bishop, Jacob of Nisibis[22] and became a 'Son of the Covenant'. He moved from Nisibis to Edessa in AD 363 when the former city was ceded by the Sassanids. He settled in Edessa, where most of his important works were written. In Edessa he was surprised to find the multiplicity of Christian sects and noted that Orthodox Christians were a minority called 'Palutians' after one of their bishops.

He wrote only in Syriac, eschewing Greek terminology and philosophy, even though he seems to have been well acquainted with them. Like Aphrahat he used Jewish typology and symbolism in his exegeses. His voluminous theological, exegetical and ascetic writings are expressed mostly in verse, and their inspiration was mainly scriptural. His hymns and other writings were translated into Greek and Armenian from a very early time, and later into Slavonic and many other European languages. Over 500 genuine hymns survive, often of great beauty and insight. They were arranged after his death into hymn cycles of which the most famous are those on faith, paradise, and the descent of Christ into hell.

Several of his hymns were also written to counter heresy. In his 'Hymns against heresies' he wrote against syncretism, astrology and magic and was specially vehement against the Arians, Manicheans and the Marcionites[23] who had a strong presence in Edessa and surrounding regions at this time. In these writings, Ephrem cites the marks of the true church as follows: first, the use of Jesus' name and title to designate the Church. Second, the importance of apostolic succession and continuity in the laying of hands from the first Apostles. Third, the possession of integral scripture along with the sacraments and the profession of the Nicene creed.

He also wrote biblical commentaries on various Old Testament books and the Diatessaron (the New Testament version in use at his time. See chapter 2, under Tatian). His commentary on the Diatessaron is of special importance since it provides much information about the sequence and structure of this lost work. His liturgical poetry had great influence on the development of Greek and Syriac hymnology. Although he considered asceticism and suffering to be at the centre of the Christian message, he was not oblivious of the poor and sick, and appreciated the importance of learning in the Christian life. During the plague he was active in relief work and, in addition to his writings, he taught in the school of Edessa which became famous thanks to him. Deservedly he is considered the most celebrated father of Syriac Christianity. He is equally revered by East and West Syrians, as he lived and wrote before their separation into East and West Syrian Churches. He was declared a Doctor of the Church in 1920 by Pope Benedict XV.

The 'school of Edessa', or the 'school of the Persians'
The origin of this school is difficult to ascertain, though some have traced it to the middle of the second century. However, it became associated with St Ephrem when he moved to Edessa in 363, after his home town, Nisibis, was ceded by the Sassanids. St Ephrem taught biblical exegesis as well as doctrinal matters, using Syriac only and avoiding Greek philosophy, although there is evidence that he was well acquainted with it.

After St Ephrem the school became sensitive to both Syriac and Greek traditions and in it many Greek works were translated into the Syriac language. Gradually the school became multidisciplinary, teaching not only theology, liturgy and biblical studies but also philosophy, medicine, natural sciences, secular history, geography, music, and languages.

In the field of theology, it took part in the Christological debates of the fourth century and defined itself within the sphere of the Dyophysite theology of the 'school of Antioch', which stressed the humanity of Jesus, as opposed to the 'school of Alexandria' which stressed His divinity. In this it followed the theology of Theodore of Mopsuestia, who was dubbed 'The Interpreter', and became the bastion of Dyophysite theology. Within its precincts, the writings of Theodore of Mopsuestia were translated from Greek into Syriac early in the fifth century, as well as other Greek works. The philosophical works of Aristotle were translated from Greek to Syriac in this period, as Aristotelian logic was considered very important in various debates.

This school became the main centre of education for members of the Church of the East. As we have seen in the theological section, the Church of the East adopted the theology of Theodore of Mopsuestia, blessed the memory of Nestorius, became independent from the Church in the West and was more associated with the Persian empire. Consequently this school began to be called the 'school of the Persians' since it provided services for members of the Church of the East who resided mainly in the realms of the

Persian empire. This name has specific connotations as it signifies segregation of East Syrian versus West Syrian schools of thought before the official separation of churches. In this school, students from the Persian empire studied while the West Syrians and the Armenians founded their own schools.

The school came under attack after the Council of Ephesus in 431. The bishop of Edessa, Rabbula, was pro-Miaphysite and attempted to change the theological orientation of the school. In his quest of conformity, in 435 he also outlawed the Diatessaron, in favour of the four separate gospels. He made commentaries on The Peshitta, which is the Syriac version of the four canonical Gospels used in Antioch, and enforced it as the official version instead of the Diatessaron.[24]

The school was formally closed by the emperor Zeno in the year 489; most of its members fled to Nisibis and founded a school there, which soon became the principal teaching centre for the Church of the East.

The school of Nisibis

The school of Nisibis was founded within the realm of the Sassanid empire after the closure of the 'school of the Persians' in Edessa at the end of the fifth century. Christianity within the Persian empire had been flourishing especially after the act of toleration in 410. The school was founded by the bishop of Nisibis, Barsoma, who selected an able principal, Narsai, gathered tutors and pupils, and found quarters for them. The majority of the tutors including the principal, Narsai, had fled from persecution in Edessa.

The school soon became the beacon of the Church of the East, where most of its clergy were educated. It was structured on the model of the 'school of the Persians' in Edessa, following the theology of Theodore of Mopsuestia.

Some of the original statutes of the 'school of Nisibis' survive, giving an insight into how the school was run.[25] The students were highly disciplined and were expected to raise their funds by working in summer. Many teachers, missionaries and leaders of monastic communities and members of the hierarchy of the Church of the East were trained in this school over the years. In fact, until the seventh century, almost every leader and theologian of the Church of the East was educated at the school of Nisbis. And within its precincts many Greek philosophical and religious texts were translated into Syriac. Narsai, the first principal of the school, was one of the most brilliant personalities and intellectuals of the Church of the East, and had the epithet: 'the harp of the Holy Spirit'. He was a great poet, preacher, exegete, and theologian, perhaps the greatest poet–theologian the Church of the East can exclusively claim, since Ephrem and Aphrahat belonged to the era before the formal division of the East and West Syriac Churches. Of the 300 homilies attributed to him, eighty are still extant.

The school of Seleucia-Ctesiphon

As the Church of the East expanded in Mesopotamia, many more centres of learning were established. Mar Aba I founded the theological school of Seleucia–Ctesiphon in the middle of the sixth century. He was a high-ranking Zoroastrian who after converting to Christianity studied in the school of Nisibis and travelled extensively. On his return to Persia he taught in the school of Nisibis, wrote many biblical commentaries and translated numerous Greek works into the Syriac language. He was a holy man with great knowledge of the Scriptures and was elected catholicos in 540.

Soon after his election as patriarch of the Church of the East, he convened a synod in 544 and succeeded in consolidating his Church.

The school of Gundeshapur

The school of Gundeshapur was founded by Khosroes Anusharwan I (531–78), and became especially famous for its medical school, which was founded by 'Nestorian' refugees from the Byzantine empire during persecution of non-Chalcedonians: it was to outlive the Sassanid state. Situated within present-day Persia, almost all of its staff were members of the Church of the East, and it continued to train generations of physicians who served several Persian and later Arab rulers. Anusharwan also granted asylum to pagan philosophers who were driven out of the Platonic academy of Athens which was closed in AD 529 by Justinian.[26]

Asceticism and mysticism

Syriac Christianity had a strong ascetic character from its early beginnings. Both Ephrem and Aphrahat belonged to the ascetic group called 'the Sons of the Covenant'. This is probably the earliest recognizable ascetic community to emerge amongst Syriac Christians. Its members included both men and women, who did not marry and lived within the community. They considered virginity synonymous with holiness and stressed the 'circumcision of the heart', a term meaning 'the elimination of all carnal desires', as a requisite before baptism. They considered themselves the backbone of the church and were involved in all its activities. Although by this time it was a common ascetic practice to live a solitary life in the desert or mountains, they did not separate themselves from the community and took an active part in helping the sick and the needy.

At the same time, hermits who lived a solitary life in the mountains and deserts flourished and became an important feature of Eastern Christianity. By the end of the fourth century, groups of them started to live together, forming the nucleus of monastic life. The traditional founder of monasticism in Mesopotamia is Mar Awgin (died 370), who is thought to have brought the idea from Egypt. With seventy brothers, he settled in Mount Izla[27] at the end of the fourth century, where a famous monastery was later built.

Through the reforms of one of its leaders, Abraham of Kashgar (d. 588), this monastery became the bastion of orthodoxy for the Church of the East and subsequently earned control of sixty monasteries within the realms of the Persian empire. He laid down the rules for the monastic life depending on the authority of scriptures and tradition of the fathers emphasizing the life of prayer, discipline, hard work, gentleness and unity in love.

Another monastery that goes back to the early fifth century in Mesopotamia is Der Mar Matta, situated north west of the city of Mosul.[28] Other monasteries still in existence around Mosul are: Der Rabban Hurmiz, Der Mar Georgis, Der Mar Mikha'il, and Der Mar Behnam. Archaeological discoveries have revealed remains of many other monasteries and churches at al-Hira, Seleucia–Ctesiphon, Tikrit and other towns in Iraq.

Two outstanding seventh- and eighth-century figures wrote treatises on mysticism.

Isaac of Nineveh

He was born in Qatar but spent most of his life in Mesopotamia. He was made bishop of Nineveh in AD 767, but relinquished his see after only five months and retired to lead a solitary life in the mountains. He later moved to the monastery of Rabban Shapur where he devoted himself to writing about his mystical experiences. Twenty-eight of his discourses have survived and collected under the title *The Mystic treatises* or *De Perfecta Religiosa*. His writings transcended ecclesiastical barriers and soon found their way to the monks of the monastery of St Saba in Jerusalem where they were translated into the Greek language. After that they were translated into Arabic, Georgian, Slavonic and Latin and, more recently, many Western European languages.

Yuhanna al-Dalyatha, or John the elder

He was born at the end of the seventh century in a small village in Iraq situated between Duhok and Zäkho. He led a solitary life in the Hakkäri mountains of southern Turkey in an area called al-Dalyatha. He faced opposition from church leaders, which led Patriarch Timothy I to prohibit the reading of his publications soon after his death. However, his writings continued to circulate among the monks, and many are still extant (28 articles, 51 letters). It has recently been shown that some of the works of Yuhanna Dalyatha have been ascribed to Isaac of Nineveh.

Both Isaac of Nineveh and Yuhanna al-Dalyatha wrote about the achievement of God's love and the attainment of the consummate union between God and the human being. They both explained the stages necessary to the achievement of the ecstasy of union with God. These included asceticism, purification, prayer, illumination and finally the beatific vision.

Both had considerable influence on mysticism, not only in Mesopotamia but on a wider scale, as their writings were soon translated into many languages, including Greek and Arabic. They were read by monks and mystics of all Christian denominations, and since they were translated to Arabic, they could have influenced early Muslim Sufism.

The reputation of holiness amongst ascetics and monks made them candidates to lead their community. Many were taken out of their monasteries to become bishops, patriarchs or missionaries. The influence of ascetics and monks had become so important early in the Christian history of the church in Mesopotamia that, during the Synod of Isaac in 410, some of the canons were directed at their control and an assistant bishop was appointed to supervise them.

II. The Syrian Orthodox Church

Introduction

When talking of the Syrian Orthodox Church, it should be noted that the term 'Syrian' in the title of this church does not refer to the country of Syria, but to the Syriac language, a dialect of Aramaic. The Christian communities that emerged in Syria, in and around the city of Antioch, were Syriac-speaking people, sharing in a Syriac culture, and the church that emerged from this background consequently takes the name 'Syrian'.

Evangelization had started in Syria very early indeed. Paul was on his way to persecute the Christians in Damascus about ten years after the death of Jesus when he had the famous vision of Jesus, leading to his extraordinary conversion (Acts 9:1–19). He was later brought by Barnabas to Antioch, the capital of the Roman province of Syria, where one of the most successful Christian communities came into being (Acts 11:25–26). Antioch soon became one of the earliest and most important centres of Christendom. It was in Antioch that the Christian message was preached for the first time to the Greeks (Acts 11:20). It was also from Antioch that the first missions were sent to the West (Acts 13:1–2), and it was in Antioch that those who believed in Jesus were for the first time called Christians (Acts 11:26).

Most of the population of Syria were pagan Aramaeans, and they were receptive to the Christian message. Antioch was an important cultural and commercial centre and a cosmopolitan city where East and West met. It was a multiracial and multilingual city in which both Hellenistic and Aramaean cultures flourished, although, in Syrian territory with most of its inhabitants Syriac-speaking, its élite thinkers had long been grounded in Greek culture and philosophy.

By the time of Constantine, Antioch had become one of three major centres of Christianity; the other two were Rome and Alexandria. During the Council of Nicea these three centres were recognised as patriarchates and apostolic sees, equal in faith and jurisdiction. Under the patriarchate of Antioch were the bishoprics of Syria, Mesopotamia and Asia Minor. Under the patriarchate of Alexandria were Egypt, Ethiopia and North Africa, while under the patriarchate of Rome were the churches of Europe. The patriarchate of Constantinople was added in AD 381, and that of Jerusalem in 451.

Antioch took an active part in the various intellectual

controversies of the time, and was one of the central and dynamic forces in the formation of doctrine and creed in the various ecumenical councils. The theological school of Antioch was unlike that of Alexandria; it was not a single institution or establishment, but consisted of several separate units each centred around a particular famous teacher. The eminent teachers of Antioch include such figures as Lucian of Antioch (martyred 312), John Chrysostom (died 404), Diodor (died 407), Theodore of Mopsuestia (died 428), and Theodoret (died 458). These theologians were well grounded in the Greek language and philosophy, and used Greek philosophical methods in their formulation of Christian doctrine and theology. However, their style of interpretation was at variance with the school of Alexandria. Antiochene theologians used a historical approach, stressing the actual reality of the text, while the Alexandrian school used spiritual and allegorical interpretation and was less interested in the historical dimensions of the text. Other theologians connected with Antioch preferred the Alexandrian theological tradition, as represented above all by Cyril of Alexandria. Among these were the Syrian Orthodox theologians Philoxenus of Mabbug (died AD 523), writing in Syriac, and Severus of Antioch (died 538), writing in Greek.

The Antiochene liturgy, one of the earliest and most beautiful to be produced in the Middle East, was sung using the West Syriac dialect. It draws mainly on material translated from the Greek liturgical texts of Antioch, but also from Edessa and Jerusalem, and includes Syriac hymns. In spite of the Hellenization of its educated élite, the Christian community in Antioch and the rest of the Middle East continued to uphold Syriac culture and language.

The establishment of the Syrian Orthodox Church as an independent church

The Syrian Orthodox Church emerged gradually as an independent community after the council of Chalcedon in

451, one of several groups of Christians in the Middle East region who did not agree with the decisions of the council. The majority of religious leaders and laity in present-day Syria, Palestine and Lebanon, as well as those in Egypt, condemned the two-nature Christology of this council and refused to abide by its decision. This eventually led to the separation of the body of the West Syrian Church and the Coptic Church from the Byzantine and Roman Churches. Later the Ethiopian and Armenian churches sided with the former, and all followed the theology of Cyril of Alexandria. The church of Mesopotamia was not represented in the council of Chalcedon and was not affected by its consequences, as it was based outside the Roman empire and was not involved in councils convened by Roman emperors.

Although the immediate apparent reason for this schism lies in theological differences, other factors – political, ethnic, cultural and social – contributed. All have been shown to be of importance in the eventual separation of these churches. The Byzantine Church was seen as the upholder of imperial policy, while a spirit of independence and self-consciousness had been one of the hallmarks of early Syriac Christianity. The Syriac cultural identity as well as the ethnic cohesion of the people seems to have been threatened by what was seen and felt to be the enforcement of an imperially-supported decision.

The West Syrian communities who refused the decisions of the council of Chalcedon were then called 'Monophysites' by their detractors, the Byzantines, in reference to the one nature Christology which they adopted. Similarly, those West Syrians who abided by the decisions of the council of Chalcedon came to be known as the 'Malkites'. This word is derived from the Aramaic word *Malka* or king, and means the men of the king. It was implied that they sided by the decisions of the king or emperor.

Both terms are misnomers and better avoided, since they were used by the opposing parties in a derogatory way and are not appropriate. The term 'Monophysite' was used to describe the Christology of a theologian called

Eutyches, whose teaching was denounced not only by the council of Chalcedon but also by the Syrian Orthodox Church. He seems to have confused the human and the divine nature of Jesus, and taught that the human nature became mingled with the divine nature after the union, and its attributes confused. According to Eutyches the humanity of Jesus is somehow absorbed by His divinity. He is consubstantial with the Father alone.

Those who rejected the decisions of the council of Chalcedon did not follow the theology of Eutyches but that of Cyril of Alexandria. The formula of Cyril of Alexandria is 'One is the incarnate nature of the Word of God'. However, his Christology ensures that Christ is fully human and fully divine, that He pre-existed in two distinct natures which united at the incarnation without mingling, confusion, separation or division, to become one nature. Accordingly, Jesus is consubstantial with the Father and with us humans, i.e. fully God and fully human. The term 'Miaphysite' is now given to this theology, as the Greek word Miaphysite expresses this composite nature, with each preserving its own characteristics, after the union.

After the council of Chalcedon the situation in Syria and Egypt became chaotic, with alternating Chalcedonian and non-Chalcedonian leaders of the church in Antioch and Alexandria. Conflict between the two communities continued at all levels within Syria and Egypt, and some theologians began to construct a compromise theology in order to appease the two parties. Such a possible solution was called 'the Henoticon', a theological formula that was prepared by Bishop Peter of Antioch. It was supported by Emperor Zeno (474–91), who found it a good compromise for both parties. Despite some initial acceptance, it met fierce opposition from the Chalcedonians and threatened schism with Rome.

After the failed attempt by Emperor Zeno to contain the Miaphysites, Byzantine emperors began to enforce the decisions of the council of Chalcedon on all the believers within their empire. Patriarch Severus of Antioch was deposed in a synod convened on the orders of Emperor Justin in 518, and was forced to take refuge with the patriarch of Alexandria in order to save his life. This was followed by the removal of fifty-four bishops from their sees during the period of 521–7. Monks were driven out of their monasteries and pressure put on many priests to conform. The turmoil that followed in the life of the communities, due to an acute shortage of clergy, led one of their bishops, Johannan of Tella, to ordain priests in a clandestine fashion. He travelled extensively between Persia, Armenia and Syria encouraging people, ordaining priests and deacons and raising the spirits of the community.

Justinian followed Emperor Justin in 527. He was a theologian of no mean merit and although his leanings were to the Chalcedonians, he was open to the Miaphysites, and was determined to restore unity. His wife Theodora shared his interest in religion, but was secretly Miaphysite. Persecution stopped, and in 531 the emperor issued an order permitting the exiled monks to return to their monasteries, and ordering bishops to present themselves at Constantinople. The community breathed a sigh of relief and the church began to consolidate itself. Empress Theodora turned over one of her palaces to Miaphysite ascetics and leaders, and this provided the setting for the theological conference that took place in 532 between the two opposing parties, the Chalcedonians and the non-Chalcedonians. Three years later Patriarch Severus was invited to Constantinople, received with honour and allowed to promote his cause. However, many remained suspicious, as the clergy and monks of Constantinople, together with the Pope of Rome, remained opposed to this reconciliatory policy of Justinian.

The pope arrived in Constantinople in 536 and together with Justinian, who seems to have been convinced of Chalcedonian theology, began to impose the decisions of the Council on all the population. The patriarch of Constantinople was deposed and a synod was convened in which non-Chalcedonian leaders were anathematized. An imperial decree followed which initiated another persecution. Patriarch Severus, whose writings were condemned to be burned, went to Egypt again, where he died two years later. Johannan of Tella was hunted, captured and put to death.

At this point the West Syrian Church went underground again and many of its members fled Byzantine rule to Sassanid territories. With the imprisonment and death of so many of its early leaders the situation was again critical. Rescue came from two important figures: the first was Johannan of Hephaistou, who escaped from Constantinople, and began his tour ordaining priests and encouraging the laity. The second was in the person of Harith bar Jabala, King of the Ghassanid Arabs,[29] who appeared in Constantinople in 542 in an attempt to obtain bishops for his Christian kingdom. He supported the non-Chalcedonians and approached the Empress Theodora, who helped in the ordination of Theodorus of Arabia and Jacob Baradeus. The first was ordained bishop of the Arabs, and the second bishop of Edessa.

Jacob Baradeus (500–78) was a strongly determined and highly educated man, who had mastered Greek and Arabic as well as Syriac. Zealous for the propagation of his faith, he dressed himself in rags and travelled from village to village throughout Mesopotamia and Syria, strengthening the believers and ordaining priests and deacons. Pursued, and with a price on his head, he travelled in disguise at night, hiding during the day, and succeeded in building up the West Syrian Church. In Iraq he consecrated a bishop named Ahudamah in 559 who seems to have resided in Tikrit. He was the first metropolitan of the Syrian Orthodox Church in the East.

Since Jacob Baradeus was of vital importance for the survival of the Syrian Orthodox community during this period, and was hunted by the Byzantines, the members of the community were named after him 'Jacobites'. This name is inappropriate since it was applied to the community by their opponents, the Byzantines, in a derogatory way, and since the Syrian Orthodox community was already in existence before his time. Although it was a common practice formerly to use this name for the Syrian Orthodox Church, even sometimes among its own members, it should now be avoided, even though the Syrian Orthodox Church revere Jacob Baradeus as one of their great saints.

The Syrian Orthodox Church had emerged as an independent church by the end of the sixth century, mainly in Syria, Lebanon and Palestine, and to a lesser extent in Iraq. Its official name today is 'The Syrian Orthodox Church of Antioch and all the East' and its patriarch carries the title 'The Patriarch of Antioch and all the East' which stresses the importance of Antioch as an early Christian centre of leadership. Antioch continued to be a vital administrative and intellectual centre for Christians, until the coming of the Muslims in the seventh century. Though the official centre of leadership continued to be Antioch, the actual residence of its patriarch moved from there in 518 to various places according to political circumstances, until it was settled in Der al-Za'faran in Mardine in the middle of the twelfth century. This continued to be the seat of the Patriarch until 1933, when it was moved to Damascus.

The Syrian Orthodox Church, the Coptic Church of Egypt, the Ethiopian, the Armenian Church and the Malankara Church in India, all follow the same Christological doctrine, and have recently come under the umbrella term of 'Oriental Orthodox Churches' to distinguish them from the Chalcedonian 'Eastern Orthodox Churches'[30] (see table 3). The Syrian Orthodox Church is also called the West Syrian Church, in contrast with the East Syrian Church, which we now call the Church of the East. Recently the Eritrean Church (which was part of the Ethiopian Coptic Church) separated and appointed its own patriarch, becoming the sixth church of the Oriental Orthodox communion.

The Syrian Orthodox Church in Iraq

The church in Mesopotamia had been recognized by the Persians in 410 at the Synod of Isaac, and became administratively independent of the Church of Antioch after the Synod of Dadisho in 424. At this point theology was not clearly defined, as both the synods which led to independence of the Church in Iraq were convened before the councils of Ephesus (431), in which Nestorius was deposed, and that of Chalcedon (451), in which the two-nature Christology was adopted, and the Western church split into those who accepted the decisions of the Council of Chalcedon and those who did not.

Severing relations with Antioch in 424 was mainly a political move to avoid complications in the relationship between the church and the state, since the Zoroastrian Sassanids were enemies of the Byzantines, who had supported Christianity since the conversion of Constantine and the adoption of Christianity as the official religion of the State in 392. Christians within the Sassanid empire were often accused of being supporters of the Christian Byzantine empire. The situation in Mesopotamia under the Persians was peculiar, because firstly, a substantial number of its church had followed a theology that was quite distinct from both Chalcedonian and Miaphysite Christologies, and secondly, its Christians were not influenced by frictions which occurred between Chalcedonians and non-Chalcedonians within the Byzantine empire. When the Miaphysites had the upper hand, under the influence of Emperor Zeno, and the school of Edessa was closed in 489, all the teachers had to do was to move to Nisibis where, under the Persians, they established the school of Nisibis which continued to teach Dyophysite theology. When Justin and Justinian began to persecute those who did not accept the decisions of the Council of Chalcedon, the Christians of Mesopotamia were not touched because they were under Persian rule. In fact, many Miaphysites took refuge in Mesopotamia during this period. When the teaching of Theodore of Mopsuestia was finally condemned in the Council of Constantinople in 553, and 'Nestorianism' became illegal within the Byzantine empire, the remnants of the 'Nestorians' in Edessa moved to the north of Iraq.

Before the definition of Christological formulae, a substantial numbers of church leaders in Mesopotamia had followed the theology of Theodore of Mopsuestia. Most members of its church were graduates of the 'school of the Persians' in Edessa, which taught Dyophysite theology. However, some communities, especially those in Tikrit, Der Mar Matta and surrounding areas between Nisibis, Sinjar and Mosul, had followed Miaphysite theology. After the closure of the school of Edessa, the centre of learning that had been established in Nisibis continued to provide Mesopotamia with learned leaders of Dyophysite confession. Its founder, Bar Sauma, and its principal, Narsai, were both followers of Theodore of Mopsuestia; thus the school of Nisibis became the stronghold of Dyophysite theology within Iraq. In 486, Patriarch Akakios convened the Synod of Seleucia–Ctesiphon, during which the Church of the East produced the first preserved Christological creed which was clearly Dyophysite in confession (see chapter 3 Part I and table 3).

Since the Sassanid shahs did not have any discriminatory policy against any particular form of Christianity, the number of West Syrians began to increase within the realms of the Sassanid empire, as many found refuge there, especially during the persecutions of Justin and Justinian. Moreover the evangelical zeal of the West Syrians led to the conversion of many Mesopotamians to their faith. Of special interest are the Arab tribes Tay, Uqail and Tnuk in Ba'arbaya[31] and Anmar, Taghlub and Ayad in and around Tikrit.

In addition, their number was increased by prisoners of war brought by the Persian shah, Khosroes I, from Byzantine territories. In 540 and 573, a large number of captives were brought and settled in various towns. The area of their settlement near the capital Seleucia–Ctesiphon came to be known as the 'new Antioch'.

Gradually the West Syrian Church emerged within Mesopotamia as a distinct community, separate from the Church of the East. It had a distinct hierarchy, administration and places of worship and continued to follow the leadership of Antioch from the ecclesiastical point of view. Before the Persian authorities, however, its people were represented by the patriarch of the Church of the East.

Rivalry between the East and West Syrian communities soon ensued, and led to conflicts that reached their peak during the reign of Khosroes II (591–628). The wife of Khosroes, Shirin, was converted to the Syrian Orthodox faith by the Shah's physician Gabriel. During a period of vacancy in the patriarchate of the Church of the East, the Syrian Orthodox community tried to institute a patriarch of its own creed through the influence of Shirin and Gabriel. Both pressurized the king to nominate a patriarch of their denomination. Members of the Church of the East voiced their objection, as a result of which the Shah asked both parties to present their case to him. The two parties argued their theological positions in front of the shah. That did not solve the problem and, as Khosroes became preoccupied with a war against Byzantium, the issue remained suspended during his lifetime.

The rule of Khosroes II ended due to a conspiracy of his general and his own son Kobad. This son, who ruled for a short period after Khosroes, had a collaborator called Shamta, an East Syrian Christian of the Church of the East, whose own father had been dispossessed of his properties by Khosroes. During his short period of office in Kobad's government, Shamta influenced the king to let the Church of the East elect its own patriarch. The college of bishops of the Church of the East met, and elected Ishu'yab in the year 628.

Likewise, members of the Syrian Orthodox Church re-organized themselves and asked to be represented separately before the Sassanid authorities. The patriarch of the Syrian Orthodox Church sent a representative, Raban Yuhanna, who met with the Sassanid government and discussed the representation of his people as an independent community. In 629 members of the Syrian Orthodox community were acknowledged by the Sassanids as a separate community, independent of the main body of the Church of Persia (that is, the Church of the East).

Rabban Yuhanna also met with the bishop of Der Mar
Matta and four bishops of surrounding towns; the whole
community decided to follow the leadership of the patriarch of Antioch. At this stage the Syrian Orthodox Church
in Iraq had twelve bishoprics, six of them under the jurisdiction of the metropolitan of Der Mar Matta, Mosul and
Nineveh and the other six under the metropolitan of
Tikrit, and all were subordinate to the patriarch of
Antioch. The bishop of Tikrit was made responsible for all
the twelve bishoprics in Iraq and Persia, and was later
called 'Maphrian'.

The first maphrian of the Syrian Orthodox Church in
Iraq was Bishop Marutha, in the year 629. He made his
residence in Tikrit, as he was not allowed to live in the
capital of the Persian Empire, Seleucia–Ctesiphon, where
the patriarch of the Church of the East resided.

Tikrit

The city of Tikrit had Christian residents before it became
the official residence of the maphrian of the Syrian Orthodox Church. Tradition indicates the presence of Christians
in Tikrit from the first Christian century. Mar Ahudamah,
its first bishop, consecrated by Jacob Baradeus in Iraq, was
from Tikrit.

The city continued to flourish as a Christian centre
during the first three centuries of Arab rule. Its cultural
centre produced great philosophers, theologians and
physicians, such as Yehya ibn Udai al-Tikriti and al-Fathel
ibn Jarir al-Tikriti.

Recent studies and excavations show evidence of at
least seven churches in Tikrit and more than ten monasteries in and around it.[32]

From the ninth century some of the Christians of Tikrit
started to emigrate north to the region of Mosul and
Nineveh, especially to the city of Mosul, the village of
Qara Qosh[33] and later to Tur'Abdin and Jezirah. From 817
there existed in the city of Mosul a church for the Tikritis.
There are many reasons for these emigrations. Some have
been attributed to misbehaviour of some of the Tikriti

Christians' leaders due to interpersonal rivalries, but they were mainly related to severe measures taken against the Christians of Tikrit by some Muslim governors who started applying the *dhimmi* rules strictly, humiliating monks, clergy and lay people. As life became increasingly intolerable, its communities started to emigrate.

Tikrit came under flagrant attack in 1089 when, under the orders of its governor, its great cathedral of Mar Ahudama or the Green Church, was destroyed and all its furniture looted. Many of its Christian members escaped to different places, and its maphrian, Yuhanna II Saliba, escaped to Mosul. Its next maphrian, Dionysius Musa, returned to Tikrit after a new moderate ruler came to be the governor. He obtained a special permission from the Caliph in order to rebuild its churches, and encouraged many of the Christian population to return and live there. However, this situation did not last long, as the city came under military attack in the early twelfth century, when Sultan Giath al-Din Muhammad bin Malik Shah[34] sent an army and the city fell after seven months of siege.[35] The situation of the Christians and the position of the maphrian became increasingly jeopardized, and this led finally to the seat of the mephrianate being moved to the city of Mosul in 1156.

Der Mar Matta, Mosul and Nineveh

By the end of the seventh century the metropolitan of Der Mar Matta, Mosul and Nineveh had six bishoprics under his jurisdiction.[36] The metropolitan who was the bishop of Der Mar Matta was officially under the maphrian who resided in Tikrit. However, from the beginning he was given certain prerogatives which limited the authority of the maphrian over him. This led to many complications over the years and severe conflicts ensued between the communities of the Der and those of Tikrit, especially when the latter started to emigrate to Mosul and surrounding villages.

When the maphrian of Tikrit escaped to Mosul in 1089, the community there caused many problems that contributed to the decision of the next maphrian to move back to Tikrit. However, after the mephrianate was finally settled in Mosul in 1156, maphrian Ignatius Li'azir unified the two metropolitanates and cancelled the prerogatives of the bishop of Der Mar Matta. His title became 'The Maphrian of Tikrit, Nineveh, Mosul and all the East'.

The character of the Syrian Orthodox Church

Missionary
Like the Church of the East, the Syrian Orthodox Church was strongly missionary, and expanded east to Persia, Central Asia and India and south to the Arabian peninsula. Michael the Syrian, one of the great personalities of this church, writing in the twelfth century, records bishops and metropolitans in Eastern Iran, Herat, Khurasan, Bahrain, and in areas around the Oxus river. At its peak the Syrian Orthodox Church in Iraq had thirty-one bishoprics under its maphrian. However, the Syrian Orthodox Church never reached the size nor had the influence and importance of the Church of the East within the realms of the Sassanid empire.

Syriac culture
Syriac language and culture were the mainstay of the Syrian Orthodox Church, and over the centuries it had a rich cultural history with great personalities and centres of learning. In Edessa there was a prestigious school, which became especially important after the school of the Persians was closed in 489. In Iraq they developed major centres of learning in Der Mar Matti, Sinjar, and Tikrit.[37] In these centres, a wide range of subjects was taught. Apart from theology, philosophy and biblical studies, there was also history, the sciences, music, medicine and languages. Both Greek and Syriac were taught, and later Arabic. Eminent scholars contributed, writing original works in various fields of knowledge as well as translations of many Greek works into the Syriac language and later into Arabic.

To mention all the scholars and great figures of the Syrian Orthodox Church is beyond the scope of this work. It has already been mentioned that early Syriac writers, such as Ephrem Syrus and Aphrahat, are claimed by the Syrian Orthodox Church as well as other Syriac Eastern Churches (see Culture of the Church of the East pp. 49–50). In later times some of the most important of these, who were born or served within Mesopotamia, were:

Severus Sabukht (died 667); he was born in Nisibis, became a monk and was educated at Qinnesrine. He was a skilful doctor, mathematician, philosopher and the first scholar of the church to explore astronomical and natural sciences.

Jacob of Odessa (died 708); an outstanding scholar who was unique in the extent of his knowledge, brilliant mind and sound judgement. His writings covered the fields of literature, grammar, history, legislation, philosophy and theology. He made a revision and commentary on the Peshitta and translated many works from Greek to Syriac. He wrote a Chronicle which was meant not only to continue the Ecclesiastical History of Eusebius, the famous father of church history, but also to supplement his work and correct some of his errors. Born in a village near Antioch, he trained under Severus Sabukht in Qinnesrine and was made bishop of Edessa in 684.

Yuhanna bin Adi al-Tikriti; born in Tikrit in 893, he studied in Baghdad under al-Farabi and Bishr ibn Matta. He mastered Arabic and Syriac and made translations of many philosophical works into Arabic. He had his own school of logic and was himself an original theological and philosophical writer.

Al-Fathel ibn Jarir al-Tikriti, born in Tikrit at the end of the tenth century; he became a prominent philosopher and physician. He mastered Syriac and Arabic and translated many Syriac works into Arabic. He also composed a medical treatise.

Michael the Syrian (died 1199): one of the great scholars, he became patriarch in 1166. His most important work is a chronicle covering the period from the Creation to

1194, which includes the first three Crusades. This work is very important for the history of the Syrian Orthodox Church, and preserves many Syriac sources now lost.

Bar Hebraeus, also called Abu al-Farag (1226–86) is probably the most outstanding figure of this church, the son of a physician who, after studying medicine in Antioch and Tripoli, turned to theological studies and the priesthood. He was consecrated bishop and became primate of the Syrian Orthodox Church in 1264. His works are encyclopaedic in character and were mainly written in Syriac, though a few were written in Arabic. They cover a wide field of subjects including theology, philosophy history, the sciences and monasticism.

Asceticism and mysticism
The numerous monasteries in Syria, Palestine, Lebanon and Mesopotamia which members of this church established are the best testimony to its ascetic and mystical character. In addition there were famous anchorites who lived solitary lives in the desert, in caves or on top of pillars. Since monks and solitaries were immensely venerated by the religious masses, it is not surprising that the care of people fell into their hands, as people flocked to see them and to ask favours and advice from them. Many were taken out of the monasteries to become bishops or patriarch, and often other sectors of pastoral office became their responsibility.

The monasteries were not only places where people sought to practise their faith and look for holiness, but also places in which they sought knowledge, since most were important centres of learning in which Greek works were translated and numerous original works were written.

In Iraq there were many monasteries in and around Tikrit, as well as in Mosul and the surrounding villages, the most famous being that of Der Mar Matta. It is one of the most ancient monasteries, founded in the fourth century by a native of Amida, called Matta. He fled the persecution of Julian the Apostate (d.363), with three other monks, to Sassanid territories, and they became hermits, living in caves where the present monastery was later to be built. Many others soon followed his example to live a similar life in neighbouring caves, thus producing a nucleus from which the monastery developed – in its golden age housing more than a thousand monks.[38] It is situated on the mountain Maqloob, twenty miles north-west of Mosul and was reached only on foot by pilgrims until the late twentieth century when a road was built in order to provide access by cars.[39] It became an important centre of learning for members of the Syrian Orthodox Church from the sixth century onwards. Many who studied in its precincts became the leaders and thinkers of the Syrian Orthodox community over the years. The most famous of its members is Bar Hebraeus, who resided there as bishop, and whose tomb can still be found to the present day.

Der Mar Matta was the seat of a bishop from 480 and for a time competed with Tikrit for the leadership of the Syrian Orthodox community. In 869 its abbot and monks recognized the authority of the maphrian of the Syrian Orthodox in Tikrit.

The monastery came under attack from Kurdish tribes four times from the beginning of the twelfth century, but it was rebuilt after each attack. In the nineteenth century rooms were added for pilgrims, who traditionally climbed the mountain to stay there for several days or weeks. Its fame for holiness, as a place where people asked favours from its famous saints, together with its unique position and tranquil atmosphere, made it an attraction not only to Christians of all denominations but also to Muslims.

Notes

1 The proceedings of the synods of the Church of the East have been preserved in the document '*Synodicon Orientale*'.
2 See Mingana, p. 302.
3 The area called west Turkestan is the Sogdian kingdom east to the Oxus river, and included such renowned cities as Samarkand, Bukhara and Tashkent.
4 See E.Hunter, *The Church of the East in Central Asia*.

5 Baum and Winkler state that in the eighth century, Kashgar was ruled by a Christian prince. (p. 49.)

6 Gillman and Klimket, p. 217.

7 East Turkestan is that area of central Asia which is west of the borders of China.

8 See Gillman and Klimket, p. 269.

9 The stele can be seen in the stele museum in Xian, China.

10 See Baum and Winkler, p. 49.

11 Marco Polo arrived in Khan Baliq (Beijing) in 1275 and stayed in China for seventeen years, reaching Venice again in 1295. He travelled along the Silk Road and recorded information on Central Asia as well as China. His father and uncle had travelled to China before him, met Kublai Khan and brought news in 1269 to the crusaders in Acre that the khan wanted the pope to send him Christian missionaries who could prove the Christian religion to be superior to other religions to those from other faiths. After delays related to vacancy in the papacy, Pope Gregory sent two friars with the Polos, Nicolas Vicenza and William, with whom he sent a letter to the khan. The party of the two elder Polos and Marco Polo together with the friars left for Acre, but the friars never reached Kublai Khan because of political disturbances in the region.

12 This story is told in a third-century apocryphal book, *The Acts of Thomas*.

13 'Hira' from the Syriac 'Hirta', meaning camp. It became the capital of the Lakhmids, an Arab vassal state within Mesopotamia. It is situated in an area south west of Baghdad, around present-day Najaf and Karbala of modern Iraq.

14 Also called 'Der Hind the Elder' as there was another monastery built by a princess called Hind called 'Der Hind the Younger'.

15 Preserved by the Arab writer Yaqut al-Hamawi in his book *Mu'jam al-Buldan or 'The dictionary of the countries'*.

16 See E. Hunter, *Syriac inscriptions from Hira* and the book *The Monasteries and Christian places in al-Kufa and its environs* by Muhammad Sa'id al-Turaihi.

17 Philip Hitti, p. 83. He also refers to tradition preserved by ibn Rustah that it was from al-Hira that Quraish acquired the art of writing.

18 These were the wars conducted by the Caliph Abu Bakir

against the tribes of the Arabian Peninsula who apostatized from Islam after the death of Muhammad.

19 The text is translated by Dr Brock: *Studies of Syriac Christianity*, pp. 133–4.

20 Gillman and Klimkeit p. 122.

21 By this time West Syrian Christians who were called 'Monophysites', had formed the Syrian Orthodox Church which had developed a distinct community in Iraq (see part II of this chapter page 66).

22 Jacob of Nisibis, the Bishop of Nisibis is known to have attended the council of Nicea in 325. Some believe that Ephrem accompanied him, but there is no evidence to prove that he attended the proceedings of the council.

23 The Marcionites were the followers of Marcion, while the Manicheans were followers of Mani. Both sects were among a multitude of other sects known as 'Gnostic sects'. Gnostic influences were widespread in the second century: they believed that special knowledge or gnosis was the means of salvation. Some gnostics believed that Jesus the man was a mere shadow, the only reality being his divinity.

24 See *The Blackwell Dictionary of Eastern Christianity*, p. 399.

25 See Vööbus, *The statutes of the school of Nisibis*.

26 See *The Cambridge History of Iran*, vol. 3 ch. 15.

27 A mountainous area between Amida and Nisibis.

28 This monastery later became and still is an important centre for the Syrian Orthodox Church.

29 The Ghassanids are Arabs who had moved from Yemen at the end of the third century and established a kingdom in Syria in the region south-east of Damascus. They were soon Christianized and Syrianized, without abandoning the Arabic language. By the end of the fifth century they were brought under Byzantine political influence and formed a buffer state under the control of the Byzantine empire. They helped the Byzantines in halting the overflow of Bedouin hordes from the Arabian peninsula into the empire and fought with them against their rival, the Sassanid empire.

30 The Eastern Orthodox Churches include the Greek, Cypriot, Russian, Romanian, Bulgarian, Czech, Serbian and Georgian Churches.

31 Ba'arbaya is the area between Nisibis, Mosul and Sinjār.

32 Ancient travellers and historians speak of ten churches in Tikrit, while official Iraqi archaeological reports found

evidence of only three churches. Qasha thinks that some of the churches could have been monasteries. In his book, *Tikrit, the headquarters of the Syrian Orthodox Church,* he gives a good review of recent findings by the Iraqi government excavations of the area as well as the work of the Dominican, Jean-Maurice Fiey, who lived in Iraq for over twenty years and made a remarkable study of its churches and monasteries.

33 Qara Qosh is a predominantly Christian town south-east of the city of Mosul which was called Bakhdeda in ancient times. Its inhabitants increased during the exodus from Tikrit during the tenth and eleventh centuries. A friend from this town told us that some people from Qara Qosh still connect with relatives in Tikrit and intermarriages still occur on occasions. It is also known that the women in Tikrit still make the sign of the cross on the dough when they make bread, without being aware of its meaning.

34 During this period the Abbasid caliphs were nominal rulers, while the actual rulers were the Seljuq Turks. Giath al-Din was the Seljuq ruler during the caliphate of al-Mustadhir.

35 The details and the dates of this incident are not very clear. Fiey in his book *The Situation of the Christians under the Abbasids* states on p 229 that the Green Church was given to the Arabs in 1106 and that the city came under siege... presumably in the same year.

36 During the Synod which Rabban Yuhanna convened in Der Mar Matta, the four bishops who attended represented the bishoprics of Sijar, Banohadra (Duhok), Barman, and Sharzoor (Sulaymaniyah). Two other bishops were later ordained for Komel and Feishabur.

37 Sinjar and Tikrit are towns in Iraq, Sinjar north of Mosul while Tikrit is north of Baghdad, midway between it and Mosul. See map 3.

38 Seven thousand, according to Abu Nasr al-Bartilli, one of its leaders who writes in 1290. The Arab biographer Yaqut of the twelfth to thirteenth century mentions a thousand.

39 A cousin of Saddam Husayn visited Der Mar Mattai as a pilgrim asking for a son. When the son arrived he ordered the road to be built and the monastery to be modernized.

4

The seventh to the sixteenth centuries

Under Arab Muslim rule – the seventh to the thirteenth centuries

Mesopotamia came under Arab Muslim[1] rule after the battle of al-Qadisiyah in 637 when the Persian armies were defeated. Syria had already fallen to the Arabs after defeat of the Byzantines at al-Yarmuk in 636. Mesopotamia was ruled by the Ummayads from Damascus until 750 when a new dynasty, the Abbasids, took over and began to rule from Iraq. Their first capital was al-Kufa, until the new capital Baghdad was built in 762.

The initial reaction of Christians in both Syria and Iraq was to welcome the Arabs, as both East and West Syrian Christians had always looked at their Byzantine and Persian masters as foreign occupiers. Eastern Christians from both denominations felt a closer kinship with the Arabs as they were of the same racial origin, being Semites,[2] while the Byzantines and the Persians were Indo-Europeans.[3] This response was particularly cordial among members of the Syrian Orthodox Church in Syria, since their church was still illegal in Byzantine territories and many of its members had fled to Iraq as a result of persecution. The Arabs were seen as liberators, by Syrian Orthodox Christians, who soon assumed the same status as other Christians within the newly-founded Arab Empire in both Mesopotamia and Syria.

Christians, together with Jews, were called 'the people

of the book' or *'ahl al-Dhimma'*,[4] by the new Arab rulers. They were not forced to convert to Islam but were allowed to practise their faith provided they paid a special tax called the *jizyah* and followed certain rules. The *jizyah* had to be paid in return for their protection by the Muslim State, since Christians and Jews were not allowed to serve in the army. The application of this tax goes back to the time of Muhammad in Arabia, when he concluded a treaty with the king and the Christian religious authorities of Najran, in which he guaranteed them the privilege of maintaining their faith in return for paying this tax. This was revealed in the Qur'an in Sura 9:23:

> Fight those who believe not in Allah nor the last day nor hold forbidden which has been forbidden by Allah and his messenger, nor acknowledge the religion of the truth from among the people of the book, until they pay the *jizyah* with willing submission and feel themselves subdued.

The third caliph, Umar bin al-Khattab, arriving in Christian Syria, had drawn up covenants at Damascus and Jerusalem between the Muslim rulers and the indigenous Christians, which permitted them to keep their churches and maintain their rites and beliefs in return for the payment of a head tax, the *jizyah*, and their readiness to submit to the Muslim rulers. This was called the Covenant of Omar. The *jizyah* was levied annually and the amount varied according to the individual's ability to pay.

The Muslim state was a theocracy and followed civil and religious rules that had their inspiration from the Qur'an. The caliph had the title *'Amir al-Mu'minin'* or the 'Commander of the faithful'. Non-Muslims were not forced to follow the same rules, but were put under the jurisdiction of their own religious leaders, who were responsible for the internal affairs of their community such as marriage, inheritance and personal disputes. However, they had to follow the rules of the contract, which in addition to paying the *jizyah* was to observe certain rules, called the '*dhimmi rules*'. There were two categories of rules, the first of which were obligatory and were meant to protect Islam, while those of the second category were not obligatory but recommended.

The origin of these rules is uncertain. The first category probably goes back to early Islam and their breach puts the person outside the protection of the Muslim ruler or state. The second category of rules can be traced to the Umayyad caliph Umar ibn Abdul Aziz (717–20). The most classical description of the *dhimmi* rules is given by the tenth-century Abbasid jurist al-Mawardi:[5]

The first category includes:

1. They (i.e. the *dhimmis*) must not denigrate or misquote the book of Allah.
2. May not accuse the messenger of Allah of lying or speak of him disparagingly.
3. Must not mention Islam with slander or calumny.
4. Must not approach a Muslim woman to commit adultery with her or with view to marriage.
5. Must not undermine a Muslim's faith or cause harm to his wealth or religion.
6. Must not help the enemies of, or spies on, Islam.

Rules of this category are obligatory and their breach means a breach of the covenant and puts the person who breaks them outside the protection of the Islamic State. The second category includes:

1. The changing of their outward appearance by imposing the wearing of distinctive special clothing and a special zinnar belt.
2. They are not to erect buildings higher than that of a Muslim, but these must be equal or lesser in height.
3. They must not allow the sound of their bells, the reciting of their book and their talk of Uzayr or Jesus to reach the ears of the Muslims.
4. They must not drink wine in front of the Muslims, display crosses or allow their pigs to be seen openly.

5. They must conceal the burial of their dead and not lament or mourn openly.
6. They are prevented from riding horses, but they are allowed to ride mules or asses.

These sets of rules were not a binding part of the *dhimmi* contract unless they were stipulated, in which case they became obligatory. If they are not fulfilled it does not entail breaking of the contract, but the *dhimmis* are held to observe them by force and are chastised accordingly for any breach.

In addition to the above rules given by al-Mawardi, other limitations suffered by non-Muslims include the punishment of apostasy from Islam by death and prohibition from holding administrative positions. Although the Qur'an is clear that there is no compulsion in religion (Suras 2:256 and 42:15), apostasy was considered as treason. The prohibition from administrative posts can be traced to a statement in the Qur'an which prohibits believers from being under the domination of Christians and Jews:

> Oh you who believe, take not the Jews and the Christians for your friends and protectors. They are but friends and protectors to each other. And he of you who turns for friendship amongst them is of them. Verily Allah guides not a people unjust. (Sura 5:51).

Rules of the first category were always taken seriously, and the *jizyah* had to be paid by all – causing the conversion of many impoverished Christians from early times. However, most of the second-category rules were rarely applied in the first three centuries of Islamic rule. Early Muslim caliphs were shrewd and benevolent. They remembered the commendations in the Qur'an of the Christians as nearest among them in love (Suras 5:82 and 2:62). They also realized the importance of non-Muslims in maintaining the structure of the state at a time when Muslims were still a minority within it. *Dhimmis* were allowed to continue in their jobs and some served in high official and administrative positions until later periods.

The Abbasid civilization and the Christians of Iraq
In spite of the *dhimmi* rules and the gradually dwindling number of Christians within the Islamic state, Christianity continued to flourish in Iraq during the first three centuries of Islamic rule, as is evidenced by the continuous building of churches and monasteries, the output of many literary works and the activities of missionaries.

The patriarch of the Church of the East, Ishuyab III (died 660), who witnessed the early years of Arab rule, took a positive attitude to the invaders and described the Muslims as 'commenders of the faith who honour the clergy, the churches and the monasteries'.[6] Faced with the apostasy of the Christians in Oman, he did not upbraid the Arabs, but blamed the laxity of his clergy. During his reign his missionaries had reached beyond the Oxus to the Turks, and to China in 635, and apparently did not feel threatened. In a letter to his monks in Qatar, he appeals to them to abide by his rulings and informs them about the successful missions in the East.

Patriarch Timothy I (780–823) writes in one letter that the Holy Spirit has anointed a metropolitan for the Turks, and he is preparing to consecrate another one for the Tibetans. And in another letter he writes that many monks crossed the sea and went as missionaries to the Indians and the Chinese. During his forty-three years of office, he worked under a total of five different caliphs, and maintained a good relationship with each of them. He promoted missionary activities in many areas and established six new ecclesiastical provinces. During his reign as catholicos, the Church of the East had two hundred and thirty dioceses and twenty-seven metropolitans. He appointed a new bishop in Yemen and a metropolitan in Turkistan. In one of his letters, he notifies his correspondent of the death of the metropolitan of China. Timothy was also a prolific writer, the author of several theological treaties and letters. Of two hundred letters attributed to him, fifty-nine are extant in the Vatican archives, and these provide glimpses into his extensive theological and philosophical knowledge as well as his pastoral efforts. He transferred the residence of the catholicos to the newly founded city of Baghdad, even though the catholicos continued to be consecrated in the church of Kokhe in Ctesiphon. The Jacobite maphrian stayed in Tikrit, which developed into an important religious and cultural centre for the Syrian Orthodox Church.

The elimination of borders between the Asiatic territories which had been under Byzantine and Persian dominion, and their unification under Arab rule, had positive consequences for the local population as a whole. Movement between these areas became easy and exchange of goods and knowledge profitable. The tolerance and strict sense of justice of early Muslim rulers, combined with an eagerness to learn from their cultured subjects, led to progress and affluence with the eventual development of the great Abbasid civilization on Iraqi soil.

Iraqi Christian scholars, doctors and scientists played a major role in the emergence of this civilization. By the time of the arrival of the Arabs, Christians not only formed a large proportion of the Iraqi population, but many of them were highly educated. As we have seen in chapter 3, many Christian cultural centres had flourished from the fifth century, within both Mesopotamia and Persia. Their scholars were acquainted with Syriac and Greek and had already translated Greek, philosophical and medical works to Syriac.

During the early Abbasid period Christian cultural centres in Iraq continued to provide facilities where teachers, doctors, translators and clerks were educated, and these served numerous Abbasid caliphs. Christian functionaries continued to serve in various professions and state institutions until the time when Muslims were to become educated and supplant them. Of course in addition to the Christians there were the Persian Zoroastrians who were forced to convert to Islam, as they were not included as one of the protected People of the Book, and they too contributed to the emergence of Abbasid culture.

Christians, however, excelled especially in the fields of medicine and the translation of Greek literature, and their role continued to be of importance well into the late Abbasid period.

Medicine

When al-Mansur, the second Abbasid caliph, became ill and no physician in Baghdad could cure him, he sent for the dean of the medical school in Gundeshapur, which was renowned as the best of its time. The dean was a Syriac Christian from the Church of the East, Georgis bin Bakhtisho. He came to Baghdad and cured the caliph, after which al-Mansur asked him to stay in Baghdad and made him the physician of the palace. Subsequently eight generations of the Bakhtisho family, as well as many other Syriac Christian physicians, continued to serve Abbasid caliphs almost exclusively for a period of three centuries. Many of them used their position in the court of the caliphs to influence events and further the interests of their church and Christian community. Physicians at court served as more than just doctors who treated the caliphs, princes and their families. They became confidential friends and advisors to many caliphs. The first to see and greet al-Rashid in the morning was his physician Gibra'il bin Bakhtisho, and when the fact that he was only a *dhimmi* caused jealousy, the caliph answered: 'But I owe my good health to him, and since the well being of the Muslims is dependent on me, their well-being is dependent on Gibra'il.'

The medical profession often became a tradition within families. Apart from the Bakhtisho family, many members of the Massawayh family and al-Ibadi family were doctors. Massawayh Abu Yuhanna prepared medicines in the school of Gundeshapur, and although he did not actually study medicine there, he was promoted by Georgis bin Bakhtisho, the dean of the school. He wrote a book about how to prepare medicines that was of vital importance to the medical profession. His son, Yuhanna bin

Massawayh, served six caliphs as a physician, wrote 44 original works and translated many Greek medical works into Arabic, and was made the first head of *Dar al-Hikma* by the caliph al-Ma'moon.

The list of these Christian physicians during the Abbasid period is considerable. Many of them wrote original works in medicine and translated medical works into Arabic. In addition, they acquired a special importance within Baghdadi society and acquired a particular prestige. This is illustrated by a story told by al-Jahiz about a Muslim physician called Asad bin Jani who answered as to why he did not have any customers:

> This year is bad with lots of illnesses, and you are knowledgeable in your medicine with lots of patience and experience, so why do you have no work?' He answered: 'First of all I am a Muslim, and people had thought before I became a doctor or even before I was created that Muslims do not succeed in medicine. Second, my name is Asad and it should have been Sliba, Gibra'il, Yuhanna or Bera. Third my surname is Abu Harith and it should have been Abu Isa, Abu Zakaryya, or Abu Ibrahim. Fourth I wear a white cotton overcoat and it should have been of black silk. Finally my language should have been that of Gundeshapur'.[7]

Translation
The second major field in which Syriac Christians contributed during the Abbasid period was that of translation of Greek works to Arabic. The Syriac-speaking Christians had already translated Greek philosophical works into Syriac, which is one of the Semitic languages. Since Arabic is also a Semitic language, their experience in translation of Greek made them obvious candidates for translating these works to Arabic. Moreover, neither the Persians who lived in Iraq, nor the Arabs that ruled the state, were conversant with Greek. In fact, translation of Greek philosophical works to Arabic was almost exclusively performed by Christian scholars. Qanawati enumerates

over sixty translators, all of whom were Christians, except for one Sabian and one Jew. To name all the Christian scientists, philosophers and translators of this period is beyond the scope of this work. Scholars travelled from all over the empire to Baghdad, and offered their services to caliphs and rich sponsors. Some sponsors are known to have paid in gold the weight of each book translated into Arabic.

The most famous of the translators was Hunayn Bin Ishaq (809–873). He was a Syriac-speaking Arab from al-Hira who belonged to the Church of the East. He mastered Arabic, Greek, Syriac and Persian. In addition to being the greatest of the translators, he was a physician with special knowledge of eye diseases, a writer, and a teacher in the academy of Baghdad. He laid down the basis of accurate translating techniques, which was of vital importance for the accurate transmission of knowledge. In one of his commentaries he states:

> Galen's works were translated before me by a certain Bin Sahda ... When I was young I translated them from a faulty Greek manuscript. Later when I was forty, my pupil Hubaish asked me to correct the translation. Meanwhile a number of manuscripts had accumulated in my possession. I collated these manuscripts and produced a single correct copy. Next I collated the Syriac text with it and corrected it. I am in the habit of doing this with everything I translate.[8]

Hunayn also laid the foundation of scientific and philosophical terminology in Arabic, which was lacking until then, and which was essential for transmitting thought and knowledge. He worked with a team who translated almost the whole corpus of Galen's medical works, as well as many of the works of Aristotle, Plato and Hippocrates. In addition, he composed many philosophical and scientific works, and an apology for Christianity, as well as a medical book that was used extensively in European universities in the Middle Ages.[9]

Two other major Christian figures stand out in this

period as translators, namely Abu Bishr Matta and Yuhanna bin Adi (893–974). The first acquired his solid grounding in Greek learning in Dayr Mar Qunna, a monastery south of Baghdad, while the second was a member of the Syrian Orthodox Church from Tikrit. Both had wide interests in philosophy, literature, theology and the sciences and translated many Greek philosophical works as well as themselves writing original theological and philosophical texts.

The importance of the translation movement cannot be overemphasized. The availability of philosophical and scientific works in Arabic and the provision of scientific terminology in the Arabic language were keys to Arab cultural awakening and the emergence of an Arab civilization. Moreover the work of these translators was of major importance for Western civilization, since Greek works reached Europe via the Arabs in Spain. Some Greek philosophical works were only preserved in these Arabic translations.

Theology and philosophy
The interaction that occurred between the Christians and the Muslims in the field of theology and philosophy during Abbasid times is quite unique. Many well-documented interfaith dialogues occurred between Christian and Muslim thinkers: the most famous is that which occurred between Patriarch Timothy I and the Caliph al-Mahdi (775–85). The latter questioned the patriarch about the Christian faith, and asked him his opinion of Muhammad and Islam. The manuscript of this dialogue is extant and shows the depth of knowledge of the patriarch, and his great wisdom. The second well-known dialogue is that between Hunayn bin Ishaq and Yehya bin al-Munajjim who was bent on converting Hunayn to Islam. Hunayn debated and wrote in defence of his faith. The third known dialogue occurred as late as 925 between the philosopher Dinkha of Tikrit and al-Mas'udi who debated in the Green Church in Tikrit and in Baghdad.

Christian and Muslim philosophers debated with each

other on issues of faith and philosophy including free will, revelation and eternity. Notable examples are Hunayn bin Ishaq, contemporary with the well-known Muslim philosopher al-Kindi, and Abu Bishr Matta who was contemporary with the Muslim philosopher al-Farabi. Both al-Farabi and Abu Bishr Matta taught the prominent Christian philosopher Yuhanna bin Adi, who established his own school where philosophy and logic were taught, while Abu Bishr Matta established the Aristotelian school in Baghdad.

Several schools of thought developed within the Muslim community, in which Christian thought and influence can be discerned. That of *al-Mu'tazila* believed that human beings have free will, and rejected the idea that the Qur'an was the uncreated Word of God,[10] though it asserted that it was revealed. The caliph al-Ma'moon belonged to this school of thought. Another was that of *Ikhwan al-Safa* or 'the brothers of purity'. This school tried to break down the barriers between faith and reason. Its members were open to Christians, acknowledged the accuracy of the Bible and quoted from it. They considered Jesus an ideal of purity and holiness, and accepted his crucifixion. Finally the *Sufis*, the mystics of Islam, spoke of experiencing the presence of God and of union with Him through love.

These schools were later outlawed. However the dogma of the Qur'an as the uncreated Word of God, which continued to be maintained, has an obvious parallel in the Christian doctrine of Jesus as the uncreated Word of God.

Christian–Muslim relations during the Abbasid period
During the first three centuries of Abbasid rule sporadic persecution of Christians took place under certain caliphs, during which churches were burnt and Christians were humiliated by the application of the social rules and other restrictions. But these were transient and there was always a Christian in high office who could defend his community and cause the orders to be reversed. When the famous caliph Haroon al-Rashid ordered the destruction of

churches and the application of the *dhimmi* rules, his physician Gibra'il bin Bakhtisho walked into the palace attired in the special dress his fellow-Christians were ordered to wear. When al-Rashid objected, the great physician answered that he also was a Christian and had to dress as his fellow brothers in faith were ordered. It was in response to this that Haroon al-Rashid revoked the order.[11]

During these first three centuries, although Christianity was vigorous and Patriarch Timothy spoke of new missions abroad and dialogued with al-Mahdi, the situation of the Christians within the Muslim world was one of gradual attrition. Some Christians were unable to withstand the effects of the *jizyah*, the apostasy laws, the marriage laws and their inferior status. Many impoverished Christians simply could not pay the *jizyah* and converted for financial reasons. In addition, the social pressure was enormous, as nearly every individual was subjected to attempts of conversion. Many could not defend their faith or were too weak to resist a change from inferior status. The laws of apostasy meant that nobody dare change his mind about his faith. Marriage laws also caused a gradual decrease in the numbers of the Christian community, since it was taken for granted that a woman who married a Muslim man would have her children brought up as Muslims. Moreover, although the woman could officially keep her faith, overwhelming social pressure often meant that she could not practise it freely. Finally, the fact that speaking against Islam was punishable by death, and that a Christian could not testify against a Muslim, meant that many could not defend themselves properly in legal disputes.

Some persecution of Christians could be traced to rivalry within the Christian communities themselves or the jealousy of an isolated Muslim who wanted advancement. Sometimes it was instigated by political events. When al-Mahdi was fighting the Byzantines he ordered the destruction of some churches. His Christian physician Isa explained to him that these churches belonged to the

'Nestorians', and that its members were hated by the Byzantines. He verified this with a Byzantine captive who told him that these 'Nestorians' ought hardly to be considered Christians. Consequently, al-Mahdi revoked his order.

Having said that, there was the paradox that many Christians were promoted to high office, as physicians of caliphs, finance ministers or translators, which made many of them rich and influential, causing much jealousy and intrigue against them.

Finally, the introduction of Christian and Greek philosophical ideas into some of the Islamic schools of thought resulted in friction between the different schools on the one hand, and between Muslims and Christians on the other. Muslim theologians, who eventually became the mainline stream, accused the Christians of introducing Greek philosophical thought into Islam and corrupting the faith. This culminated during the reign of al-Mutawakil (847–61) with a systematic attack on the Christians. Al-Jahiz wrote *'al-Rad ala al-Nasara'* or 'In response to the Christians' and al-Tabari wrote a systematic attack on the Christians in his book *'al-Din wal Dawla'* or 'The religion and the state'. In this book al-Tabari reminded the Christians that they were only *dhimmis*. These attacks on the Christians and Christian thought demonstrate how important the Christians had become. Not only were they rich and influential, but they had managed to introduce Christian elements into Islamic thought.

The rigidity in the application of the *dhimmi* rules reached its peak during the reign of al-Mutawakil. The Mu'tazila and Ikhwan al-Safa schools were finally outlawed, the Sufis persecuted, and the schools that followed al-Sunna and al-Shari'ah[12] were followed.

By the end of the ninth century, Arab religious tolerance had practically ended. Several factors can be recognized for the change in their dealing with the Christians.

First, the continuous growth in the numbers of educated Muslims rendered the caliphs less dependent on Christian functionaries. Thus, during the reign of al-Mutawakil, we read of the dismissal of a large number of Christians from office for no pretext other than religion. Many Christians converted to Islam just to keep their jobs. Consequently, the number of influential Christians, who in the past had pleaded with caliphs to protect their fellow Christians and their church, decreased, and there remained nobody to speak for them.

Second, the increasing use and strength of the Arabic language that followed the translation movement meant that there was less need of Syriac. From the beginning of the ninth century the move amongst Christians away from Syriac to Arabic became more noticeable and by the end of the first millennium, Arabic was clearly displacing Syriac amongst the Christians.

Third, the church became impoverished financially, partly because of a decrease in the number of believers, and partly because there was no other source of income. Thus it was impossible to maintain its various centres of learning, and so Syriac learning continued mainly in the monasteries solely for the instruction of the Christian clergy.

Fourth and finally, the weakness of subsequent Arab rulers and the rise of the influence of Turkic and Iranian elements proved to be detrimental for the Abbasids. Various dynasties ruled the empire through nominal Abbasid caliphs.[13] Their treatment of Christians varied, but in general conditions worsened, and overt persecution occurred under later rulers. From the tenth century onwards, rulers applied the *dhimmi* laws rather strictly. Humiliated Christians converted to Islam, leaving increasingly impoverished churches of all denominations. In fact the tenth, eleventh and the twelfth centuries can aptly be described as the age of decline for Syriac Christianity within the whole of the Arab Empire. Great Christian centres such as those in Seleucia–Ctesiphon, Tikrit and al-Hira had vanished. This does not mean that Syriac learning ceased. Christians moved north and learning continued in monasteries. As late as the eleventh century al–Biruni mentions the 'Nestorians' as civilized and learned.

By the twelfth century the Mongols were gaining increasing control in the eastern part of the empire, and in 1258 Arab rule came to an end in Iraq, when the Mongol Khan Hulago entered Baghdad and terminated the Abbasid dynasty.

Under Mongol, Turkoman, and Safavid rule – the thirteenth to the sixteenth centuries

It is paradoxical to find that there was a period of relative peace and stability for Christians in Asia under Mongol rulers, given their military ruthlessness and brutality. Many of them had Christian mothers and/or wives. In fact, three of the great khans were sons of the Christian queen Sorghoqtani: Mongke, Hulago and Kublai Khan. Despite some Christian sympathy, however, these khans did not convert to Christianity and continued to adhere to their hereditary shamanistic beliefs, including the belief in a higher state of being, heaven.

Both Hulago and Kublai Khan are known to have been favourable to the Christians, while the only khan who is known to have converted to Christianity is the khan of Russia, Sartak.

When Hulago conquered the Abbasids and sacked Baghdad in 1258, the Christians were spared. Among his armies were many members of the Church of the East, one of whom became his general, Kitbuqa. Christians of all denominations saw the Mongols as avengers of an oppressed Christianity and welcomed the fall of the capital of Islam. During Hulago Khan's rule, Christians benefited as the *jizyah* tax was removed, churches were built and Christians were no longer barred from high offices which had authority over Muslims. Hulago Khan's wife, Doquz-Khatun, was a particularly pious woman who had her children baptized. She became a patron of East Syrian Christianity and a special adviser to her husband, who is said to have taken her counsel before any major decision. Acting on her advice he sent an army to Syria, which conquered Nisibis, Edessa, Harran and Aleppo. When Damascus was seized in 1260, Christians celebrated the conquest of the city as a victory of the Cross over Islam. However soon after this the Mamluks of Egypt re-conquered Syria: the Christians paid a great price for their alliance with the Mongols.

In Iraq, after the conquest of Hulago, Christians for the first time faced the prospect of life free from the pressure of an officially discriminatory rule. This policy among the Mongols probably gave origin to the legend of Prester John, the Christian king who would save Christianity after the defeat of the crusaders.[14]

However, in 1294 Kublai Khan died, and a year later the Mongol khan of Persia, Ghazan, converted to Islam. The conversion of Ghazan brought the Persian section of the empire to Islam, soon followed by most of Asia from China to Iraq. Up to this time, all ruling Mongol khans had protected the Christians. Now they were subject to retaliation by the Muslim population.

The conversion of Ghazan to Islam in 1295, marked a particularly ominous time for non-Muslims. Ghazan reinstated the *jizyah* and ordered many churches to be burned. He also enforced the *dhimmi* rule for non-Muslims and turned a blind eye to mob violence against them. During the next one hundred years numerous churches and monasteries were destroyed in many places, and mob attacks led to the elimination of entire Christian communities in many cities of Iraq. Two prominent massacres occurred in Arbil and Amida in 1310 and 1317 respectively, during which many people, including women and children, were killed or enslaved, and others fled to the countryside and the mountains.

The final destruction came in the fourteenth century under the rule of Timur Leng. He was an outsider, not of royal Mongol blood, more Turk than Mongol, from Central Asia. He claimed descent from Genghis Khan himself and with his hordes he initiated a long series of campaigns. In 1393 he overran Mesopotamia and captured Baghdad. He persecuted both Christians and Sunni Muslims and left mayhem everywhere until his death in 1405.

After the Mongols, Iraq came under Turkoman dominance,[15] during which it fell to new levels of misery and poverty. With weak central governance, feudal divisions reached their highest level during this period. Instability and low productivity brought famine and disease in their wake. Bubonic plague broke out several times and large cities were abandoned.

Turkoman rule was followed by Persian Safavid rule in 1508. The Safavids were Shi'ah[16] Muslims, and their entry into Baghdad was accompanied by a massacre of Sunni Muslims and Christians. They were defeated by the Ottomans in 1538.

During these turbulent times the Christians were reduced to small communities which survived in isolated areas of northern Mesopotamia. Some of them settled in the plain that extended from Mosul to Aleppo, an area called Jezirah. Others settled in the mountains of northern Iraq, southern Turkey and north-west Iran. Members of the Church of the East were concentrated in the Hakkäri mountain heights of southern Turkey, Urmiya in northwest Iran, and the mountainous area of north Iraq such as Alqosh, Zäkho and Amadiyah. Members of the Syrian Orthodox Church were mainly concentrated in Aleppo, Mardin, Diyarbakir and the mountainous heights of Tur'Abdin, though there was a significant population in Mosul and some surrounding villages.

The seat of the patriarch of the Church of the East moved from one location to another, depending upon where he believed he would be most secure.[17] From the middle of the fourteenth century the Church of the East vanished from Central Asia.[18] In China, after a period of revival under Mongol rule during the Yu'an dynasty, it came under attack when the Ming dynasty came to power in 1368.

By the middle of the sixteenth century, Christian centres had no more presence in such previously important cities as Baghdad, Tikrit and Nisibis. The Church of the East had dwindled to the region between Mosul, Lake Urmiya and Lake Van.

Wedged between two hostile empires, Persia and Turkey, and living next to Kurdish and Yazidi[19] tribes, Christians had a precarious existence for centuries, isolated from the outside world and out of contact with urban civilization. Under such restriction, the ancient tradition of scholarship declined. The patriarch of the Church of the East had to become a secular as well as a religious leader. In 1450 the elected patriarch enacted a law which restricted his office to members of his own family. Since the primate could not get married, incumbency passed to a brother or a nephew, who might sometimes be too young to rule, and authority was weakened by nepotism.

The seat of the patriarch of the Syrian Orthodox Church also moved from one place to another until it was established in Mardin by 1171. Situated at the outer peak of the Jabal Tur range, Mardin overlooked the vast plains that stretched from Urfa to Jezirah and Mosul where the West Syrian community had settled.

By this time, there was no communication between any of the Eastern churches and the Western church in Rome. In fact the Roman Catholic Church did not know of the existence of the Church of the East, since the latter had developed independently after severing its relations with the Church of Antioch in the early fifth century. While the Church of the East was expanding eastwards, the Western church in Rome was devoting its efforts to evangelizing Europe and apparently had no news of the church in Iraq until the time of the Mongols.

News of the Church of the East started to filter to the West by the end of the crusades through the legend of 'Prester John', the priest-king who was to save the Christians from the Muslims. When the Mongols were invading Eastern Europe, Pope Innocent IV (1243–54) sent two Franciscan friars to discuss peace with the Great Khan Kuyuk. They were the first to report the presence of the 'Nestorians' among the Mongols, and brought some news about the Church of the East to Europe. The Franciscan friars had also reported to Pope Innocent the predisposition of the Patriarch Sabrisho V towards the Roman Church. The pope answered the patriarch with a letter congratulating him on his faith. The Patriarch replied acknowledging the authority of the pope. His letter was sent together with two other letters; one was from the metropolitan of Nisibis, Ishu'yab Bar Malkon, signed by him and three of his bishops, and a statement of their faith was included. The other letter was from China.

The Church of the East also contacted the western Roman Church when the Patriarch Yahballaha III sent his friend, Bishop Bar Sauma, to the Pope Honorius IV in 1287, together with a message from the Mongol King Argun. The Il-Khan Argun wrote to the Pope that the great Khan Kublai had commissioned him to liberate the 'land of the Christians'.

Both Patriarch Yahballaha III and Bar Sauma were monks from China. Rabban Sauma was the son of a wealthy nobleman from Peking who became a priest and served in the church of Peking, before renouncing the world to become a monk. He distributed all his property to the poor and lived in an isolated cell for several years, then moved to a cave in the mountains where he lived as a hermit. People began to go to him and hear him teach. One of those who visited him was Mark, the son of a Nestorian archdeacon who later became a monk himself and lived with Bar Soma as a hermit. Together they set on a pilgrimage to the Holy Land in 1275–6. On the way, they met Hulago's son Abaqa and when they reached Maragha they met the Catholicos Dinkha I. They then travelled past Arbil to Mosul and Nisibis, visiting monasteries and shrines, and stopped in Ctesiphon at the patriarchal basilica of Kokhe. However, they were not able to reach Jerusalem, because it was under the control of the Mamluk Sultan Baibar, and there was war between the Mongols and the Mamluks. They tried to travel through Armenia and Georgia to reach Palestine by sea, but the patriarch ordered them back, as he planned to entrust to them the leadership of the church in China. He consecrated Mark, who adopted the name Yahballaha, as Bishop of Cathay (northern China) and Bar Sauma was made vicar general. As the wars in Central Asia made their immediate return impossible, they passed two years in a monastery near Mosul. During this period, the patriarch of the Church of the East, Dinkha I, died in 1281 and the East Syrian bishops elected Bishop Yahballaha as Patriarch Yahballaha III, head of the Church of the East. This seems to have been a political move as Yahballaha did not have good command of Syriac, nor did he know any Arabic, but it was thought that his knowledge of the Mongols was an advantage. He came close to converting the Tartars and the Turkic people *en masse*. The failure to evangelize Turkestan properly contributed greatly to the collapse of the Church of the East a decade later.

Bar Soma traveled through Constantinople to Naples, then to Rome, where he was welcomed by the pope. From Rome, he travelled to Paris, then to Bordeaux, where he met King Edward I of England. He then journeyed back to Rome, where in the meantime Nicolas IV had become pope. The pope allowed him to participate in all the religious ceremonies of Holy Week and personally offered him Communion. He was sent back with presents to the patriarch, and the document of faith of the universal Church. In 1304 the patriarch answered and sent back the article of faith which was carried by the Dominican Ya'qub. However, neither the sought-after alliance with the Mongols nor the attempt at union with the Church of Rome materialized.

Notes

1 Islam is a religion founded by Muhammad, who claimed to be the last of the prophets, the first being Adam, who was followed by many of the Old Testament prophets such as Abraham and Moses, and Jesus of the New Testament. All those prophets preached the same message at their own time, but their message got corrupted by the people, so there

was a need for a final prophet who would give the right instruction. 'Islam' denotes submission to God and the Muslim is the one who submits to the will of God.

The message which Muhammad preached is believed to have been revealed to him in a series of revelations which were later recorded in a book, *The Qur'an*. The Muslim performs prescribed acts of worship and strives to fulfil good works within his community. The five pillars of Islam comprise: 1.The profession of faith: 'There is no God but one God and Muhammad is the prophet of God' 2. The observance of a sequence of prayer five times a day 3. Fasting during the month of Ramadhan 4. Giving alms to the poor 5. Performing the pilgrimage to Mecca at least once in a lifetime.

2 The name Semite takes its origin from the biblical name Shem, the son of Noah, who is believed to have populated the Middle East area after the deluge. Semite refers to various groups of people who inhabited the Middle East and the Arabian desert, who have common physical features and speak languages that belong to the same linguistic family. The latter include the Babylonian, Akkadian, Assyrian, Aramaic, Hebrew, Arabic and Ethiopian languages.

3 Indo-European languages are the descendants of a single unrecorded language, believed to have been spoken over 5,000 years ago in the steppe regions north of the Black Sea and to have split into a number of dialects. These were carried by migrating tribes to Europe and Asia, and developed in time to separate languages, a number of which have left written records of their various stages. These languages, past and present, can be grouped into the following main branches: Anatolian, the major representative of which is Hittite; Indo-Iranian, including Sanskrit, modern Hindi and Persian; Greek; Italic including Latin and its modern representatives, French, Italian, Spanish, Portuguese and others; Germanic, including Gothic, modern English, German, Dutch, and the Scandinavian languages; Armenian; Celtic including Irish and Welsh; Albanian; Slavic including Russian, Czech, Polish Serbo-Croatian and others.

4 The word *dhimma* is an Arabic word that means responsibility and is somehow related to honour. So *Ahl-al Dhimma* are those non- Muslims who the Muslims claim to be in their *dhimma*, thus responsible for their protection. Since the beginning of Islam they were usually the Christians and the Jews.

5 I have given these rules nearly verbatim as found in 'Al-Ahkam as-Sultanyyah' or 'The laws *of Islamic Governance'* by al-Mawardi, pp. 210–12.

6 In Brock 'Syriac views of emerging Islam', p. 15.

7 See Jean Fiey, *The situation of the Christians during the Abbasid Caliphate*, p. 148.

8 Rosenthal, p. 20.

9 This book is called 'Book of Medical Questions for Beginners' and was widely known under the Arabic title of 'Kitab al-Masa'il al-Tibbiyya' or 'The book of Medical problems'. In Latin, it was given the title 'Isagoge Johannitus'.

10 One of the basic tenets of Islam established by the eighth century is that the Qur'an is the uncreated Word of God, present with Him from eternity.

11 See Jean Fiey in his book, *The situation of the Christians during the Abbasid Caliphate* p. 94.

12 Al-Shari'ah is the canon law of Islam based on the Qur'an, while al-Sunna is the traditional customs and practices based on Muhammad's words and acts as written in the *Hadith*. On the bases of these, medieval Muslims developed the elaborate science of jurisprudence called *al-Fiqh*. When these two sources were found to be inadequate to deal with all legal problems, two other sources were used, these were *qiyas* or analytical deduction and *ijma'* or consensus of opinion. Four orthodox schools of jurisprudence emerged which vary in the strictness of applying al-sunna, al-shari'ah and the other two sources. These are al-Hanafi school, al-Madina school, al-Shafi'i school and al-Hanbali school. They provide an elaborate system of laws and regulations which govern all aspects of life within the Muslim community, including ritual and worship as well as civil and legal obligations.

13 These included the Tahirids, the Saffarids, the Sammanids, the Ghaznawids, the Buwayhids and finally the Seljuq Turks. See Hitti, pp. 461–83.

14 This legend was carried to the West by the crusaders. It told of a Christian king from the East, beyond the land of Islam, who would lead to the triumph of Christianity. It is thought that the original model of the priest–king John is Togril the king of the Kerait, one of the tribes in Central Asia. He had converted to Christianity and though he himself did not lead a particularly Christian life, his three daughters were devout Christians. Togril in his fight with his uncle was helped by

Genghis Khan's father. Togril's three daughters were married to Genghis Khan and his two sons Jochi and Tolui. Being devout Christians they influenced their husbands and sons in favour of Christianity. Other khans also had Christian wives, mothers and advisers and may have been alternative original models of the priest–king Prester John.

15 Two Turkoman federations ruled Iraq after the Mongols and the death of Timur Lang, the Qara Qoyunlo meaning 'Black Sheep', and the Aq Qoyunlu, meaning 'White Sheep'. They were evicted from Iraq by the Persian/Safavids.

16 Sunni and Shi'ah are the two major branches of Islam. Sunnis constitute the majority in most Muslim countries other than Iran, where the Shi'ah predominate. Commonly described as Orthodox, Sunni Islam differs from Shi'ah Islam in the interpretation of the Sunna and in recognizing the legitimacy of the first four caliphs as Muhammad's successors. The Shi'ah, on the other hand, consider that authority begins with Ali and that the first three caliphs were usurpers. There are other differences in community organization and legal practices, but doctrinally they generally adhere to the same body of tenets.

17 Initially the patriarch lived in Maragha. When this was plundered he moved to Arbil. Dinkha II (1332–64) resided in Karamles, a village near Mosul, while his successor Shimon II resided in the city of Mosul. The exact period any leader spent in office is not known .

18 Archaeological research has shown tombstones from Central Asia dating from 1345 and 1368, and on the borders of China dated 1361 and 1371/2. See Wilhelm Baum, p. 104.

19 The Yazidis are a Kurdish-speaking religious group which has an oral-based transmission of religion. They believe in a creator God, but also worship the sun and Melik Tawus (Peacock angel). It incorporates the universal principles of faith, cosmology, reincarnation and prayer. It is thought to be the original religion of the Kurds with added elements from Islam and Zoroastrianism, and with some connection also to Christianity. For example, Yazidis baptize their children at birth. They may have been influenced by Christian ascetics in north Iraq. The founder of the Yazidis, Sheik Adi, never married, and one of their shrines may be a converted Christian church, whose origin may be linked to the persecution of Ghazan.

Photograph taken at the Syrian Orthodox Cathedral in Damascus on
Sunday 6th May 2001 during the official visit of His Holiness Pope
John Paul II to Syria. From the left:
1. His Beatitude Mar Rufail Bidwid, Patriarch of the Chaldean Church
2. His Holiness Mar Ignatius Zakko I Iwas, Patriarch of the Syrian
Orthodox Church of Antioch
3. His Holiness Pope John Paul II
4. His Holiness Mar Ignatius Hazim IV, Patriarch of the Greek Orthodox Church of Antioch
5. His Eminence Mar Gregorius Yohanna Ibrahim, Archbishop of
Aleppo, Delivering the welcoming speech of the Syrian Orthodox.

King Faysal II with religious leaders greeting Cardinal Tappouni
(left), the late Patriarch of the Syrian Catholic Church.

The Chaldean Patriarch, Poulis Shekho (centre) and the bishop of the Syrian Catholic Church, Bunni, in a wedding ceremony.

The late Patriarch of the Chaldeans, Mar Rufail Bidawid (right), with the Patriarch of the Church of the East, Mar Dinkha (left).

The inauguration ceremony of Patriarch Bidawid.

The Armenian Orthodox Church in Baghdad, 1956.

Der al-sayyida, the monastery of Our Lady in Alqosh.

Monastery of Der Mar Behnam, the main door of the church.

Monastery of Der Mar Behnam, middle façade of the church.

Monastery of Der Mar Behnam, main gate.

Monastery of Der Matta, exterior.

Monastery of Der Matta, a monk with an ancient book.

Monastery of der Rabban Hormiz, stylized cross.

The chaplain of the Syrian Orthodox in London, celebrating Mass.

The chaplain of the Chaldeans in London, celebrating Mass.

The chaplain of the Church of the East in London, celebrating Mass with his deacons.

The chaplain of the Syrian Catholics in London with his deacons.

The house of the Chaldean bishop in Mosul, before bombing.

Suha Rassam (centre), with Fr Robert Beauly – one of the Carmelites who established the St Joseph's Centre and Christian Cultural Club in Baghdad.

The house of the Chaldean bishop after its bomb damage, 7 December 2004.

The Xian-fu momument, top with cross on lotus.

The Xian-fu momument, the sides of the monument with the names of those who had served in China from the arrival of the first Christian monk, Alopen, in 635 AD to the time of its inscription in the 8th century.

5

The sixteenth to the twentieth centuries – under Ottoman rule

The Ottoman empire

The Ottoman Turks had moved from Mongolia to Asia Minor, where they founded a small principality during the early fourteenth century, under their first leader, Osman. After conquering the Seljuk Turks, the Ottomans expanded at the expense of the steadily-declining Byzantine empire. Constantinople was taken in 1453, and the Ottoman Turks then proceeded to establish an empire that extended from Hungary to Yemen, and from Algeria to Tabriz, with Istanbul (the former Constantinople) as its capital.

The Ottomans were Sunni Muslims, who portrayed themselves as the unrivalled leaders of Islam, with the Sultan carrying the title *Amir al-Mu'minin*, or 'The commander of the faithful'. He was an absolute monarch, who considered his rule divinely established, and himself answerable only to God.

To the Sunni Ottomans, Shi'ah Islam was not only a heresy, but a threat to their self-image; this led to an inevitable clash with the Shi'ah Safavids who had reached eastern Asia Minor. The Ottomans defeated the Safavids in Azerbaijan in 1514, and proceeded to take control of Kurdistan and northern Mesopotamia during the next two years. Baghdad was conquered in 1534 and the south of Iraq, with Basra as the centre of resistance, was taken in 1546, by which time all of present-day Iraq had come under Ottoman rule.

Contact with the outside world was initially very limited, as Ottoman rule was articulated as *Dar al-Salam* 'the realm of peace', while all the outside world was seen as *Dar al-Harb* or 'the realm of war', which in theory did not allow for diplomatic relations. However, trade and politics made communication and some form of representation a necessity.

The Venetians were the first to establish a trading base within the Ottoman empire. They had a presence in Aleppo as early as the fourteenth century. Sultan Sulaiman 'the Magnificent' made an alliance with France in 1536 granting it commercial privileges within the Ottoman empire. This was followed by a similar arrangement for the British in 1581 and for the Dutch in 1613.

Ambassadors were received from Western Europe around the middle of the sixteenth century, when western countries started to be represented by consuls in the capital, Istanbul, as well as in many of the provinces of the empire. It was, however, not until 1793, that the Sultan established any permanent embassy to represent him outside his domain. In order to promote trade and diplomacy, the Ottoman regime made concessions to many Western governments which allowed consular representatives and resident merchants to protect themselves and those of their nation's subjects working for them. These concessions were extended to the protection of whole groups in major ports and cities, and later to religious communities. The French acted as the protectors for Roman Catholics, while the British spoke for the Assyrians.

The political exchanges that followed on trade led to an encounter with Western culture. Through the influence of the consuls it became possible to obtain a *firman* or an 'official decree', from the Ottoman authorities which made it possible for religious and scientific missions to be established. Latin religious orders were permitted to exercise their religious functions, and some of their members were even appointed as consul. Organized Roman Catholic missions started to reach the area from the beginning of the seventeenth century[1] and became an important avenue of contact with Western culture. Scientific, archaeological and exploratory missions followed in the eighteenth century. In 1625 an Italian nobleman brought back to Europe bricks found at Ur and Babylon, on which was writing with previously unknown characters. The first scientific mission to the area was sent in 1761 by the king of Denmark to collect information on various matters including archaeology. Many others were to follow.

Between 1839 and 1876 the Ottoman government introduced a series of reforms that were collectively known as *tanzimat* (regulations for reform). These included areas of administration, defence, economics and land ownership; all were designed to centralize authority and secularize the government, and stressed equality of citizens before the law regardless of religion. The *hatti humayun* in 1856 provided that the temporal affairs of each community were to be placed under the control of a council chosen by the community. Each *Vilayet* or province had a local administrative council, which represented the community at the Parliament in Istanbul, and different religious communities were represented in this council.

The activities of the scientific and religious missions, together with the economic improvements that resulted from trade, were instrumental in inducing enormous changes within all the communities of the Ottoman empire, whether Christian or Muslim. However the changes that occurred within the Christian communities, especially within Turkey amongst the Armenians and the East Syrians, was to have disastrous consequences for them. Attempts at secularization and modernization were interrupted during the autocratic rule of Abdul Hamid in 1878. He reinstituted pan-Islamic rule and governed with an iron hand as a dictator. The Young Turk movement in 1908, which reinstated secularization and other aspects of the *tanzimat*, removed him. After World War I, Turkey emerged as a strong nation through the strong nationalistic leadership of Mustafa Kemal, even though it had lost all its colonies.

Iraq under Ottoman rule

Early Ottoman rule had divided Iraq into four provinces or *vilayets*: Baghdad, Mosul, Shahrazur and Basra, each represented by a local ruler called the *pasha*. From the point of view of defence, Baghdad was the most important; consequently the pasha of Baghdad was of the first rank with the title of *wazir*, while that of other provinces were governed by lower-rank pashas. This allowed Baghdad to exercise control over the other provinces, with the right to appoint or remove Kurdish princes. Later, with a constant Persian threat and insurrection by Kurdish leaders, Shahrazur and Basra were placed under the direct administration of Baghdad, while Mosul continued to be a separate province – though losing much of its territory to Baghdad.

In general, the first period of Ottoman rule in Iraq benefited overall economic and social development, contrasting with the destruction that accompanied Mongol rule and the chaos that followed unstable Turkoman and Safavid rule. Gradually, in spite of setbacks due to recurrent epidemics, floods and recurring wars with the Persians, production and trade increased, the population grew and cities expanded. However, the general level of education and the distribution of wealth remained far from satisfactory until the nineteenth century, when radical changes within the Ottoman government and contact with the Western world had began to have positive effects.

First, the gradual integration of the area into a European-dominated world economy improved the economic situation of all the inhabitants. From 1723, the East India Company had a permanent trading base in Basra and became the main trading agency in the Gulf. The opening of the Suez Canal in 1869 rendered the base of the East India Company in Basra even more important, and the Iraqi economy accelerated. Improvement in communication followed, such as the use of steamships between Baghdad and Basra in 1861, and a telegraph service was instituted between Baghdad and Istanbul.

Second, the introduction of the *tanzimat* caused enormous changes within the administration of the Iraqi community. Seventeen men represented Iraqi provinces in the 1908 Ottoman parliament, in which there was one Christian and one Jew. In Istanbul they met representatives from other provinces of the Ottoman Empire and discovered a sense of solidarity based on their common problems.[2] An army was organized that owed its allegiance to the central Ottoman government in Istanbul.[3]

Third, education resulted in producing individuals who could fill government posts, and an élite of indigenous intellectuals who would transform society in their region. Madhat Pasha, one of the most progressive figures of the Ottomans during the period of the *tanzimat*, was the ruler of the province of Baghdad between 1869 and 1872. He established a technical academy and a secondary school designed to provide civil servants as well as two military schools, all of which were free. He also established a printing press in 1869. A junior high school for girls followed in 1899, and a primary teachers' academy in 1900. The only higher education institution established during Ottoman rule was a law college.

Religious missionaries also provided education. Catholic missions had arrived in Iraq from the first half of the seventeenth century. The Capuchins were the first to arrive, followed by the Carmelites and the Dominicans. The Carmelites opened the first primary schools in Baghdad in 1721, St Joseph's primary school, while the Dominicans opened primary schools in Mosul and surrounding villages soon after they arrived in 1750. They also introduced the first printing press into Iraq in 1860. French Dominican nuns arrived in Mosul in 1873, and began to teach young women writing as well as sewing and other domestic skills. The Jews also had one of the earliest modern schools in Iraq, established in Baghdad by *Alliance Israelite Universelle* in 1865. It had teachers from many parts of the world, and accepted non-Jewish students.

Fourth, scientific and archaeological missions which began to explore the hidden treasures of Iraq led to a vital transformation in the understanding of its history. Discovering the remains of the Assyrians and the Babylonians and deciphering their cuneiform writing led to major revelations, not only about the ancient history of Iraq but also with regard to the Bible and the origins of other civilizations. One of the early archaeologists, Sir Henry Layard, who excavated Nineveh in 1845, had a Christian helper from Mosul, Hormiz Rassam, who became an archaeologist in his own right. A scientific mission led by the president of the National Geographic Society, Mr Ainsworth, was sent to explore the suitability of navigation along the Euphrates. Isa Rassam, the brother of Hormiz Rassam, acted as interpreter to Mr Ainsworth in this mission.

Finally, the spread of the Arabic language, through many new publications and through the Arab literary societies that were emerging in Damascus, Beirut and Cairo, had its own positive influence. Christian thinkers were in the vanguard of the revival of the Arabic language, especially in Egypt and Lebanon. Long before the rise of political Arabism, a literary revival had been initiated.[4] In Iraq, one such famous figure stands out: Anastasius the Carmelite (Anastasius Maria of St Elias). He was born in Baghdad in 1866, and after becoming a Carmelite priest, he returned to Baghdad, where he spent most of his life until his death in 1947 and was buried in the Old Latin Church of Baghdad. He was an Arabic linguist and published articles in Arabic in no less than sixty-two periodicals: he himself edited *Lughat al Arab* or 'The Language of the Arabs'. Christians and Muslims alike, many of whom came to be in the forefront of Iraqi thinkers and intellectuals, attended his evening study circles. The Arab Academy in Cairo elected him among its first members in 1932.

Christians under the Ottomans

The position of Christians varied at different times and in different places throughout the Ottoman Empire. Before the introduction of the *tanzimat* in the nineteenth century, Christians were second class citizens who were required to pay the *jizyah* and followed the *dhimmi* rules. The patriarch of the Greek Orthodox Church was nominated as the official administrator of all Orthodox Christians within the Turkish Empire, while the Armenian patriarch represented all other Christians of the Orient. This situation continued till after 1830 when other denominations were given similar administrative rights. The term *millet* was introduced for the non-Muslim communities.

Within Turkey, Christians were allowed to continue in their jobs, although administrators and officials were identified with the Sultan and had to Islamize. At variance with the prescriptions of the usual *dhimmi* rules, the administration started to enlist by force children from the Christian peasantry and turn them into janissaries, the special army of the Sultan. This military policy predominated in the European field of Turkish conquest and was less frequent in Arab lands.[5]

In Mesopotamia, most of the Christians had moved to the northern villages and surrounding mountainous areas. They lived in four main areas:

Urmiya, in northwest Iran: Christians were under Persian domination and paid the *jizyah*. Apart from occasional oppression by local landlords they lived comparatively comfortably in villages governed in feudal style by landlords who were generally Muslims. All were members of the Church of the East

The Hakkäri mountains in southeast Turkey: Christians were nominally under Ottoman rule and fell under the governor of the *Vilayet* of Erzerum. Since they lived in remote and scarcely accessible areas, they were not within the bounds of Ottoman civil administration and no government troops entered these regions, nor did the tax collectors. The Christians lived under the control of their tribal chiefs or *maliks*, with the Patriarch Mar Shimon as overall head. They enjoyed a considerable amount of autonomy and did not have to pay tribute to anyone except their patriarch, who was a theocrat. Most of these regions were mountainous and isolated from the civilized world. Consequently the majority of the inhabitants led a tribal life depending chiefly on livestock for their living. These Christians lived alongside Kurdish tribes with whom they learnt to coexist. All the Christians who lived in this area were members of the Church of the East.

South-west Turkey bordering Syria, particularly in the regions around the cities of Mardin, Diyarbekir as well as the mountains of Tur'Abdin: here the majority of this Christian population was Syrian Orthodox.

Northern Iraq, especially in the town of Mosul and the surrounding villages and mountainous areas such as Amadiyah, Zäkho and Alqosh: Christians who lived in the villages were Syriac-speaking, while those who lived in the town of Mosul spoke Arabic.[6] These Christians of northern Iraq were under direct Ottoman rule within the *vilayat* of Mosul and had to pay the *jizyah* and follow the special *dhimmi* rules. The majority belonged to the Church of the East, though a significant number were Syrian Orthodox Christians.

Although the Christians living in the first three regions fall outside the boundaries of present-day Iraq, and the first was itself under Persian rule, they are mentioned here for two reasons. First, they are all in areas of what is called Mesopotamia, and shared in the development of Christianity in what would become the modern state of Iraq. Second, a large number of Christians from these areas had to take refuge in the modern state of Iraq at the end of the nineteenth and the beginning of the twentieth centuries.

During the four centuries of Ottoman rule, up to the formation of the modern state of Iraq in 1920, several changes took place within the Christian communities of Mesopotamia. These changes led to a radical transformation in their nature and the emergence of new denominations. Until the beginning of the sixteenth century there were only two communities, the Church of the East and the Syrian Orthodox Church. Both had learned to live peacefully within the limits of foreign and Islamic rule and to coexist with their Kurdish and Arab Muslim neighbours. During the nineteenth century, the political and structural changes that occurred within the Ottoman government, as well as foreign influence, led to disturbance of this balance. The rise of nationalism, as well as contact with traders, politicians, travellers and missionaries brought about these changes. Having tolerated the inferior *dhimmi* status for centuries, Christians were more than ready to welcome the *tanzimat* and co-operate with missionaries and scientists who brought them learning after decades of suppression. However, this caused a backlash against the Christian communities as the Ottoman authorities started to see the danger of separation and fragmentation within their empire. By the end of Ottoman rule, the Syriac Christians had endured several onslaughts by both the Kurds and the Turkish government, and became divided. Major demographic changes followed the massacres of Armenians, East and West Syrians, all of which communities sought refuge in neighbouring countries. Members of the Church of the East, came to perceive themselves as a nation, descended from the Assyrians, with claims to sovereignty and independent rule.

Contact with the Roman Catholic Church

The communication that occurred between the Church of the East and the Roman Catholic Church during the Mongol period provided the latter with the first glimpses of the presence of the Eastern churches. During the crusades some information started to filter through, including the legend of Prester John. At the end of the crusades, further contact occurred with the Eastern Christians in Cyprus. This island was under the rule of the French from 1192 to 1489, and played a unique role for the Christians of the Middle East throughout the Middle

Ages. It became a citadel for Western powers to which they retreated after their defeat during the crusades and became a refuge for many Eastern Christians who suffered as a result of these wars. There were the Maronites,[7] Greek Orthodox, Armenians, as well as East and West Syrian communities in Cyprus, all with their priests and bishops. Franciscan and Dominican missionaries came to Cyprus and became acquainted with the various Eastern churches. Further contact with these and other Catholic missionaries took place later when they established missions within various cities of the Ottoman Empire.

As the Roman Catholic Church became aware of the Eastern Christian communities, it started initiatives to bring them within its fold. In 1222 Pope Honorius III issued an order to the bishop of Jerusalem and the missionaries residing in Cyprus to bring back 'the schismatic Eastern Christians to obedience to the Pope'. In 1340 Pope Benedict XII convened a provincial synod in Cyprus for Eastern Christians, and during the Council of Florence (1438–45), more formal contact took place.

As a result of all these activities Uniate churches emerged, formed between the Catholic Church and the several Eastern Churches. Contact and union occurred with the two Iraqi Christian communities, the Church of the East and the Syrian Orthodox Church.

The Church of the East

The first serious attempt at union between the Church of the East and the Church of Rome occurred on 7 August 1445. It was established at the Council of Florence by the East Syrian bishop, Timotheos of Tarsus, who attended the council and the term 'Chaldean' for this uniate Church was used. However the union did not materialize.

During the sixteenth century, a considerable degree of dissatisfaction arose among members of the Church of the East with the leadership, especially over the hereditary system of succession of the patriarchate. The bishops of Arbil, Urmiya and Salmas voiced their opposition, and in 1552 they elected John Sulaqa, the abbot of the monastery of Der Rabban Hormiz as anti-patriarch. He adopted the name John VIII, established contact with the Franciscans and travelled to Rome. He accepted the Catholic creed in the presence of Pope Julius III, who consecrated him patriarch in 1553 and gave him the pallium. The Pope sent him back with two Dominicans who were to instruct the East Syrian Christians in the Roman faith.

On his return, John Sulaqa was recognized only by the faithful of Mardin and Diyarbakir. The patriarch of the Church of the East, Shimon VIII Dinkha, declared his election illegitimate, and on his orders John Sulaqa was arrested by Ottoman authorities soon after his arrival, and murdered in 1555.

After the death of John Sulaqa, the Uniate community elected Abdisho IV. He could not travel to Rome until 1562, when he received recognition by Pope Pius IV. A copy of the creed written in Syriac in Abdisho's own handwriting is preserved in the Vatican. In 1565 the Pope granted the Chaldeans the retention of traditional rites and customs, and two subsequent patriarchs of the Sulaqa line followed. However, it was hard to maintain contact with Rome because of difficult political circumstances. Moreover, there was friction between Rome and this newly formed Uniate community in Iraq regarding the East Syrian Church in India. When the Portuguese took control of India, they attempted to place the East Syrian Church under the jurisdiction of the Latin Church. Since the East Syrian Church of India had always been under the jurisdiction of the Church of the East, such a move created negative repercussions for the newly-created union, and it was dissolved in 1672. The patriarch of the Sulaqa line, Shimon XIII Dinkha, severed ties with Rome and founded the new 'Mountain Nestorian' patriarchate at the monastery of Kotchannes in the Hakkäri mountains. This community continued to represent the Church of the East as it was previously before union with Rome.

In the meantime, and before the patriarch of the Sulaqa line went to Kotchannes to form the Mountain Nestorians, the original patriarch of the Church of the East himself began to negotiate union with Rome. In 1606, two messengers of Patriarch Elias VII appeared in Rome to prepare for the union, but this was not achieved. Various other overtures were made, and there was a line of Chaldean Catholic patriarchs based in Amid/Diyarbakir from 1681–1828, all named Joseph except the last (Augustin Hindi 1804–28).

Between 1751 and 1772 negotiations regarding a new union of the Mountain Nestorians with Rome were recommenced; however, this did not last long and relations with the Mountain Nestorians were finally severed.

In 1830, Rome acknowledged John VIII Hormiz as the 'The Patriarch of Babylon over the Chaldeans',[8] and this Uniate church came to be called 'The Chaldean Church'. Since then, the Chaldean Church in Iraq has been stable and relations with Rome cemented.

Despite difficult relations during the seventeenth and eighteenth centuries between Rome and the East Syrians, much scholarly work was initiated. The Maronite Joseph Simon Assemani (1687–1768), became the most important patron of Syriac Christianity in Rome. He presented the first systematic study of East Syriac literature for a European audience, and his four-volume work is still consulted today by scholars as a major source.

In 1844 this Uniate Church obtained recognition from the Turkish authorities as an independent *millet*, distinct from the Church of the East.

The patriarch of the Chaldean Church initially resided in Diyarbakir, then in Der Rabban Hormiz, a monastery in Alqosh, a small town to the north of the city of Mosul. The patriarchate later moved to the city of Mosul until the middle of the twentieth century when it settled in the capital, Baghdad.

The Syrian Orthodox Church
Several sporadic attempts at union between the Syrian Orthodox Church and the Roman Catholic Church occurred from early times.[9] Intra-community friction had caused rivalry between various leaders, and led many of

them to seek help from the Catholic Church. During the first century of the crusades, a rival of Patriarch Michael the Syrian brought a large proportion of the Syrian Orthodox community of Jerusalem to the Catholic faith, but no further steps were taken and the community that converted merged with the Latins or Maronites. In 1237, the patriarch of the Syrian Orthodox Church, Ignatius Dawud III submitted to Rome, but when he could not bring the rest of the community with him, he resigned his office and joined the order of the Friars of the Holy Land.

The direct contact that occurred between members of the Syrian Orthodox Church and the Roman Catholic Church during the provincial synod in Cyprus (1340), and during the Council of Florence (1438–45), was followed by the submission of individuals to the Catholic faith, but no greater movement materialized.

After the middle of the sixteenth century the Patriarch Nimat Alla Asfar had direct contact with Pope Pius IV and his successor Pius V, and signed a profession of Catholic faith. On his return to his people he met with strong opposition, and was arrested and accused of collaboration with the Sultan's enemies.[10] His nephew Dawd Shah obtained recognition as patriarch from the pope, but on his return was not allowed to meet the papal representative, as there was talk that he had come to make an alliance between the Christians of the Middle East and European troops against the sultan.

All these failures reflect a combination of both readiness for and resistance to union with the Roman Catholic Church, the aetiology of which has many factors. On the one hand there was much dissatisfaction amongst church leaders, many of whom sought union with Rome to solve their problems. On the other hand, there was pride amongst the community in their long-established churches which had survived centuries of difficulty and persecution, and union with Rome was seen as the dissolution of their identity.

However, many were sincerely attracted to the Catholic Church after contact with its missionaries, who had begun to flood the area from the first half of the seventeenth century.[11] Under the influence of Capuchins, Carmelites, Jesuits and other orders, many families from the Syrian Orthodox Church in Syria and Mesopotamia converted to Catholicism.

In Aleppo,[12] the number of those who converted to Catholicism had become substantial, which led the Maronite Patriarch Yuhanna al-Safrawi to consecrate the deacon Andrew Akhejan as a priest for that community. Andrew Akhejan was the son of a Syrian Orthodox merchant from Mardin, who had settled in Aleppo. He was attracted to the Catholic faith, studied its doctrine and practice and was received into the Maronite Church. He was sent to Rome in 1646, where he completed his studies for the priesthood. In 1656, he was consecrated bishop of Aleppo for the Syrian Catholic community. However, friction with the patriarch of the Syrian Orthodox Church caused him to leave for Lebanon, only to return when the latter died. He was consecrated patriarch in 1662 and sent back to Aleppo, where he led both Syrian communities for a time: those who were united with Rome and those who were not. Further friction caused him to leave for Constantinople, where he conducted talks at high levels that enabled him to return and lead the new Uniate community till he died in 1677.

The next bishop, Shahbadeen, encountered similar difficulties, which led to his imprisonment along with a number of priests and monks. They were banished from Aleppo, and on their way to Constantinople two of them died, including the patriarch. Those who survived took refuge in Lebanon where they received help from the Maronite patriarch. They were given land where they built the monastery of Der Mar Ephrem in 1730.

Following that, further trouble resulted in the Patriarch Nimat Alla Jarwa escaping to Lebanon in 1781. In Beirut, he built a centre for the patriarchate and a monastery, over a hill called *Sharfat Dar'oon*, named '*Sayidat al-Najat*' or 'Our Lady of Succour'. From there, he consolidated the communities that wanted to unite with the Roman

Catholic Church, whether those in Syria, Diyarbakir or Iraq. In 1785 he was given the title 'Patriarch of the Syrian Catholic Church' and Rome recognized his community as a self-ruling Uniate church with retention of its rites and customs.

The Syrian Catholic Church was formally recognised as separate *millet* by Ottoman authorities in 1843. After cementing relationship with Rome this Uniate church grew in strength, which led its patriarch to move his residence to Mardin in 1854, where a large number of his community resided. The centre of the patriarchate, however, was moved back to Beirut in 1930 by Cardinal Tappouni.

The first bishop for Syrian Catholics in Iraq was consecrated by Ni'matalla Jarwa in 1790. That can be considered the foundation of the Syrian Catholic Church in Iraq, when Bishara Akhtal was given the name Qorlis Behnam (Cyril Behnam), and consecrated Bishop of Mosul, Bakhdeda and der Mar Behnam. He was, in fact, responsible for all the Syrian Catholics in Iraq, including those in Baghdad and Basra. At the turn of the century the number of Christians who moved to the cities increased, and Baghdad became the centre of another bishopric. During the hectic period around World War I, its believers were augmented by refugees received by Iraq from southern Turkey, where many of the Christians came under attack from both the Kurds and the Turkish authorities.

Contact with the Church of England and American Protestant missions

Little was known about the Eastern Syriac churches by British and American Christians before the beginning of the nineteenth century. Information started to filter from India, Lebanon and Iraq through the East India Company, and from the political representatives of Western countries in these areas. This stimulated interest in the Eastern churches and missions began to be organized.

British and American missionaries initiated their activities in Malta, making it the base for their preparations for the evangelization of the East. In the United States, the American Board of Commissioners for Foreign missions (ABCFM), and the Episcopal Board of Missions prepared to send missions to the Middle East. The first was an establishment of the Congregational Church of New England, the second of the Episcopal Church. The British had three main organizations that became interested in evangelizing the Middle East, namely the Society for Promoting Christian Knowledge (SPCK), the Society for Propagation of the Gospel in foreign parts (SPG) and the Church Missionary Society (CMS).

A mission station was established in Malta in 1810, to train missionaries who would work in the Middle East, as well as preparing translations of books in the Arabic and Syriac languages. A printing press was brought first to Malta, then to Beirut, and the Bible and a number of other religious books were translated. It was in Malta that an Iraqi Christian, Isa Rassam[13] was employed in translation work. Among other books, he translated *The Pilgrim's Progress* into Arabic and revised the Arabic text of a prayer book.

Unlike Roman Catholic missions, the American and British missions did not aim to convert Eastern Christians to their own denominations. They made their objective clear from the beginning: their aim was to take the Christian message to all, Christians and non-Christians. Since evangelization of the Muslims was forbidden, their plan was to invigorate the Eastern churches, who would in turn evangelize the Muslims. They thought that by educating the local Christians and strengthening their churches, the latter would in turn be in a position to take the Christian message to non-Christians.

With the simultaneous arrival of different missions, some unforeseen events occurred. Competition between British and American missions as well as between both themselves and Roman Catholic missions took place, leading to a weakening of the Eastern churches rather than their being strengthened. In addition, contrary to their original plan, few Protestant denominations emerged from amongst the Eastern churches. The result was a destabilization of the various Christian communities, which affected their own relations with their Muslim neighbours.

The Church of the East

The first Protestant mission to the Church of the East was set up in Urmiya, Persia, in 1834 by the ABCFM, under the direction of the Revd Justin Perkins. Schools were opened and religious books in the Syriac language were brought, including the Bibles and prayer books.

After the establishment of the American mission in Urmiya, the ABCFM sent Dr Asahel Grant to start a mission in Mosul and the Kurdistan mountains. He set off in 1839 from Mosul to Amadiyah, where he reported that all Christians there had embraced Catholicism. From Amadiyaj, he traveled to the Hakkäri mountains where he met with Mar Abraham Shimon XVII, patriarch of the Church of the East. He stayed five weeks with him and discussed extending the mission of the ABCFM to the Hakkäri area. He also warned him of Catholic missionaries who were trying to win over the 'Nestorians' to the Catholic faith. On his way back, Dr Grant met with Nour al-din, the Kurdish Amir of Hakkäri, with whom a friendship had developed. Grant made another visit to the area in 1840 and met Mar Shimon and the deputy of the Amir of Hakkäri, who was with Mar Shimon, and discussed the mission again.

In Britain, the SPCK approved in 1838 a grant that would help to explore the situation of the Church of the East and other Christians in the area.[14] It was meant to be only a fact-finding educational mission. The secretary of the SPCK wrote specifically stressing that the Society did not seek to interfere with the affairs of any of the Christian denominations in the area but was anxious to afford them any assistance as it could, consonant with its own principles, in order to improve their condition.

The exploratory mission arrived in Kotchannes in 1840,

just one month after the visit of Mr Grant of the American mission. They met with the patriarch of the Church of the East, and gave him the message that the SPCK hoped to open schools and to print Syriac Bibles and other church books. In their report to the Church of England, news of the American mission in Urmiya and the visit of Dr Grant to Mar Shimon were not mentioned.

The visits of an American missionary, followed by that of the British, were not received positively by the Kurds but worsened the relationship between them and the East Syrians. During this period, the Ottoman government had started to apply its reforms by means of the *tanzimat* that included the centralization of its power and representation of different regions in local councils. The Kurds and the East Syrians, who had lived harmoniously beside each other for generations and were only nominally under Ottoman rule, now started to vie for power. Nour al-din, The Kurdish Amir of Hakkäri, wanted to subjugate the East Syrians to his rule, and felt threatened by the European and American interest in them: he suggested to Mar Shimon that the latter relinquish his political authority over his local tribal leaders, as *al-Malik*, and instead accept Nour al-din as the overall ruler. In 1841, when they did not reach an agreement, Nour al-din, in an attempt to subdue the patriarch, attacked his residence and burned it down, but the patriarch escaped to a neighbouring friendly village. Mar Shimon then started to negotiate with the Ottoman government to be accepted as the sole representative of his people.

While the Kurds were fighting the Ottomans in a bid for independence, the 'Nestorians' were temporarily forgotten. During this period Mr Grant managed to build an extensive complex on the summit of an isolated hill at Ashita. Rumours started to spread among the Kurds that this was an establishment for defence rather than a mission station. When Mar Shimon asked Mr Grant to provide protection against the Kurds, the latter answered that he had no political power and that it was his policy not to interfere in politics.

In October 1842, one month after Mr Grant left Mar Shimon, an Anglican mission supported by the SPCK and the SPG arrived. It comprised of the Revd Percy Badger together with a layman called J. P. Fletcher and it carried greetings from the Archbishop of Canterbury, William Howley, and the Bishop of London, C. J. Blomfield. Badger offered Mar Shimon help in opening schools and other educational facilities, and warned him about the American missionaries in respect of differences in doctrine and church discipline. The patriarch, being aware of these differences, asked what other help the British might offer apart from what the Americans were proposing, that is, in opening schools and in giving material help. The patriarch wanted assistance in his claims against the Kurds. Badger asserted that they would be protected. He even wrote to the British Ambassador in Istanbul, endorsing the patriarch's wish to be confirmed as the Ottoman government's exclusive civil ruler of the areas of Hakkäri, subject only to the sultan and independent of the Kurdish chiefs.

Just as Grant had warned Mar Shimon about the Catholics, so Badger warned him about the Americans. Badger also tried to win some Chaldean Catholics of Mosul to the Anglican Church. He thought that encouraging the defection of the Chaldeans from the Catholic Church would help him win over the 'Nestorians'.

All this was not in the agenda of the SPCK and SPG, as neither wanted to compete with American missionaries. They were not even ready yet to support a permanent mission, neither were they prepared to sanction the principle of direct interference in the affairs of the Eastern Churches.

In 1843, while Badger was with the patriarch, two men carried a letter from the Amir of Hakkäri, Nour al-din, to the patriarch, asking him to specify a place where they could meet in order to resolve the problems of leadership between them. The patriarch refused to accept the invitation, purportedly at Badger's suggestion. Nour al-din considered the refusal of the patriarch to meet him to be an affront to his authority, and a massacre ensued in July

1843. Nearly ten thousand East Syrian Christians were killed by the Kurds, and many were taken captive. Badger and Rassam, the latter by then the British vice-consul in Mosul, gave refuge to Mar Shimon and many others who escaped the massacre in Mosul. Both Badger and Rassam continued their onslaught against the American missionaries. Mr Grant, who was in the area before the massacre, had met another Kurdish Amir, Badr Khan, who was with his friend Nour al-din. Before his departure, hundreds of East Syrian Christians had come to kiss his hands, hoping that through this visit there might be security for them. Grant, true to his principle of non-interference in politics, promised no such thing. He had spent ten days with the Kurdish Amirs and even witnessed preparations for the invasion of the East Syrian area. Mar Shimon eventually boycotted him and even demanded the expulsion of the whole American mission.

The missionaries, specifically Badger and Grant, were blamed for precipitating this disaster by interfering in the delicate balance of civil power in eastern Turkey. Badger was dismissed and called back to England, where he continued to plead for the East Syrians. Grant, who was thought to have been able to avert the disaster, was accused of having done nothing to avoid it. Both were seen as instrumental in inspiring fallacious hopes and exciting dangerous prejudices.

By 1850 the two Kurdish Amirs, Badr Khan and Nour al-din, who were trying to establish independent Kurdish rule and who were the direct cause of these atrocities, were captured and exiled by Ottoman authorities. Ottoman rule was then firmly established in the area.

Although after this the East Syrians had some respite and the patriarch was in charge of his people, the area remained unstable since they still had to handle affrays of Kurdish brigands and the corruption of petty Turkish *mudirs*.

While the patriarch continued to ask the British government for help, some of the East Syrians turned to the Russians, when they saw that Britain was not doing enough to improve their condition. In response to this, and after much negotiation in political circles, the British appointed military consuls to ensure that justice was done in the area.

During this period, Archbishop Tait established a new mission of the Church of England under the leadership of Edward L. Cutts. It had the official title 'Assyrian Christian Aid Fund'. For the first time the epithet Assyrian was used in connection with the Church of the East, while previously the term 'Nestorian' had been used.[15] From this time 'Assyrian' replaced 'Nestorian' in the formal Anglican vocabulary when talking about the Church of the East.

Although Cutts's main assignment was to the Church of the East, he also advised the mission to contact the Chaldean Christians in Mosul and to communicate with the Syrian Orthodox patriarch, Mar Ignatius Peter III, who resided in Mardin, and to enquire of their needs there.

Mar Shimon responded by a letter to Archbishop Tait outlining his acceptance of the mission's plan of opening schools, restoring churches and supplying books and a printing press, but also asked for protection against aggression. Bishop E.W. Benson, who succeeded Archbishop Tait, took the Assyrian cause to heart and established the Archbishop's Mission to the Assyrian Church. Again the principle of the mission was to educate the Assyrian Christians and not to change their allegiance or faith. Arthur John McLean and William Henry Brown led the mission which was sent in 1887. Primary schools were opened, and a printing press brought in order to prepare books in the Syriac language. Later, a school for educating priests and deacons was established, and the mission of the Sisters of Bethany inaugurated schools for girls, while medical personnel established a medical department for the mission.

By the end of the nineteenth century, as a result of all these activities, the East Syrian Christians started to see themselves more as a nation than a church. They perceived themselves as the descendants of the Assyrians, and claimed rights to self-rule within a country of their own. Relations with them became more political than ecclesial. In addition, an independent body eventually emerged in 1872 under the name of 'The Assyrian Evangelical Church', contrary to the initial aim of the Protestant missions – as the Revd Justin Perkins had put it: 'Our aim is not to convert members of the Church of the East to our own faith'.

The Syrian Orthodox Church

The Episcopal Board of Mission established a Protestant mission targeting the Syrian Orthodox Church in 1839. It was headed by Horatio Southgate, who reached Istanbul together with John G. Robertson in 1840, and was meant to serve the Syrian Orthodox Christians in the areas of Diyarbakir, Mardin and Mosul. Southgate toured the area for three months and stayed with the patriarch of the Syrian Orthodox Church at Der al-Za'faran in Mardin for three weeks. After that he went back to Istanbul and decided to run the mission from there. He invited the bishop of the Syrian Orthodox Church in Mosul, Behnam, to stay with him in Istanbul, where he gave him instruction in theology and helped him in obtaining books in both Arabic and Syriac, then encouraged him to return to his diocese and open a school there. He also delegated a priest, Michael Jamala, to work amongst the Christians in Mosul, and a congregation started to gather around him. However, no further help came from Southgate, as he had clashed with his superiors who wanted him to move to the area of Mardin and conduct the mission himself among the community from there, while he continued to argue that it was better to conduct the mission from Istanbul. Consequently the mission was terminated in 1850.

In Mosul the priest Michael Jamala, together with another local evangelical, Mikha al-Naqqur, turned to the ABCFM for help. Justin Perkins, who was stationed in Urmiya, visited Mosul in 1849, and organized a mission to the Syrian Orthodox Christians of Mosul, Mardin and Diyarbakir that was called 'The Assyrian Mission'. The first Congregationalist (from the ABCFM) to arrive in Mosul was the Revd Dwight W. Marsh who, after touring the villages, noted that the most important thing to do was to win the hearts of the people. In order to do that he suggested sending a physician who would treat the sick and be able to influence not only Christians but also Muslims. Dr Lobdell was sent and the Congregationalists started to exploit the people through the medical help they offered. The crowd of patients had to listen to their preaching before treatment was given. Since many Muslims came to obtain treatment, they too had to listen to the sermon, which created problems with the Muslim authorities. The Congregationalists also clashed with Bishop Behnam who got on very well with the Episcopalian Southgate. He wanted them to open schools and let the people and hierarchy practise their faith according to the rites and tradition of their church. Bishop Behnam considered himself capable of preaching the Gospel, whereas the Congregationalists insisted on doing the preaching and showed disregard of church rites and local customs. Consequently church authorities started to fight the missionaries and to excommunicate those who followed them. This led to secession and the formation of a separate Protestant denomination which became recognized by the Turkish authorities as a separate *millet*.

In 1860, the 'Mission to the Assyrians' was closed and the areas of Mardin and Diyarbakir merged with 'The Missions in Eastern Turkey'. Mosul was kept as a mission station in name only, and was visited from Mardin. At the end of the nineteenth century it was turned over to the Presbyterians, who in turn handed it to the British CMS.

Contact between the Syrian Orthodox Church and the Church of England also occurred through the personal endeavour of its Patriarch Peter IV (1872–94), who is notable for his efforts in reviving his church and bringing her up to date. Apart from his efforts in renewing ancient churches and monasteries and laying the foundations for new ones, he encouraged publications by bringing in a printing press. In order to secure his authority over the

Syrian Orthodox Christians in India, he travelled to London in 1872, as Britain was the imperial power there. He met with the Archbishop of Canterbury, Campbell Tait, British officials and Queen Victoria and showed them the *firman* from the Ottomans that gave him full authority over his believers within their domain, and asked for similar rights in areas under British rule. He stayed for nearly a year as a guest of the Archbishop of Canterbury, and although he got no positive response to this specific request, a warm relationship developed between him and Queen Victoria. She asked him to pray over the tomb of her deceased husband aloud in Syriac and remarked in her diary that the Patriarch looked just as she had imagined our Father Abraham had looked.

Other Protestant missions
Other Protestant missions sent to Iraq, were those of the 'Church Missionary Society', the London Society for Promoting Christianity among the Jews, (SPCJ)[16] and that by the Reformed Dutch Church of the USA.

In 1883, the Arab Turkish mission was established by the Church Missionary Society, which organized stations in Baghdad and Mosul. They opened schools for boys and girls in Mosul and Baghdad, an outpatient clinic in Baghdad and a small hospital in Mosul, as well as bookshops for religious books. The mission was closed by the beginning of World War I, because of political and security problems.

The SPCJ arrived in Baghdad in 1844, represented by Joseph Wolff. Although meeting much resistance from the local Jewish community, he opened a school, an outpatient clinic, a bookshop and a printing press.

The Reformed Dutch Church of the USA established the Arab Mission, which opened its first station in Basra in 1891. After that they expanded their work to Imara and al-Nasiriyah as well as to some areas of the Gulf. Their main work consisted of the distribution of the Bible and other religious literature, together with preaching and trying to convert other Christians to their own denomination. They also provided some medical services and opened a school in Basra for both boys and girls called 'The High School of Hope'.

Changes within Ottoman rule, World War I and their influence on the Christian communities

All Christian communities within the Ottoman empire welcomed attempts at secularization of the state, and the elimination of the *dhimmi* status that followed the *tanzimat*. For the first time in their history, apart from a short period during Mongol rule, the Christians of Mesopotamia were considered equal citizens before the law. Their involvement in the local ruling councils alongside other communities gave a tremendous boost to their morale.

Within the provinces of Baghdad and Mosul, many Christians as well as Jews and Mandaeans[17] started to move back to the cities, to acquire a general education, and to contribute to society as artisans, traders and professionals in law, medicine and education. Most traders employed by the East India or other trading companies were Christians and Jews. Consequently many became wealthy, especially Armenians[18] and Jews, who became merchants, financiers and bankers. In the eighteenth century the Jewish population of Baghdad is estimated to have constituted about twenty-five per cent of its population, many of whom excelled also in the professions. One of the Jews who practised law during the late Ottoman period became Iraq's first Finance Minister. Both Christians and Jews had been exposed to Western culture quite early, as they were more readily inclined to work with foreign traders and to attend missionary schools.

The effects of the second aspect of the reforms that were aimed at centralizing Ottoman rule were variable. For many provinces, the influences were positive, strengthening the cities and decreasing the control of feudal rural sheiks, a process that led to greater prosperity. However, for the Christians of the Hakkäri area who lived alongside the Kurds the situation was different. Both the Kurds and the East Syrians had enjoyed a practically autonomous existence for nearly four hundred years. In their attempt to maintain their status, they vied for authority, a struggle that often ended in tragedy.

Contact with the West had not only involved educational, scientific and economic change, but had also introduced the idea of nationhood amongst all communities. Within Turkey, the rise of nationalistic movements amongst Armenians, Kurds and the East Syrians led Sultan Abd al-Hamid to reverse the *tanzimat* and reinstitute pan-Islamic rule in 1878. He began the suppression of all nationalistic movements, the biggest being that of the Armenians, followed by the Kurds. After crushing the Kurdish insurgence in 1880, he acknowledged Patriarch Shimon XVIII Ruben as the leader of his community.

When Christian nationalistic movements began to be seen as a threat, Sultan Abd al-Hamid made a Kurdish–Turkish alliance and started to turn the Kurdish tribes in a systematic way against both Armenians and East Syrians. By 1890, Kurdish tribesmen were officially conscripted, dressed in uniform, armed, and given the name of the sultan – the Hamidiya Cavalry. They were to be a match for the Armenian and East Syrian revolutionaries, whom the sultan thought were being supported by Western powers. This led to a situation of general lawlessness, frequent raids and robberies, ignored by local governors, which made life impossible for the Armenian and East Syrian communities during the last decade of the century. Sizeable Armenian massacres occurred in several places (in 1894 in Sazun, 1895 in Istanbul, and 1896 in Van). The Turkish government sent messages to Mar Shimon and his people asking them to oblige the missionaries to leave their neighbourhood. The fact that the representative of the Archbishop of Canterbury had resided permanently at Patriarch Shimon's village since 1886 did not help, and there were raids against his people. As late as 1908 the British ambassador in Turkey stated that in the summer of that year a Kurdish raid upon 'Nestorian villages' left eleven thousand victims homeless.

When the Young Turk movement removed Sultan Abdul Hamid in 1908 and reinstated secularization and other aspects of the *tanzimat*, it was thought that the situation of the Christians within the Ottoman Empire would improve. Instead, a new policy of Turkification aggravated the situation for the Armenians and Assyrians, and further massacres and displacements occurred. Persecution then ensued, in the name of nationalism, and any claim of rights or resistance to the policy of Turkification was equated with treason. Kurds as well as Armenians and East Syrians suffered from the Turkish government, but the Christians suffered in addition at the hands of the Kurds. The Kurds initially wanted the East Syrians to fight with them against the Turks. When the East Syrians refused and wanted to be their own masters, they were attacked by Kurds as well as by the Turkish government. Moreover, the Turkish government found it to its advantage to see the Kurds attacking the Armenians and the East Syrians, and so did nothing about the atrocities committed by them against both communities. During this period, many Armenians as well as East and West Syrian Christians found refuge in Iraq as well as other neighbouring countries, as a result of these events.

At the onset of World War I, the Patriarch Shimon Benjamin was summoned to Van to meet the *Wali*, who asked him to be neutral and not to side with the Russians because Turkey was entering the war. After consulting with all the *maliks* and notables of his people, the patriarch decided to wait and see how far the Turks would fulfil their promise of protection. When attacks by the Kurds continued and the Turks proclaimed *jihad*, the East Syrians decided to enter the war against Turkey in alliance with the Russians, in April 1915. The East Syrians of the Hakkäri Mountains continued to defend themselves against Turkish attacks, but as winter was nearing, life in the alpine regions became difficult. Fearful of further massacres, they decided to join their brethren in Urmiya. The Russians had occupied the area in 1909 and had established a mission for the 'Nestorians'. Some East Syrians had even joined the Russian Orthodox Church.

When Russian troops withdrew temporarily, thousands of villages were depopulated and their inhabitants escaped to Russia, only to return when the latter regained control of the area in 1915. In March 1917 the Russian Revolution broke out, and in the summer all Russians withdrew from Persian soil. Having lost their chief support, the East Syrians were isolated. The question facing them was whether to escape to Russia while they could, or to hold on until the arrival of the British. They finally decided to side with the British, who sent a military officer to organize them. To complicate matters, the patriarch was murdered treacherously by the Kurdish Agha Simco in March 1918. The latter, who had been an ally of the patriarch, invited him to negotiate strategies against the Turks. After talks were finished, and as Mar Shimon was leaving with his men, he and his accompanying party were shot in cold blood. His brother Poulus was consecrated patriarch after him.

Delays in the arrival of British forces, with both Turks and Kurds arrayed against them, led their leadership to decide, in August 1918, to move the whole population from Urmiya and march south to meet British forces at Hamadan. During this journey, it is estimated that fifteen thousand out of the sixty thousand who set out on the march perished, including the representative of the American mission, Mr Shedd. The American mission in Urmiya had continued to have a presence during Russian occupation, and assisted the East Syrians during the critical period after the withdrawal of Russian forces in the summer of 1917. During a period of just over a year, until the decision was made to march down to meet the British in 1918, the American mission helped them in supplying sustenance for their resistance against the Turks and Kurds.

From Hamadan in West Iran near the border with Iraq, they were moved by the British forces to a camp in Ba'qubah, a town situated about forty kilometres northeast of Baghdad. They were temporarily settled by the

British occupying forces in Iraq, and given immediate medical attention and general care. Negotiations were then started about their permanent resettlement. The war had finished and the Allies had already divided the Middle East between themselves. They had not fulfilled their promises to secure independence for the Arabs, Kurds or Assyrians. The mission of the Archbishop of Canterbury had withdrawn its members at the beginning of the war. When news of the plight of the Assyrians reached the Archbishop, he sent back the Revd W. A. Wigram to help the British authorities in Iraq to settle the Assyrians in their own country in the Hakkäri or in another suitable place. This was not achieved and the East Syrians continued to struggle for an independent state.

During World War I, further massacres and the deportation of Armenians from Turkey led to a large number of them reaching Iraq as refugees. Many West Syrian Christians living in the areas of Mardin, Diyarbakir and Tur'Abdin suffered a similar fate, in spite of the fact that unlike the Assyrians and the Armenians, they had not taken any active political role, nor did they make any claim for independence. The communities were a mixture of Syrian Orthodox and Syrian Catholics, although Tur'Abdin remained a stronghold of the Syrian Orthodox. One of the prominent Iraqi figures during this period was Gibra'il Tappouni. Born into a well-known Syrian Catholic family in Mosul, he was the bishop of the Syrian Catholic community and resided in Mardin. Turkish authorities imprisoned him in 1918 with other clergy accused of spying for the British. After spending three months in jail, during which he was condemned to death, he was rescued by the efforts of Pope Benedict XV and the intervention of the Austrian Empress, Zita.

Notes

1 In 1627 Capuchin and Jesuit missionaries established a base in Aleppo, to be followed by the Carmelites a year later. During the next few years French Capuchins gained a firm

foothold in Baghdad where the mission was allowed to practise medicine.

2 Contact between the members of the administrative council in Istanbul with similar members from other Arab countries, as well as members of other communities demanding nationalistic rights, was important in awakening Arab nationalistic feelings. This feeling of Arab nationalism led eventually to the formation of political movements aimed at ending not only Turkish rule but also any form of Western dependence. The Arab nationalistic movement in Iraq came at a later stage, especially when compared with nationalistic movements within Turkey among the Armenians, the Kurds and the Assyrians.

3 Thabit Abdullah in his book, *A Short History of Iraq*, states that by 1912 there were an estimated 1200 Iraqi officers serving in the Ottoman army.

4 Christian figures who were at the front of this revival include the Lebanese lexicographer Putrus al-Bustani (1818–83) who produced a comprehensive dictionary in Arabic, 'al-Muhit and an encyclopaedia, 'Dar al-Ma'arif'. He pioneered in modernizing the style and the vocabulary of the Arabic language, which was necessary for both literature and education. The Egyptian writer Jurgi Zedan (1861–1914),was a prolific author of historical essays and novels, which aroused a sense of Arab pride in their past. The poets, father and son, Nasif and Ibrahim al-Yazaji (1800–87 and 1847–1906), wrote poetry, hymns and prose through which they brought a new quality in Arabic expression and invigorated Arabic journalism.

5 Though I remember my great-grandmother who lived in Mosul telling us stories about Ottoman rule. One of these stories was of how they had to save money diligently in order to have their Liras ready so as to bribe the Turkish gendarme who came to take their young men for the army. It was well known that once they were taken they never came back.

6 The Arab-speaking Christians who lived in Mosul did not speak the Syriac language, neither did any of the ancestors that they could trace (my great-grandmother who was born in 1870 could not remember any of her ancestors speaking the Syriac language). The origins of these Arab Christians is difficult to ascertain. It is quite possible that some of them are

descendants of the Arab tribes of Mesopotamia who had converted to Christianity during early centuries and who did not convert to Islam. Of special importance were those who lived at Hira and Tikrit and who were forced to leave their homes following war and persecution from the tenth century onwards. The majority however are probably Syriac-speaking Christians who became assimilated into Arab culture and lost their Syriac tradition and language over the years.

7 The Maronites are among the earliest Syriac Eastern Christians to unite with Rome. In 1182 they united with the Roman Catholic Church, retaining their rites and customs, as well as maintaining a considerable degree of autonomy. The Maronites originally dwelt around Apamea in northern Syria, but during persecution by Byzantine authorities, moved to Beqa'a valley in Lebanon. They gradually extended their settlements to inhabit most of Mount Lebanon by the middle of the nineteenth century. At a certain stage they formed just over half of the population of modern Lebanon, but this has changed in recent years due to emigration and an increase in the number of Muslims.

8 The term 'Chaldean' was used long before the Roman Catholic Church used it as a title for its patriarch, and before the establishment of the uniate church, by members of the Church of the East in reference to their church. The expressions Chaldea and Chaldean had been popularly used for Babylon and Babylonian, a usage influenced by the Old Testament. However, it is the geographical location of the patriarch that led the East Syrians to be called Chaldeans; whether located at Seleucia–Ctesiphon during Persian rule or Baghdad during Arab rule, this area was the domain of the Babylonians. The famous British archaeologist, Henry Layard, reported that in the chapel of Der Rabban Hormiz, where the patriarch once resided, there were tombs of patriarchs of the Church of the East bearing the title 'Patriarch of the Chaldeans of the East'.

9 John Joseph mentions that as early as 709 the bishop of Myafarqin had made a profession of the Catholic faith, followed by the bishop of Haran and his successor. At the beginning of the eleventh century a group of bishops made a move towards union, including the secretary to the patriarch John Bar Abdun.

10 During this period the pope was organizing the Spanish –

Venetian alliance against the Ottomans which ended in the victory of the Spanish and Venice in 1570 at Lepanto. The pope was thus considered the enemy of the sultan. On his arrest, the patriarch not only denied these charges, but apostatized to Islam in order to save his life. Subsequently he made his way to Rome and received absolution from Pope Gregory XIII; he remained in Rome until his death, writing and translating Syriac literature.

11 Pope Gregory XV founded the Congregation of Propaganda Fide in 1622. The Capuchins, a branch of the Franciscans, were the first to put themselves under its direction: they sailed to Constantinople and established a mission in Aleppo in 1626. During the succeeding decades they established missions in many places throughout the region. The Carmelites founded a mission in Aleppo in 1627 and the Jesuits and Dominicans followed. See John Joseph, p. 36.

12 The city of Aleppo was a cosmopolitan city with a flourishing trade and an exciting international environment. It had a sizeable Christian population with Armenians and Greek Orthodox forming the majority, followed by the Syrian Orthodox. Another important community was that of European merchants who were looked after by their respective consuls. Many of the indigenous Christians became traders, associated with Catholic missionaries and became attracted to Catholicism. Moreover, there was an advantage in being a Catholic, as the Europeans favoured their co-religionists.

13 Isa Rassam was born into a Chaldean family in Mosul in 1808. He left his home town and headed for Rome in order to prepare for the priesthood. In Cairo, where he stopped to visit an uncle, he met a German missionary of the Church Missionary Society (CMS), who converted him to Protestantism. Since he was fluent in both English and Arabic, he was offered a job as a translator in Malta, where he met another employee of the CMS, Percy Badger, whose sister he married. Both Rassam and Badger changed their allegiance to the High Church wing of the Church of England when they came in contact with William Palmer ('the Deacon') in Oxford. They became opposed to both Protestant and Catholic missions when they were sent to report on the East Syrian Christians in Mosul and the Hakkari area.

14 The Society for Promoting Christian Knowledge was a foundation of the Church of England, with the Archbishop of

Canterbury as president. The grant was given to Mr Ainsworth of the National Geographic Society who was assigned by the East India Company to explore the suitability of the River Euphrates for navigation. Isa Rassam was in England at the time and he was nominated to the SPCK as a suitable companion to Mr Ainsworth. Rassam was appointed as a translator in this exploratory mission.

15 Coakley, in his book *The Church of the East and the Church of England*, states that Archbishop Tait was seriously ill and that the wording of the report had signs that it was the work of Badger. Although the East Syrians never liked to be called Nestorians, they did not call themselves Assyrians until this date. Moreover although the patriarch and bishops in each area acted as temporal as well as religious leaders of their communities, they did not conceive themselves as a nation. In fact, it was the famous British archaeologist Henry Layard who, after unearthing the remains of the Assyrian capital Nineveh, exclaimed that the Chaldeans and the Nestorians were indeed as much the remains of Nineveh and Assyria as the heaps and ruined palaces he was excavating.

16 There was a sizeable Jewish community in Iraq. They were mainly concentrated in Baghdad, forming about one third of its population by the beginning of World War I. Jews were also to be found in Mosul, Basra and the Kurdistan mountains.

17 A small Monotheistic religious Gnostic sect whose community live in southern Iraq around the river Tigris and south west Iran around the river Garon. They believe in a creator God, 'the living eternal one' and the afterlife of the soul. Adam, the first man, is created from mud, then Eve. They do not have a singular figure as prophet or founder of their religion, though they believe that the book they have is revealed to one of the enlightened, who are many, from Adam to John the Baptist, and to whom God communicate his message through heavenly beings or angels. Their sacred literature is written in the Mandaic dialect of Aramaic, the chief of which is the Ginza or 'Treasure'. Their doctrine is based on a dualistic opposition between the World of Light and the World of Darkness. The soul is imprisoned in the body and is only freed by the redeemer, Manda de Hayy, the personified 'knowledge of life'. The Mandaeans denounce violence and practise various rituals such as fasting, prayer and

almsgiving. One of their main rituals is baptism which is performed in running water and which is practised several times on various occasions. This explains their dwelling near running water. The other important rite is the Mass for the dead which assists the soul in its ascent to the World of Light. Their origins may go back to a Gnostic sect living west of the River Jordan in the first and second century AD who practised repeated baptisms.

18 The presence of Armenians in Iraq can be traced back to the seventeenth century when Shah Abbas transferred a large number of them as artisans from their homeland to his new capital, Isfahan. They soon became the empire's most important long-distance merchants, with links stretching as far as far as Western Europe, Russia, India and China. Through their control of the silk trade to Ottoman territory, many of them came to settle in Baghdad, Mosul and Basra, adding a new denomination to the Iraqi Christian community.

6

The twentieth century – the modern state of Iraq

Iraq under British rule and mandate 1918–1932

British forces landed in Basra as soon as World War I was declared in 1914. They fought their way up to Baghdad and had subjugated all of present day Iraq by 1918. Before the end of the war, Britain and France agreed on dividing the Fertile Crescent area between themselves,[1] even though they had promised independence to the Arabs, Kurds and Assyrians in return for their support during the war.

In 1920, the newly-established League of Nations declared that the Fertile Crescent should be divided into a number of mandates. Syria and Lebanon were entrusted to France, and Iraq, Jordan and Palestine to Britain. The fate of the province of Mosul was not settled until 1925, when the League of Nations finally awarded it to Iraq. Debate took place over whether it was to become part of Turkey or Iraq as it was conquered by Britain after the Armistice with Turkey. After a referendum, in which the Christian community of *vilayet* al-Mosul played a major role in combination with British influence, it was declared to be part of Iraq.

In the same year that the League of Nations granted Britain mandate rule in Iraq, an uprising broke out against the British, mainly in the southern provinces, which was later called the 'Revolution of 1920'. This movement forced the British administration to form an interim Iraqi government with King Faysal I, son of Sherif Husayn, as king.[2] He was crowned king of Iraq in August 1921. The Iraqi kingdom, under British mandate, continued to have a British military presence until Iraq was declared a sovereign state in 1932, and was formally admitted to the League of Nations.

The territory of Iraq was one of the least-developed in the region and contained a number of peoples divided by ethnicity, religion and tribal loyalties. The population of Iraq did not exceed three millions, 90% of whom were Muslim. About 55% of the Muslim population were Shi'ah, the rest being Sunnis. Of the remaining 10% the majority were Christians, followed by Jews, Yazidis and Mandaeans. The bulk of the population were Arabs (75–80%), the remaining 15–20% being Kurds, Turkomans, Assyrians and Persians. The proportion of the Christians was given in the census of 1947 as 3.1%, while in that of 1951 as 6.4%.[3]

Almost all factions of society warmly welcomed the king and organized parties in his honour. Amongst the most notable were the parties given by the Ja'fari private school in Baghdad, Madrasat Sharfat Iranian, the Catholic, Orthodox, Armenian and Jewish communities. During a party given by the Jewish community, the king stated: 'I do not want to hear that this country contains Christians, Jews or Muslims because we are all Semites forming one nation called Iraq, and what I want from my Iraqi citizens is to be nothing other than Iraqis'.[4]

In spite of the warm welcome the king received during this period, he had a difficult task uniting the various factions of the country into one nation, the new Iraq, especially since various nationalistic movements, as well as the Communist Party, caused many disturbances.

Arabic replaced Turkish as the official language and the Ministry of Education began to build the foundations and superstructure of a new educational system. The discovery of oil in Kirkuk in 1927 was a major event that was to transform the country. Although, under a special treaty, the British secured most of the revenues, Iraq nevertheless became a rich country and could spend more on education, the army and construction. With affluence, the overall population of the country increased, the proportion living in the cities escalated, and the general standard of living started to improve.

The Christians of Iraq

During World War I, the Christian Arabic-speaking leaders within Iraq distanced themselves from any move to look to the Europeans as protectors. At the same time they made it clear that they did not seek an independent existence or any form of autonomy. Consequently they did not face any special difficulty, either during the war or under the newly-formed government. They welcomed King Faysal as their leader and soon integrated within Iraqi society, serving in various fields.

Refugees enhanced the numbers of Christians in Iraq who fled from Turkey before, during and after World War I. These included Assyrians, Armenians and West Syrians. The latter included a combination of Syrian Orthodox and Syrian Catholic Christians from the cities of Mardin, Diyarbakir, Tur'Abdin and the surrounding areas, all of whom had taken no political side during World War I, nor did they seek an independent political existence, in spite of which they suffered from Kurdish and Turkish persecution. After the war, the Turkish government granted permission to all Christians to leave Turkey. This led to yet another wave of emigration, in panic, in 1922. This flight included a combination of Christians of all denominations who had not yet left Turkey, or who had gone back to their homes there at the end of the war. Syrian Orthodox as well as Syrian Catholics, Chaldeans and Armenians left in haste, bringing to an end many centuries of Christian presence in such cities as Adana and Urfa.

The Catholic Church with its two communities, the Chaldeans and the Syrian Catholics, made up the majority of Christians, most of whom were in Mosul and its surrounding villages. These started to organize themselves as soon as the war ended, restoring old churches, building new ones and establishing schools for general and ecclesiastical education. Schools for girls and boys were established in which religious education could be given, as well as fulfilling the national curriculum.

Catholic missionaries who had already established missions in Mosul, Baghdad and Basra were encouraged to continue their activities. The Dominican fathers, who had been in Mosul since 1750, had many primary schools in Mosul and the surrounding villages, dispensaries, a printing press and an orphanage, as well as a training college for the priesthood. They proceeded to establish an intermediate and a secondary school for boys. A branch of Dominican nuns[5] had arrived in Mosul in 1873 and had opened primary schools for girls in Mosul, and a dispensary. They also had an orphanage, and organized workshops in the villages where they taught young girls sewing and embroidery. Another daughter house was opened in Baghdad in 1881, where they set up a primary school for girls in the old central Christian district of Baghdad, together with workshops and a dispensary. In 1907 they established branches in Basra and Imara, where they provided similar services.

The Carmelites, who had arrived in Basra in 1721, then in Baghdad in 1722, had a school in Basra, two boys' schools in Baghdad, a press, an orphanage and a dispensary. The church they built in these early days still stands in a central part of the old city. During the modern period they built another church and monastery in a new area of Baghdad (Karradat Maryam) and were preparing to move their school and establish a centre that would serve for other activities.

The Syrian Orthodox Christians of Iraq also adjusted well to the new state and welcomed King Faysal as leader. The majority spoke Arabic, and almost all their leaders were well acquainted with the Arabic language. It was under the leadership of Patriarch Ignatius Ilias III (1917–32), who had played an important role in helping the Christians in Mardin and Diyarbakir by meeting with the last of the Turkish sultans, and with Mustafa Kemal, the President of the Republic of Turkey. The Syrian Orthodox Church soon established its own schools and ecclesiastical educational facilities.

The Assyrians, who arrived at the Ba'qubah camp in 1918, soon realized that they had not been taken into consideration when the region was divided, and that they would not have an independent existence. Mar Poulis Shimon, the leader of the community, died of tuberculosis in the Ba'qubah camp in May 1920. His successor was his young nephew Eshai aged eleven years. The Revd W. A. Wigram, the last member of the Archbishop of Canterbury's Mission to the Assyrians, who was helping in their resettlement, took the young patriarch with his aunt Surma,[6] and the rest of their family to their old house in the mission at Bibaydi before returning home. His assignment was officially terminated at the end of 1921, and although the revival of a further mission for the Assyrians was discussed by the new Archbishop of Canterbury, nothing ever materialized. The Archbishop had no political power and as the Assyrians were only interested in political independence, he spoke for them as the representative of the British Christian conscience rather than in ecclesiastical matters. In 1924 the Mission committee agreed to pay for the young Mar Shimon Eshai XXI to come to Britain, and arrangements were made for him to be educated in Canterbury and then in Cambridge. He returned to Mosul in August 1927 where he resumed the leadership of his community and continued to plead for an independent nation for his people.

A number of Assyrians had begun to emigrate to the United States and the United Kingdom in the nineteenth century after contact with American and British missionaries. From the Ba'qubah camp some were in touch with relatives and friends in Western countries, and from there they continued to plead with the British government and the League of Nations for a return to their original homeland in the Hakkäri area, where they wanted to live as a self- governing nation.

When plans for mass resettlement in a certain area failed,[7] the Assyrians agreed with British officials in Iraq on a policy of gradual dispersal. Individuals were given grants to settle wherever they could and the camp at Ba'qubah was closed in the summer of 1921.

From the Ba'qubah camp, the Assyrians were transferred to the Mindan camp near Mosul from which they were settled in three main areas: those who were originally from Urmiya were allowed to go back to their homes with the agreement of the Persian government; those whose original homes were south of the border with Turkey and within the borders of modern Iraq went back to their own villages. As for the Hakkäri mountainpeople, some returned to their homes in the Hakkäri area, including Mar Shimon and his sister Surma. At the time they met no resistance, but returned to Iraq again when the Turkish government expelled them in 1924. The majority, however, settled in Mosul and the surrounding villages. It is estimated that about nine thousand settled in Amadiyah and its northern districts, and eight thousand in Duhok, Zäkho, 'Aqrah and Shaykhan. A small number chose to live in the cities where they found suitable employment.

During this period, many of the Assyrian refugees joined the levy forces, a British controlled force in the British army that operated during British mandate rule. This force included Arabs and Kurds as well as Assyrians, but since the latter proved to be able fighters more were recruited. In 1919 two battalions of Assyrians were formed out of the refugee camp in Ba'qubah and were used in operations against the Kurds in Amadiyah. A further fifteen hundred Assyrians were recruited in 1922, and this policy continued: it created a feeling of intense jealousy from the Iraqi army, and hatred from the town inhabitants. Assyrians were considered to be protégés of the British, and so were equated with British imperialism. From 1926 the number of Assyrian levies started to be reduced, and by June 1932 there were only eight hundred, employed mainly in the British Royal Air Force.

During this period, a new American Protestant mission

was established in 1923, the United Mission of Mesopotamia, later changed to the United Mission in Iraq.[8] Members of the mission arrived in September 1925, opening modern schools and hostels for both boys and girls. Their stations extended from the capital, Baghdad, to Mosul, Kirkuk, Duhok, Bahshiqa and Hillah. They worked mainly among the local Christians but in Bahshiqa they targeted the Yazidis. While many of their missionary stations faltered and later closed, that in Baghdad continued.

In addition to converting a few Christians to Protestantism, one of their main achievements was the establishment of a high school for girls. The American School for Girls in Baghdad, started as a primary school and a nursery, but later became exclusively an institution for intermediate and secondary education covering both literature and the sciences. Because of the high level of education it provided, and the success its students achieved in the final exams, the school expanded to include three hundred and twenty students by the time it was placed under Iraqi government jurisdiction in 1972.

Independent Iraq under the monarchy

After four centuries of Turkish rule and fourteen years of British rule and mandate, Iraq finally became an independent nation. In 1932 it was formally admitted to the League of Nations with King Faysal I as leader. The king did not live long, dying of a heart attack while in Geneva in 1933. He left the throne to his twenty-one year old son Ghazi, who in turn died in 1939 in a car accident.[9] Ghazi's successor was his seven-year-old son Faysal II, who ruled with his uncle Abd al-Ilah as regent until the monarchy was toppled by a military coup in 1958.

The constitution of Iraq was democratic, with a two-chamber parliament, the House of Deputies and the House of Senators; Christians and Jews were represented in both houses. In 1935, there were eight Christian and Jewish representatives out of eighty-eight deputies. This was increased to twelve Christians and six Jews in 1954, when the number of deputies was increased to one hundred and thirty-two in order to match the increased number of the population.

Although Islam was the official religion of the state, other religious groups were given full rights. The constitution ensured

> complete freedom of conscience and free exercise of all forms of worship subject only to the maintenance of public order and morals. No discrimination of any kind shall be made between the inhabitants of Iraq on the grounds of race, religion or language, and the government shall secure the right of each community to maintain its own schools for the education of its own members in its own language, while conforming to such educational requirements of a general nature as the government of Iraq may impose ... [10]

Christians had equal rights for admittance to the universities, some of which had already been established when Iraq was under British mandate. Officially they had equal access to all jobs, and a few held senior positions and were representatives in parliament. Yusif Ghanima, the patriarch of the Chaldeans, represented the Christians in the House of Senators, while several prominent Christian lay people were representatives in the House of Deputies. One of them was the leading intellectual, writer and journalist, Rufa'il Butti, who was later made Minister of State – his newspaper was the most widely read. However, administrative positions in general continued to be the prerogative of Muslims, even at the lower scale such as administrator of a village or director of a hospital.[11] Due to these restrictions, Christians excelled in the professions and served as doctors, nurses, engineers and teachers as well as craftsmen and business people.

All Christian communities, except the Assyrians, gave their loyalty to the king and organized celebrations in his honour. The Chaldeans, Syrian Catholics and Syrian Orthodox Christians proclaimed their loyalty to the Iraqi government, emphasizing that they claimed no temporal power for themselves. When the provisional constitution of Iraq provided for representatives in the chamber of deputies, the Syro-Chaldean hierarchy opposed it, maintaining that they sought no special rights and that they trusted to the goodwill of their Muslim brethren that they would be treated as equal citizens to the Muslims. What happened to the Christians, whether Armenians, Syrian Orthodox or Syrian Catholics, during the last few decades of Ottoman rule was still vivid in their memory. The massacres of these communities were partly attributed to Western European policies and the failure of the Europeans to stand by their promises to them. One of the Iraqi newspapers warned: 'Do not forget the fate of the Armenians and the Assyrians who put their trust in Christian powers and were practically exterminated in the process'.[12]

Although foreign intervention may have protected the Christian communities on certain occasions and provided education at a time when this was not provided by the state, in the end it led to tragedy, and it complicated relations between Christians and Muslims. The Christians were seen as collaborators with the Europeans and identified with their policies. Such associations continued to have a detrimental effect until later times.[13]

The Minister of the Interior, Muzahim al-Amin al-Pachachi, addressed a group of various religious and ethnic minorities in Mosul promising that they would be treated with equality and that 'our non-Muslim fellow countrymen are partners with us without distinction or privilege as regards religion or sect'.[14]

He asked the Chaldean patriarch to continue to give the help and support that he had already given to the Iraqi government and to influence the Vatican to support the policy that the Iraqi government was following. He warned that certain groups were endeavouring to destroy the country's unity at the time when Iraq was entering a new era and was about to be freed from British influence. He exhorted the leaders present during the meeting to work as brothers in unity. Both Christian leaders and the Vatican's Apostolic Delegation in Iraq expressed their satisfaction with the policy Iraq was pursuing, and their support.

Churches of all denominations who respected the king continued to flourish under the monarchy. By this time the largest community was that in communion with the Roman Catholic Church, namely the Chaldean and the Syrian Catholic Churches. Next in size was the Syrian Orthodox Church, then the Church of the East (or the 'Assyrian Church of the East') and the Armenian Churches. There were also small Protestant, Latin, and Greek communities.

Since the period when Iraq was under British mandate, existing Christian missions expanded and new ones were established. This continued under the monarchy and missionary schools became an asset to both Christians and Muslims. The latter were willing to send their children to these schools, since there was no attempt at evangelization.

In 1928 the Dominican Sisters of the Presentation opened a private primary, intermediate and secondary school for girls, and an orphanage in a modern district of Baghdad, Bab al-Sharqi. This was the first private school for girls, and was unique in the high standards of education and discipline it offered. It was highly prestigious and sought after by Muslims as well as Christians. It accepted students from provinces outside Baghdad, as it offered special accommodation facilities. It continued to be popular until it was put under government jurisdiction in 1974.

Between 1912 and 1937 the Presentation Sisters worked in the government hospital of Baghdad[15] as nurses and teachers of nursing technique. The first Iraqi nurse was a member of their order and trained by them. In 1937 they started building a private hospital which was inaugurated in 1950 by the name of the Hospital of St Raphael. A nursing school followed this in 1962, where hundreds of nurses trained and graduated to serve in the government sector.

The Carmelites moved their primary school from the old district of Baghdad to a modern part of the town and enlarged its facilities. The grounds where the new school was built also included 'The Centre', in which facilities for other Christian activities were provided, such as the '*akhawiya* of our Lady', or 'The Fraternity of our Lady', the 'Women's Charity Society' and the 'Christian Cultural Club'. This centre was established mainly by the efforts of two young Carmelite priests who had arrived to Iraq in 1956, Father Robert Beulay and Father Raymond Charbonnier. In this club Christian college students from all denominations met socially, in the spirit of ecumenism brought forward at that time by the Second Vatican Council. The emphasis was on cultural activities such as the study of history, literature or poetry, as well as social activities. There were monthly lectures given by experts in their field, small weekly study groups and yearly plays. I was privileged to have been a member of this club, as I have mentioned in the introduction.

A Jesuit American mission arrived in 1932, coinciding with Iraq independence. Initially four Jesuits arrived and established a small secondary school for boys, Baghdad College, in a rented accommodation in the centre of Baghdad. Two years later, plans were made to build an extensive campus in Sulaikh, a northern district of Baghdad. Some twenty-five acres of land was bought in which nine major buildings and some minor buildings were constructed. Soon after they moved to this new complex in the year 1938–9, the number of admissions climbed and the school became a major feature of modern Iraq. Its doors were open to all, and many notables, ministers and Arab sheiks had their children educated at it. The school was not only a model in its curriculum which encompassed the sciences and the humanities, but it also excelled in sports, on which the Jesuits put much of their emphasis. The secondary school programme was first published in 1926 and provided for a four-year course until 1932, when it was lengthened to five years at two stages: the intermediate in three years and secondary level in two years. Intermediate level graduates could choose between two tracks in the secondary school, the sciences and the humanities.

Although in Baghdad a modern university had been established which had colleges that gave courses in most scientific and literary fields, the Jesuits decided to open a university. They were granted official permission from the Ministry of Education in 1955 to start two four-year courses, one in physics and the other in business administration, as they felt that experts in these two fields were urgently needed. They were given one hundred and sixty-eight acres of land in Za'faranyia, an area fourteen miles south of Baghdad where they established a fine university. This university was very successful and its courses were recognized in Western countries.

The Syrian Orthodox Church flourished under the able leadership of Ignatius Efrem I Basaum (1887–1957). He was born in Mosul and became patriarch in 1933. He mastered several languages and was a respected scholar of both Arabic and Syriac. His writings covered the areas of religion, languages, history and culture and he made several translations from Syriac to Arabic. He had a prominent role in the Paris peace conference of 1919 where he gave a speech putting forward the rights of the Arabs; this made people call him 'The Bishop of Arabism'. He ordered the building of several churches, established St. Efrem's clerical college in Zāhlah, which he moved to Mosul in 1945, and published *The Patriarchal Magazine*.

The Armenians who had escaped the massacres of Turkey, together with the original small Armenian community that had resided in Iraq from the seventeenth century also organized itself and was represented in two churches: the Armenian Orthodox Church and the Armenian Catholic Church.

New Protestant denominations also emerged as a consequence of Protestant missionary activities.

By contrast, the refusal of the Assyrians to co-operate led to tragedy. When the British handed full rule to the Iraqi government, the Assyrian levy system was dissolved, but the tribesmen were allowed to retain their arms, the argument being that this would enable them to defend their villages until the Iraqi government was in full control. When this finally happened, Mar Shimon XXI Eshai was asked to relinquish any claim of temporal power and to order his armed men to hand in their weapons and to join the Iraqi army.

Extended negotiations followed between Mar Shimon, his *maliks* and tribesmen on one hand, and Iraqi government officials and British mediators on the other hand. Many of the Assyrians could not adjust to the new situation in which they found themselves. Mar Shimon himself was only eleven years old when he became patriarch in 1920. He had spent the next seven years in Britain where he was educated, and actual leadership was in the hands of his aunt Surma. His tribes had enjoyed a more or less independent self-rule within the Ottoman Empire, and had been promised independence by the British alongside whom they fought. Consequently, they felt betrayed by the new stance of British officials who were trying to convince them to co-operate with the Iraqi government.[16] This led to division within the Assyrian community. A proportion of the Assyrians under the leadership of Malik Khoshaba resigned themselves to settlement in Iraq, considering the leadership of Mar Shimon erroneous, while the party of Mar Shimon continued to cause problems. One of their leaders, Yaqo, started touring the villages of north Iraq with armed men promoting the cause of the Assyrians for an independent existence.

The Iraqi government, taking advantage of the absence of the king, who left the country on an official visit to Britain on 20 June 1933,[17] reacted abruptly by calling Mar Shimon to Baghdad and asked him to sign a document giving full allegiance to the king, and relinquishing any temporal power he had been claiming. Mar Shimon answered with a detailed letter arguing about a certain point in the document that was sent to him. He was summoned to Baghdad on 24 June 1933 and put under house arrest. His followers were given the choice of leaving the country or signing their full allegiance to the government. Some of them accepted and settled in Iraq, while a group of them decided to leave the country. On 4 August, some eight hundred armed Assyrians arrived at the border with Syria, without having negotiated any agreement with the French authorities, who were still in mandate control over Syria. Consequently they were refused admission to Syria, and were sent back to Iraq. A battle ensued with the Iraqi army at Derabun, causing the death of many on both sides, and the internment of some Assyrians by the Iraqis. About five hundred men went back to Syria, where they were interned by the French government and were later given the choice of settling in Syria or leaving.[18]

These events were represented as a dangerous movement, and that the British were behind them. Anti-Assyrian measures taken over the next few days included the hasty arming of Kurdish irregulars, the search of all roads for stray Assyrians who were shot on the spot (no fewer than a hundred Assyrians were shot this way), while Kurdish and Arab tribes started looting and ruining nearly all the Assyrian villages in Zäkho and Duhok and Shaykhan areas. Refugees, penniless and hungry, poured into Mosul and the large central area of Alqosh and Semmel seeking protection. In Semmel, Assyrians had clustered around the police station for protection. Their terror increased when tribesmen were allowed to enter the village of Semmel and loot their homes. On the morning of 11 August 1933, under the leadership of Bakr Sidqi, the military commander of Mosul (although he himself took care to be absent on that day), a detachment of the Iraqi army carrying machine guns entered the village of Semmel in a motor vehicle, and under the order of its officers methodically massacred every man in the village. The work was complete by the early afternoon, and the army withdrew in their vehicles, leaving a total of three hundred and fifteen dead, including six women and four children. The Iraqi army announced the incident as a defeat of an uprising, and the government announced it as a timely anti-British measure. The newspapers and the people on the streets hailed Bakr Sidqi and the army as heroes. Amir Ghazi and al-Gaylani were hailed as nationalist heroes, while the king was completely ignored. This incident has been considered a blot on the history of the Iraqi army, because many of the men killed had put down their weapons. The Iraqi government was apologetic at the United Nations, although it tried to put the blame on Kurdish and Arab tribes. The military in charge were not condemned.[19]

The Patriarch Mar Shimon Eshai was deported to Cyprus in August 1933. From Cyprus he moved to Geneva, Paris and London, during which period he continued to plead the cause of the Assyrians with the United Nations. He finally joined the community of Assyrians in the United States of America. Some of the Assyrians had emigrated to the USA from the early nineteenth century when they had come in contact with American Protestant missions. However, the majority emigrated after World War I. With the help of the American Episcopal Church, the Church of the East consolidated around the leadership of Mar Shimon in Chicago. The Assyrians who were interned by the Iraqi government were deported in 1936 to Syria where the French government allowed them to settle in the region of Khabur in the plains of Jezirah (an area between the upper Euphrates as it turns up to Turkey and the Tigris).

The community of the Assyrians that stayed accepted the authority of the king, received Iraqi nationality and contributed to the building of modern Iraq. The church began to organize itself under the leadership of Metropolitan Mar Yosip Khananisho. Those Assyrians who continued to serve in the British RAF took a conspicuous part in the operations that put down the military uprising of 1941.[20] During this period all Christians felt specially vulnerable, since it was Rashid Ali's government and the Army that conducted the massacre of Semmel.

The republic of Iraq

An army coup with General Abdul Karim Qasim as leader of the free army officers toppled the monarchy on 14 July 1958. Several reforms were introduced and an effort was made to represent the different communities. However, numerous coups and plots plagued the regime, which was finally overthrown in 1963, when Qasim was killed, and Abd al-Salam Arif became President. The Ba'ath[21] party played a major role in this coup and its organized 'National Guards' started to wreak havoc in the country, detaining and killing mainly the communists. The Ba'ath party was displaced in October of the same year and Abd al-Salam Arif continued to rule as President until he died in a helicopter accident in 1966 and his brother Abd al-Rahman succeeded. Neither belonged to an official party but both considered themselves as Arab Nationalists. During this period, the Ba'ath party had gone underground and started to organize itself and consolidate its influence. On 17 July 1968 it gained full control after a bloodless coup with Ahmad Hassan al-Bakir as President and Saddam Husayn Vice-President of the Revolutionary Command Council. They ruled together until Saddam seized total power in 1979.

Saddam Husayn ruled as a ruthless dictator, with three sets of police and security machines spying on each other and on individual citizens. Several attempts to overthrow him failed and the average individual had no option but to comply. Those who voiced any objection were ruthlessly treated.[22] Every individual was asked to register as a Ba'athist and those who did not were disadvantaged. With rare exceptions, those who held administrative positions had to be confirmed Ba'athists. The slogan to explain away the few citizens who would not join the party was 'Every decent citizen is a Ba'athist even though he has not joined the party'. Every single institution in the country including schools, hospitals, the ministries and general administration had to reiterate Saddam's slogans and celebrate his birthday. The cult of Saddam the individual became a phenomenon that weighed heavily on every decent person who did not want to take part in these celebrations. Nobody could avoid them as they took place during official office work – it was the duty of every individual to be at work on the birthday of Saddam, and absence was recorded.

During the thirty-four years of Ba'athist rule the country passed through several crises. The first was the Iraqi–Iranian war which lasted eight years (1980–8); the second was the invasion of Kuwait in August 1990, and the third was the bombing of Iraq in 1991 by coalition forces and the introduction of sanctions which had lasted twelve years, until April 2003, when a coalition led by the Americans invaded Iraq in April 2003.

The Christian Iraqi community was generally fairly treated by the regime, as long as they toed the line. In fact some of them were specially favoured because they were trusted, as they were less likely to cause trouble. Their religious institutions were respected, and even supplied with free electricity. Many Christian cultural events were encouraged. In 1974 a conference celebrating the great Christian Arab physician and translator, Hunayn ibn Ishaq was organized by the Iraqi government, and between 1984–5 a centenary celebrating the fifteen hundredth anniversary of the establishment of Der Mar Behnam was officially supported. A sense of belonging to the country as an Arab, an Iraqi and a Christian was encouraged but only through being a Ba'athist.

However, the Christians suffered equally with their Muslim brethren, whether from the totalitarianism of the Ba'athist regime, the despotism of Saddam Husayn, the carnage that accompanied the two Gulf Wars or from the sanctions imposed by the United Nations on the country from 1991 until the removal of Saddam.

The abolition of private education

When the Ba'ath regime seized total power in 1968, one of the first steps to be taken was to place all private schools under government jurisdiction, whether they belonged to Christians or to Muslims. The Ba'ath party saw education as one of the exclusive functions of the state, and was opposed to any form of private education, as was stated in Article 45 of the constitution of the Ba'ath party: 'Teaching is one of the exclusive functions of the state. Therefore all foreign and private educational institutions are abolished'.[23]

The Ba'athists had their own agenda of making every Iraqi individual an Arab nationalist, including Kurds, Turkomans, Assyrians or any other small ethnic minority. Every single individual had to be involved in what they claimed was the struggle against imperialism and Zionism, and this was to be achieved through the education system. In actual fact, the schools became the tools of propagating the cult of Saddam Husayn, the national hero.

Christian schools had been in operation from the eighteenth century, and had made a substantial contribution to the education of the nation. They were also the main avenues where Christian religious education was given. Many of them were established, owned and run by Iraqi churches and their teachers were all Iraqis. Yet these too were placed under the control of the state.

The first move was made against al-Hikma university, and the Jesuit fathers teaching there. In September 1968, a decree from the council of command of the revolution decreed that al-Hikma university was to be 'Iraqized'[24] and placed under the direct supervision of the government in all respects. In October the Jesuit fathers were dismissed and given five days to leave the country. Twenty-eight Jesuits departed and the grounds of al-Hikma university were taken. Nine months later, in August 1969, the government took possession of Baghdad College and similarly dismissed thirty-three Jesuits. In spite of threats, hundreds of students, both Muslim and Christian, went to the airport to bid the Jesuit fathers farewell.

By 1972, all private schools in turn were put under the

control of the state, even though native Iraqis and local churches owned them and they were run by Iraqi staff. Iraqi teachers were allowed to continue teaching their general subjects, but religious lessons were no longer allowed. All headmasters and headmistresses had to belong to the Ba'ath party and all children and students had to reiterate the slogans of the Ba'ath party and Saddam Husayn.

The taking over of the schools dealt a major blow to the Christian communities, mainly because it deprived them of a system of education they appreciated and loved, and it took away their freedom regarding methods of educating their children. Moreover, the Ba'athist regime considered their system tantamount to Westernization, against the spirit of Arab nationalism; consequently it was an indirect accusation of complicity with Westerners and Western imperialism. This was actually far from the case, since most of the schools, especially the primary schools, were owned by the Iraqi churches and classes were taught by Iraqi teachers, who loved their country and conveyed this feeling to their students. In the Jesuit school, it was the policy of the administration and teachers to encourage their students to value their country and their ancient heritage. Many of their teachers spoke fluent Arabic and some of them were Arab scholars who taught in Arabic and encouraged the use of the Arabic language. A notable example was Father Richard McCarthy, a dedicated teacher in Baghdad College, who was fluent in Arabic and an authority on Islamic philosophy and theology. In fact one of the reasons given by the Jesuits for starting al-Hikma university was to provide higher education in subjects that were not fully provided by the University of Baghdad in order to avoid students leaving the country for further education at a young age. My experience with the Carmelites in the Christian Cultural Club was exactly that. They fostered in all students they encountered a feeling of belonging to the country, and a pride in being Iraqi and Christian.

Having lost their schools, the Christians soon adjusted

to the new situation. Churches began to organize a system of religious education for their parishioners within the churches, usually on Fridays, the official holiday of the week. The Christian Cultural Club continued to operate under close supervision of the government until it was closed down in 1986.[25] The Carmelite fathers retired to their monastery and began a fraternity for college students which concentrated on religious rather than cultural aspects of education. They were amongst the few foreigners who were not expelled by the regime.

Internal migration and emigration

The governorate of Mosul had the largest proportion of the Christian population of Iraq at the beginning of the twentieth century. This gradually changed due to movement of the Christian population from the city of Mosul and its villages over the next few decades.

This movement began soon after the 1958 revolution. The communist party, which had been suppressed during the monarchy, now started to be active. In 1959, in a show of force, the party decided to convene the national congress of Ansar al-Salam (Peace Partisans) and organized a massive rally in the city of Mosul, though most of the population was against it. The city was divided and the Christian community as a whole was classified wrongly as 'communist sympathizers'.[26] The commander of the city garrison, Colonel Abd al-Wahhab al-Shawaf, sensing the tension, pleaded with Qasim to prevent the convention and the rally from taking place. The colonel was an Arab nationalist and was supported by Abd al-Nasir and the United Arab Republic, the transitory republic which was the result of union of Egypt and Syria. When Qasim refused the request, he declared a mutiny, and launched an armed movement against the central government in Baghdad. Qasim's government put down the mutiny in five days, and al-Shawaf was killed. During the following weeks the communists took control of the city, set up their own kangaroo court and committed many atrocities. As a consequence Qasim changed his policy and suppressed the communists. There was a backlash of intimidation and assassinations during which the Christian community was targeted indiscriminately. This was followed by a wave of migration of Christians from Mosul to Baghdad, which changed the proportion of Christians present in these two major cities.[27] Whilst in the census of 1957 more than half of the Christians were in Mosul, this was reversed in the census of 1977.

In northern Iraq, the Christian communities which had lived in villages alongside Kurdish ones were affected when the Kurdish movement began, soon after Qasim's government was toppled in 1963. The Ba'ath party with its ideals of pan-Arabism did not have sympathy for Kurdish national aspirations. Although Ba'athist rule was interrupted in October of the same year, the rulers that followed, Abdul Salam Arif and Abdul Rahman Arif, who were not Ba'athists, also spoke of Arab nationalism. The Kurds asked for national rights, and when negotiations failed the army launched several offensives, all of which ended in stalemate, with disastrous consequences. The war dragged on for several years during which the Christian villages suffered greatly. The Kurds wanted the Christian villagers to support them in their fight against the government. The majority refused co-operation with the Kurds and consequently were attacked by them, while the few who co-operated were attacked by the government. Caught between two hostile camps, large numbers fled from their homes to the cities, mainly Baghdad and Mosul. As a consequence a large numbers of purely Christian villages were emptied. Many of these villagers ultimately joined their friends and relatives in Europe and the United States.

After the Iraqi–Iranian war a common response amongst all communities, whether Christian or Muslim, was to leave the country if possible. During hostilities many young people left because they did not want to lose their lives in a war they did not believe in. Other individuals left due to persecution by the regime, or because of extreme economic hardship. The phenomenon of emigration was aggravated after the invasion of Kuwait and the institution of sanctions. The departure became an exodus. People left in droves, as they had lost the hope of anything beneficial happening to their country. At first, having lived through eight difficult years of the Iraqi–Iranian war (I remember this very vividly), people were expecting relief and affluence when the war came to an end in 1988. When they saw no improvement in the general situation, they began to question the policies of the government. Nobody ever imagined that Iraq would be invading Kuwait, particularly so soon after of a war at the end of which nobody was a winner.

Moreover the cruelty of Saddam and his gangs was worsening and, knowing that several attempts to topple the regime had failed, people lost hope when the world coalition did not remove him. Many who had never dreamt of leaving the country left their property and affluence behind, seeking life in any country that would accept them. Over the next ten years the diaspora of Iraqis stretched from Europe and Canada to Australia, New Zealand, Yemen, Malaysia and other parts of the world. Being resourceful and intelligent, the majority started to make a good living, but some lost their lives during the process, especially the poor. Many people, prosperous and well-educated in their own country, were reduced to the status of refugees.

Christian–Muslim relations

There had been a record of positive Christian–Muslim relations since the creation of the modern state of Iraq in 1932. The constitution had stressed the equality of all religious groups before the law, in opportunities for education and work, and their identical responsibility for the defence and building up of their country. During the last seventy years anti-Christian feelings had rarely been voiced, and the majority emphasized what was in common between the two religions rather than the differences. Muslims from all over the country and from all social classes began to be engaged in education, and accepting non-Muslims as equal citizens became more or less the norm. They met their Christian compatriots in schools and at work, and strong friendships developed. Socialization between Christians and Muslims became a common phenomenon, and any discussion on religious matters was carried on in a spirit of friendship.

Of course, it was difficult to wipe out centuries of prejudice and hard feelings. The long Ottoman rule and its treatment of the Christian as second-class citizens left a deep scar in the collective consciousness. Moreover, the tragedies that followed the involvement in politics of the Assyrians and the Armenians moulded their behaviour for a long time after the Ottomans had gone. Soon after they were recognized as equal citizens by the new Iraqi government, the incident of the massacre of the Assyrians in Semmel, and the response of the Iraqi population, reopened a wound that had begun to heal. Consequently Christians were in general timid, easily subdued, and avoided involvement in politics. All these factors made competition for higher jobs difficult. Moreover, undisclosed rivalries at work, in which religion was used as a pretext in order to get the upper hand, were fairly common. However, during the monarchy, barriers began to be overcome and we find a few Christians becoming government ministers: Yusif Ghanima became finance minister several times, and Hanna Khayat health minister. After Qasim's revolution there was an attempt to include Christians: Najib al-Saig became ambassador for Iraq in Lebanon, and Da'ood F. Sarsam was appointed minister of municipality in Naji Talib's government. Naji Talib himself was the first Shi'ite premier. Hanna Razooqi al-Saigh served as deputy prime minister in the ministry of finance during the rule of Qasim, Arif and Saddam, and practically ran it for several years, but did not become a minister, because he did not want to get himself involved in politics. During the Ba'ath regime, many Christians were given administrative positions, the most well-known being Tariq Aziz, the minister of foreign affairs. However, it was not credentials or efficiency at work that mattered during the Ba'ath regime, but allegiance to the party and later to the cult of Saddam Husayn.

On the social level, laws regarding conversions and mixed marriages continued to cause problems. The story of a well-known doctor in Baghdad is representative of how the pressure of the community continued to dominate and limit freedom of religious practice. He was a secular person, but had converted to Islam when he wanted to divorce his first Christian wife. He later married another Christian wife of a different denomination. Before his death he went to the United States for treatment, met with his family, asked to be buried with his father in Baghdad, and was given the Catholic last rites before he died. On the arrival of the coffin to Baghdad, it was received by the Muslim community who wanted to make sure that he was buried the Islamic way even though he was to be buried in a Christian cemetery. The cortège left from the medical college, and the wake had to be in a mosque. It was said that in his house his second, Christian, wife had to endure people who enforced the recital of the Qur'an, and who expressed views that it was their duty to make sure that the children were brought up as Muslims. The story exemplifies the fact that once a Muslim, there is no possibility of changing one's mind, even if the conversion to Islam was in lightweight manner. It is an attitude welded into the fabric of the community, which will take a long time to change. Another story is that of a prominent civil servant from Basra whose Christian wife left him and married a Muslim. He was a devout Christian and made sure that his only daughter was brought up a Christian. In fact, I met her aged eight at the dormitory of the Presentation nuns in Baghdad where she was sent to do her primary education. When it came to official documents, she had to be registered as a Muslim. Her father had to obtain special permission that allowed his daughter to follow the faith in which she had been brought up. These are two stories from eminent Christian families. The occurrence of similar social pressures amongst the poor and the defenceless are innumerable. I have personally come across many young nurses who had married Muslim men. Not only was it taken for granted that their children would be brought up as Muslims, but many of them were not allowed to go to church or to practise their faith. The Christian community feels very intimidated by such incidents, and for many in such situations the only way to maintain one's faith is to leave the country.

During the rule of Saddam everybody suffered from his totalitarian regime, but he did not tolerate specific anti-Christian activity. However some incidents began to take place during the last few years of his rule, as he started to use Muslim fundamentalists to sustain his regime. Moreover, his plans of resettling the population, in an attempt to solve the Kurdish problem, led to the destruction of large number of villages in the north of Iraq, many of which were entirely Christian.

Notes

1 Known as the Sykes–Picot Agreement in 1916, in which the French and the British met before the end of the war and agreed to divide the Fertile Crescent between themselves after the war. France was to receive the territory of modern Lebanon, Syria and *vilayet* al-Mosul, while Britain would receive the *vilayet* of Baghdad and Basra, Jordan and Palestine.

2 Sherif Husayn of Mecca, a Hashemite descendent of the prophet Muhammad, was governor of Mecca when he sided with the British and declared a revolt against the Ottomans in 1916. He personally led the Bedouins in the Arab revolt against the Ottomans and organized an army led by his son Faysal. Faysal's forces, with the help of the famous Lawrence of Arabia, entered Damascus at the head of Allenby's British forces which freed Syria, and Palestine. He was acclaimed king of Syria and led an interim government there in 1918, but was obliged to leave when the French entered Syria, as the French did not want him as king. These events have been immortalized in the famous film *Lawrence of Arabia*.

3 These figures are obtained from *A Short History of Iraq* by Thabit Abdullah, p. 123, except the figure for the Christians which comes from the census of 1951 in *Al-Iraq* vol. I, by Hanna Batato, p. 219.

4 *The Jews of Iraq* by Ya'qub Goriyya, p. 31.

5 The full name is: The Dominican Sisters of the Presentation of the Virgin Mary. They were simply called the 'Presentation Nuns'.

6 Surma was the aunt of Shimon XXI Eshai and the sister of the murdered Patriarch Shimon XIX Benjamin and of Patriarch Shimon XX Poulis. She was a remarkable woman, who together with her brothers was educated by the missionary W. H. Browne, of Archbishop Benson's mission to the Assyrians. She went to England in the autumn of 1919 in order to plead the cause of the Assyrians, and met with the Archbishop of Canterbury and some British officials. She asked for her people to be returned to their original home in the Hakkäri mountains and wrote a book with the help of the Revd W. A. Wigram entitled *Assyrian Church Customs*. She acted as the leader of her community until the young Patriarch reached the age of eighteen when he resumed official leadership.

7 During the Paris peace negotiations in 1919, five Assyrian deputations put their claims before the conference, aiming at the establishment of an Assyrian State. Deputations came from Iraq, Turkey, Persia, the Caucasus and the USA. These requests were discussed at the Treaty of Sèvres (10 August 1920), which had a clause that was meant to guarantee the protection of the Assyro-Chaldeans and other ethnic and religious minorities, and a commission was entrusted to visit the area so as to determine any adjustment that needed to be made in the Turkish and Persian frontiers that would guarantee their freedom. At the Conference of Lausanne (24 July 1923), the Assyro-Chaldeans were not represented and Turkey refused to provide an allowance for them to have schools that taught in their language or other measures to maintain their traditions and customs. The treaty only included a series of provisions relating to the protection of non-Muslim communities in Turkey. At the Conference of Constantinople (9 May 1924), the British commissioner in Iraq defended the Assyrians and their right to be established in a compact unity that had some sort of local autonomy.

However, when the League of Nations (16 December 1925) finally awarded the *vilayet* al-Mosul to Iraq, the Hakkäri area, which the Assyrians were claiming, was awarded to Turkey.

8 This mission was the first of Protestant missions that included several Protestant bodies that were integrated to work together. Initially a committee represented the United Reformed Church and the Church of the Elders in the United States. In 1934 the United Reformed Church united with the Evangelical Synod of North America forming the Evangelical and Reformed Church, and in 1957 the latter joined the Republican Churches of America leading to the formation of 'The United Church of Christ'.

9 Ghazi was driving his car on the night of 3 April when he crashed into an electric post near his palace. Many believe that Ghazi's death was not an accident. He has been described as frivolous, impatient of protocol and advice and lacking in wisdom and charm. He had embarrassed members of his government and was discourteous to many of his subjects. He had also shown clear signs of Pan-Arab nationalism, a strong support for Palestine and had claimed sovereignty over Kuwait. As the war with Hitler grew near, Ghazi appeared to be giving support to Germany. Nuri al-Sa'id, the pro-British prime minister of Iraq, is said to have investigated the possibility of removing Ghazi in favour of another Hashemite king. Others have speculated that it was part of a Nazi propaganda scheme to discredit the British.

10 *Independent Iraq*, by Majid Khadduri, pp. 14, 16. The above clause was part of Article 3 of the Anglo-Iraqi Treaty of October 1922. The Iraqi Constitution of 1932 included this article of the Treaty as well as Article 22 of the League of Nations, Article 30–36 of the Treaty of Lausanne and the organic law of 21 March 1925.

11 My father told us a story about the hospital in Mosul where he worked as a consultant surgeon. Nearly all the employees, including the cleaners and nurses as well as doctors were Christians, but the administrator was a Muslim. It was so almost entirely Christian that he used to comment with resentment, that 'this is not a hospital but a church, which only needs the ringing of bells to become fully so'.

12 From John Joseph's book *Muslim-Christian relations and inter-Christian rivalries in the Middle East* p. 115. He refers to the

Current History magazine, November 1924, p. 243, al-Najm 8 January 1936, pp. 134–9.

13 A story may better demonstrate this issue: While on holiday in Greece with a dear Muslim family, my ten-year-old son was told by the son of Muslim friends, who was of similar age, 'Why don't you go and live in your own country?' My son told us the story and asked which is truly his country? We were certain that these comments did not come from his parents, as we were certain of their sincerity and friendship and in considering us equal citizens of Iraq and not some foreigners that should one day return to their country *'The West'*. The comment presumably came from some ignorant or prejudiced teacher in school.

14 From John Joseph's *Christian–Muslim relations and inter–Christian rivalries in the Middle East*, p. 116.

15 Initially called al-Majidi Hospital (by the Ottomans), then the Royal Hospital (by the kingdom of Iraq),and the Republic Hospital (after the 1958 revolution that toppled the king).

16 The king himself met with Mar Shimon and tried to convince him that he would have all the rights other Christian leaders had and that his people would enjoy full citizenship and protection. But he maintained claims of temporal leadership of his community, which the king tried to explain was impossible in the context of the modern constitution of Iraq.

17 The state visit had been scheduled some time before and could not be postponed as it was of importance for Iraqi international relations. He left Iraq with three of his most trusted ministers and the British ambassador to Iraq, Sir Humphry Davies. His twenty-one-year-old son Ghazi, was to take his place.

18 Hearing of the escalation of the Assyrian problem while in Britain, the king communicated with his prime minister Rashid Ali al-Gaylani and advised him to release Mar Shimon and solve the problem peacefully. As his advice was not heeded, and sensing the gravity of the situation, he interrupted his visit in spite of feeling ill, and returned to Baghdad on 2 August. On his arrival, he was struck by the cool reception he received, in contrast to applause for his son and the generals. Information was concealed from him; ill and dispirited, he could not influence events. Realizing his isolation and impotent to do anything, he was deeply grieved and his medical condition worsened. He left for

Switzerland for treatment on 2 September where he died a few days later.

19 It has been argued that Prime Minister Rashid Ali al-Gaylani's government, taking the opportunity of the absence of the king with three of his important ministers and the British ambassador to Iraq, Sir Humphrey Davies, staged an intended propaganda coup portraying the Assyrians as a dangerous threat to the country, leading a rebellion backed by the British. News of the massacre was concealed from the public, who were instead deceived by stories of the gallantry of the Iraqi troops and the treacherous designs of Great Britain. This propaganda succeeded in creating a violent anti-Assyrian as well as anti-British feeling amongst the people. The Prime Minister, Ghazi and Bakr Sidqi emerged as heroes resisting British hegemony, and the army as able fighters who crushed a rebellion. In Mosul both anti-Assyrian and anti-Christian feelings were intense. See Abd al-Majid al-Qaysi, *The political and military history of the Assyrians*. This argument is plausible as al-Gaylani proved to be a Fascist: he was party in the insurgence against the King in 1941, and stood with Germany during World War II.

20 On the 1 April 1941, four generals and the acting chief of staff Amin Zaki Sulayman met to proclaim a state of emergency and marched troops to Baghdad to the palace. The regent escaped and the generals proclaimed the formation of a 'Government of National Defence', which included themselves and Rashid Ali al-Gaylani as the head. The movement was crushed within two months by British forces and both king and regent returned to full power on 22 May 1941.

21 The Ba'ath Party is a political organization formed in Syria in 1944 by a Christian Arab, Michel Aflaq. A few years later, it merged with the Arab Socialist Party and changed its name to 'The Arab Ba'ath Socialist Party'. Its ideology can be summarized by the slogans 'One Arab Nation with an eternal mission' and 'Unity, Freedom and Socialism'. Although secular in its tenets and considering that Christians can be fully Arabs just like Muslims, it emphasized the Qur'an as an essential inspiration for Arabism. Aflaq reiterates in his book *In the pursuit of Ba'ath* and in his milestone lecture delivered in Damascus to a packed audience entitled 'In memory of the Arab prophet', the link between 'The Prophet', Islam and the formation of the Arab nation. He

emphasizes that the soul of Arabism is Islam, but he defined an Arab as 'any individual who speaks the Arabic language and shares the history, destiny and aspirations of the Arab nation'. The Ba'ath party believe the Arabs as a nation carry a unique and immortal message. This party was attractive to many intellectual Christians and progressive Muslims, since for the Christians it gave them a feeling of recognition and belonging; for the Muslim it combined the importance of Islam nationalism and socialism. After gaining political control in both Syria and Iraq, the misuse of human rights practised by both regimes as well as their split in 1960, caused disillusionment in many sincere members. From the beginning fundamentalist Muslims were against it, not only because its founder was a Christian, but also because it is not a unified Arab *state* that they are interested in, but a unified Muslim *world*.

22 Examples of his ruthlessness are innumerable and out of the scope of this book. However, I choose one story as an example: after he came to power one of his policies was to make sure that no communist would voice an objection, however insignificant, and every suspected communist was made to sign a statement that he denounced his previous activities. One student apparently had some such association. Nobody knows what went on between him and the officials; the worst was that he failed to sign the document. The next thing we heard was that both he and his younger brother, who had no association with the communists whatsoever, did not come home. There was no warrant of arrest nor any response to the mother who went to the authorities asking the whereabouts of her two sons. No answer was ever given.

23 J. F. MacDonald *Jesuits by the Tigris*, p. 235.

24 When the grounds of al-Hikma university were taken, it was specifically called 'Iraqization' and not nationalization. The argument was that nationalisation meant transfer from the private sector to the public sector while 'Iraqization' was a purely administrative measure which had for its aim the placing of the institution under direct Iraqi administration and supervision. That meant that the al-Hikma university would remain the property of the Iraq-American association and so the ownership would not be transferred to the Iraqi government as a result of 'Iraqization' without compensa-

tion and without claiming ownership.

25 I helped in the administration of the Christian cultural administration for five or six years before its closure. I used to invite speakers to give us talks on various cultural subjects, Christians and Muslims. During these years the atmosphere was restrained and we had to watch what we said. One day we had a Christian Ba'athist speaker with whom I was discussing various aspects of culture. When I spoke of our Christian culture and heritage, he curtly stopped me and said: 'You should not speak of Christian culture. There is only Arab culture.' When I asked about those who speak Syriac, the answer was that these are also Arabs. It was the policy of foreigners to distinguish between Arabs, Aramaeans, Assyrians or Babylonians. The actual reality they argued was that these were all Arab and scholars were ordered to rewrite the history of the region, renaming all these ancient people of Mesopotamia as 'The old Arab nations'.

26 The origins of this phenomenon is difficult to explain. Although there were a number of Christians who belonged to the communist party, and some of them had important roles to play, they were by no means the majority. As a matter of fact, one of their major organizers who was executed under the monarchy was a Christian. My explanation is that being a minority they came easily under the spotlights and consequently became easily victimized.

27 Both my family and my husband's family moved from the city of Mosul to Baghdad during this period.

7

The twenty-first century

I. The churches in Iraq at the beginning of the twenty-first century

In this section I will be giving a brief description of the situation of the churches and their activities as known at the beginning of the third millennium, before the collapse of the Ba'athist regime of Saddam and the invasion of the country by American and Allied forces.

The churches in Iraq at the beginning of the twenty-first century can be categorized as follows:

The Church Of The East
    1 The Ancient Church of the East
    2. The Assyrian Church of the East

The Oriental Orthodox Churches
    1. The Syrian Orthodox Church
    2. The Armenian Orthodox Church
    3. The Greek Orthodox Church or al-Rum al-Orthodox

The Catholic Churches
    1. The Chaldean Church
    2. The Syrian Catholic Church
    3. The Armenian Catholic Church
    4. The Latin Church
    5. The Greek Catholic Church or al-Rum al-Cathulik

The Protestant Churches
- 1. The National Evangelical Church
- 2. The Assyrian Evangelical Church
- 3. The Armenian Evangelical Church
- 4. Jehovah's Witnesses
- 5. The Seventh-day Adventists
- 6. Other small groups

The Anglican Church

The Greek Orthodox Church

The Coptic Church

The Church of the East

The Church of the East was organized in Iraq after the deportation of its Patriarch Mar Eshai Shimon XXI in 1933 by Metropolitan Mar Yosip Khannanisho. In 1963 he transferred his see to Baghdad and exercised his office as patriarchal vicar over the dioceses of the Middle East. Additional bishops were then consecrated for Arbil, Mosul and Syria.

Mar Eshai Shimon joined his community in Chicago in the USA, after his efforts to secure an independent homeland had failed. From there, he started to reorganize the Church of the East in the United States of America and other regions of the diaspora. He could not visit his community in Iraq until 1970, when he was recognized by the Iraqi government as the religious head of his church.

The Church of the East was split in 1964, when Mar Eshai Shimon issued a decree in which he announced reforms to the liturgy, shortening the period of Lent and using the Gregorian calendar instead of the Julian calendar. Opposition to these changes came from Baghdad: it led to fracture of the church and the emergence of an independent patriarchate. The opposition party, led by a priest, Ishaq Nwiya, appealed to Mar Thomas Darmo, Metropolitan of India, who travelled to Iraq in 1968 and consecrated three bishops for Iraq; he himself was acknowledged patriarch for the new community. However, he died one year after his consecration and no patriarch was consecrated until 1972, since there were attempts at reconciliation with the community of Mar Shimon. When these attempts failed, the community in Iraq chose Mar Addai II Giwargis as patriarch in 1972. He was consecrated as patriarch of the new community, which came to be known as 'The Ancient Church of the East', and has been the head of this church until the present time.

The community that followed the new reforms changed its name to the 'Assyrian Church of the East'. Its patriarch, Mar Eshai Shimon, resigned his office in 1972 and married in 1973. Following the death of Mar Shimon, who was assassinated by a disgruntled relative in 1975, the bishops of this church met in a synod, decided to abolish the hereditary succession of the patriarchate, and introduced the canonical election of the patriarch. They met in October 1976 in London and elected Mar Dinkha IV Khnanaya as patriarch, and successor of the seat of Seleucia–Ctesiphon. Initially he had his seat in Tehran, until after the onset of the Iraqi–Iranian war in 1980, when he transferred it to Chicago; he has been the head of this church until the present time.

The number of the faithful at the beginning of the twenty-first century belonging to the Assyrian Church of the East under Mar Dinkha was estimated to be around 385,000, and the number belonging to the Ancient Church of the East under Mar Addai to be 50–70,000.[1]

Presently, the Assyrian Church of the East has twelve dioceses: three in the USA, including the patriarchal diocese whose centre is in Chicago; two in Iraq, including the metropolitanate in Baghdad; and one in each of Canada, Australia and New Zealand, Europe, Iran, Hassaka, Lebanon and Syria, and India (the last two are meropolitanates).

The Ancient Church of the East has two metropolitans in Iraq (Mosul and Kirkuk) and three bishops, one in each of Syria, Iraq and the USA.

Functioning churches for the Assyrian Church of the East include four in Baghdad, three in Duhok, five in Arbil and surrounding villages, four in Barwari, and one for each of Mosul, Basra, Kirkuk, Sarsank, Kanibalaf, Dere, rekan, and Ramadi.

Functioning churches for the Ancient Church of the East include two in Baghdad, and one for each of Mosul, Basra, Duhok, Kirkuk, Telkaif, Sharafyya, Karanjok, Dashkotan and Hezani.

Ecumenical dialogue

Since 1948, the Church of the East has been a member of the World Council of Churches (WCC)[2] and has participated in multilateral dialogue with Catholic, Orthodox, Oriental, Anglican, Reformed and Lutheran Churches. However admission to the Middle Eastern Council of Churches (MECC) has been repeatedly opposed by the Coptic Orthodox Church. In addition, both branches of the Church of the East have been active participants in the Syriac dialogue at the Pro Oriente foundation in Vienna since the middle of the 1980s.[3]

Dialogue with the Roman Catholic Church has been specially fruitful and achieved positive results. Mar Dinkha had met Pope John Paul II on his inauguration in 1978 and the two seem to have got on fairly well. In 1984 Mar Dinkha made an official visit to Rome together with the two other leaders of his Church, in order to inaugurate a process of theological dialogue. Lengthy discussions over ten years led to the historical common Christological Declaration on 11 November 1994. Further dialogue on sacramental theology followed from October 1995 and in October 2001 the Pontifical Council for Promoting Christian Unity published guidelines for admission to the Eucharist between the two churches.

On the basis of the common Christological declaration between Mar Dinkha IV and John Paul II, the Church of the East began to dialogue with the Chaldean Church. In 1996 the patriarchs of the two corresponding churches inaugurated an official process of co-operation between the two churches on pastoral and other practical levels.

Attempts to bring the two sister churches of the Church of the East together have also been on the way. Since 1984 the patriarch of the Assyrian Church of the East, Mar Dinkha, and the patriarch of the Ancient Church of the East, Mar Addai, have agreed on a reunion. In a synod of the Assyrian Church of the East convened in 1999, Mar Dinkha recognized all previous ordinations of the Ancient Church of the East from reader to patriarch.

The Syrian Orthodox Church

The original centre of the Syrian Orthodox Church is the city of Antioch and its patriarch carries the title 'Patriarch of Antioch and all the East'. The current patriarch is Mar Ignatius Zakka I Iwas, the 121st Patriarch of Antioch for the Syrian Orthodox Church. Born in Mosul, he joined its theological school of St Ephrem, where he trained and later taught. After serving in various positions in Iraq and Syria, and obtaining a doctorate in theology from the Episcopal General Theological Seminary in New York, he became patriarch in 1980. At present he resides in Damascus, and claims around half a million faithful under his leadership throughout the world.

The Syrian Orthodox Church has ten archdioceses (three in Syria, three in Iraq, one in Tur'Abdin, Holland, Beirut and Sweden) and thirteen patriarchal vicariates (two in Lebanon: Zahle and Beqa'a, and Mount Lebanon; two in Turkey: Istanbul and Mardin; two in the USA: East USA and West USA; and one for each of Jordan and Jerusalem, Germany, Sweden, Canada, Australia and New Zealand, Argentine and Brazil). Moreover there are parishes served by a priest who is directly linked with the patriarch in each of Austria, Belgium, France, Britain, and Switzerland.[4]

In Iraq the community is estimated at about 50–70,000 faithful. They live mainly in the cities of Mosul and

Baghdad and in some villages in the north of Iraq. They are distributed among three bishoprics; the largest is the bishopric of Baghdad, followed by that of Mosul, which also includes the city of Kirkuk and some surrounding villages; and the third is the bishopric of Der Mar Matta, which include the villages of Bahshiqa, Bahizzani, Bartella and a few other villages.

Churches and monasteries

There are several functioning churches throughout Iraq. In Baghdad there is a big cathedral and six other churches, in Mosul, six churches, in Qara Qosh three, in each of Bartella and Bahshiqa two, and in each of Sinjār, Kirkuk, Bahizzani and Mergi, one church.

Der Mar Matta is one of the oldest and most famous monasteries of Mesopotamia, which used to house over a thousand monks; it has three monks living in it at the present time. It has been recently rebuilt and modernized to provide the faithful with a sanctuary for quiet prayer and meditation, or even as a place of retreat or long break from the turmoil of life. There is also Der Mar Daniel in Bartella and Der Youhanna al-Delaimi in Qara Qosh which are being reconstructed.

There is one order for nuns: 'the nuns of Ya'qub al-Barad'i'. Two of these nuns presently reside in a convent in Baghdad, and there are twenty-five Iraqi nuns in Syria.

Educational and cultural activities

The seminary of Mar Ephrem was established in Mosul in 1945. Individuals study in preparation for the priesthood for four years. There is close co-operation with other Christian denominations who often collaborate in giving lectures and seminars in their subjects of interest.

The Syrian Orthodox Church has established schools and orphanages with every church in Mosul, Baghdad, Sinjar, Bahsheqa, Bahizzani, Bartella, and Qara Qosh. In the schools, religious instruction was given in addition to the national curriculum. When schools were taken over by the State in 1972, alternatives were found, and religious instruction was offered for the faithful in many parishes. The Mosul parish publishes a magazine called *Sada al-Mahabba* or 'Echoes of Love'.

Ecumenical dialogue
The Syrian Orthodox Church is a member of the World Council of Churches and of the Middle Eastern Council of Churches, and has been at the forefront of the ecumenical movement.

The first dialogue in which the Syrian Orthodox Church was involved was that with the Eastern Orthodox Churches. It began unofficially in 1964, and both agreed on the essence of the Christological dogma that Christ is perfect God and perfect man and that the different terminologies used by each side express the same truth.

Dialogue with the Roman Catholic Churches started unofficially at Pro Oriente Foundation in 1971; this led to the formulation of the famous 'Vienna Christological Formula', which became the basis for official dialogue. This was followed by the joint declaration between the patriarch of the Syrian Orthodox Church Mar Ignatius Ya'qub III and His Holiness Pope Paul VI on 27 October 1971, which was the first of its kind. His Holiness Pope John Paul II consolidated this agreement with Mar Ignatius Zakka I Iwas in 1984, and drew on it for the development of dialogue with His Holiness Pope Shenouda III.[5]

During these meeting theological discussions revealed that the separation of the churches was mainly related to terminological misunderstanding, and it was agreed that they all unite in professing that Christ is fully God and fully human in one person without confusion, change, separation or division. The steps that followed were to remove anathemas from their vocabulary, and to avoid invective and polemical language when referring to differences with each other.

The fruitful result of these dialogues had been foreseen by the great leader of the Syrian Orthodox Church Bar Hebreus who wrote in the thirteenth century:

When I had given much thought and pondered on the matter, I became convinced that these quarrels among the different Christian Churches are not a matter of factual substance, but of word and terminology; for they all confess Christ our Lord to be perfect God and perfect human, without any commingling, mixing, or confusion of natures ... thus I saw the Christian Communities, with their different Christological positions, as possessing a single common ground that is without any difference between them.[6]

The Syrian Orthodox Church has also conducted fruitful dialogue with the Anglican Church, and with various Reformation churches, though these have been on practical rather than on theological issues. Dialogue with other churches of the Syriac tradition, namely the Chaldean Church, the Syrian Catholic Church, the Maronite Church and the Church of the East, has also proceeded, facilitated by Pro Oriente. Given the spirit of ecumenism, the Syrian Orthodox Church has been active in the Council of Christians of Iraq.

The Chaldean Church

The first bishop to be consecrated for this uniate Church was John Sulaqa in 1553; however, it was not until the nineteenth century that relations became stable. On 5 July 1830 Pope Pius VIII confirmed John Hormiz as 'The Patriarch of Babylon of the Chaldeans' and since then relations have been stable. The seat of the patriarchate moved between several places over the centuries until it settled in Mosul in 1830. It was moved to Baghdad in 1950 by Patriarch Yusif Ghanima in view of the mounting importance of the capital, and the increase in the number of Christians living there. Patriarch Ghanima was followed by Poulis Skeikho in 1958, at a time of political upheaval for all Iraqis, as it coincided with the overthrow of the monarchy. Patriarch Sheikho had to deal with the question of military service for the priests, the nationalization of the schools and the displacement of the Christians from the north after the Kurdish movements. He also introduced semi-nary reforms and ordered the construction of twenty-five churches in Baghdad to serve the increasing Chaldean community in the capital. In 1989, Rafael I Bidawid became Patriarch; he spent fourteen years as head of the Chaldean Church. After the Gulf War, he founded '*Akhwiyat al-Mahabba*' or Caritas Iraq, an organization that helped all Iraqis, Muslims and Christians of every denomination during the long years of sanctions. He obtained official permission from the Iraqi government for publication of *Najm al-Mashriq*, an important quarterly religious magazine, and established the Babylon College for Philosophy and Theology. He was also founder of the Council of Catholic Patriarchs and Bishops in Lebanon, of the Council of Catholic Bishops of Iraq, and the Council of Christians of Iraq. He represented the Catholic Church in the fourth General Assembly of the Council of Churches of the Middle East in Cyprus, and advocated that the Catholic Church become a member of this Council. He died in Beirut on 7 July 2003.

After Bidawid's death, the College of Bishops of the Chaldean Church elected Bishop Emmanuel III Deli as patriarch on 3 December 2003. He is presently helped by three assistant bishops, one responsible for cultural and educational affairs, the second for pastoral matters and the third for international relations. He has eighteen other bishops under his jurisdiction, who together with about one hundred and thirty priests run the various bishoprics. In Iraq there is one bishop for each of the cities of Arbil, Zäkho, Amadiyah, Basra, and two for each of Mosul, Alqosh and Kirkuk (two of whom are retired). Outside Iraq there is one bishop for each of Lebanon, Syria, Egypt, Iran, Turkey, and Canada and two for the United States of America (a total of 21 bishops apart from the patriarch).

Pastoral centres served by a priest include the United Kingdom, France, Holland, Denmark, Italy, Germany, Greece, Sweden, Georgia and Jordan.

The Chaldean Church claims the largest number of believers in Iraq, about 75% of all Christians, estimated at about half a million. The majority live in the capital city, Baghdad, followed by Mosul, Arbil, Basra, Duhok and Kirkuk. A small number of families live in each of Hillah, Imara, Ba'qubah and Sulaymaniyah. There is an equal number of Chaldean Christians outside Iraq, the biggest community being that of the United States of America followed by those of Europe, Canada, New Zealand, and Australia.[7]

When union with Rome was cemented in the nineteenth century, the Chaldean Church was given the right of retention of its original rites and traditions. The Mass follows the original East Syrian tradition according to the rite of Mar Addai and Mari. In areas where the community speaks Aramaic, the Mass is said in the Eastern Syriac dialect, and in the cities in a mixture of Arabic and Aramaic. In recent years it has been translated to English in order to serve the growing number of Chaldean Christians in the United States and other western countries who do not speak the Syriac language.

Churches and monasteries
There are twenty-four churches that hold regular services in Baghdad, twelve in Mosul, twelve in Arbil, six in Alqosh, four in Kirkuk, five in Duhok, two in Zäkho, two in Basra, and one in each of Imara, Hillah and Ba'qubah.

Outside Iraq there are sixteen churches in the USA, five in Syria, four in Canada, three in France, two in Australia, two in Iran and one in each of Jordan, United Emirates, Egypt, Lebanon, Holland, Sweden and Turkey. In other countries where Chaldean Catholics are looked after by a priest, an arrangement is made with a local Catholic church where mass is said at a convenient time by the priest representing the community, and other services such as baptism and funerals are offered.

There is one monastic order for men, the Monks of Saint Antun and Hormiz for the Chaldean Church,' and two for women, The Nuns of the Sacred Heart of Jesus, and the

Nuns of Our Lady of the Immaculate Conception.

There are three functioning monasteries for men. The first is in al-Dora near Baghdad where twenty monks live, the second one is in Alqosh, 'Der al-Sayida', and the third in Mosul, Der Mar Giwagis. As for nuns, they have numerous convents in several cities, towns and villages of Iraq, as well as outside Iraq. In Iraq there are nine convents in Baghdad, three in Mosul, two in Arbil and one for each of Basra, Zäkho and Kirkuk. Outside Iraq, there are convents of Chaldean nuns in Lebanon, Jordan, United Emirates, Rome, Paris, USA and Australia. It is estimated that altogether there are over 200 Chaldean nuns who belong to both Chaldean orders for nuns, the Sacred Heart and the Immaculate Conception.

In addition to monks and nuns who belong to Chaldean orders, several Chaldean monks and nuns belong to other orders of the Catholic Church. These include Dominicans, Carmelites, Franciscans, Redemptorists, Salesians, the brothers of Focolare and the Little Sisters of Jesus.

Educational activities

1. The Chaldean seminary for training of the priesthood has been established since 1860. Although originally for the Chaldean priesthood, it accepted candidates from the Syrian Catholic community . It was first established in Mosul but was moved to al-Dora, near Baghdad, by Patriarch Sheikho. It includes two-level schools:

At level 1, Students are given the usual national curriculum of intermediary and secondary education as well as a program for religious education and instructions in the Syriac language. Accommodation facilities are provided for those students who come from outside Baghdad. Graduates of this level would proceed to level 2 or become deacons or catechists. At level 2, full-time instruction is given in philosophy, theology, liturgy, biblical studies and church history. Presently this is being given in Babylon College.

There are at present 50 seminarians preparing for the priesthood in Baghdad.

2. Babylon College was established in 1990 by the late Patriarch Bidawid and by the efforts of its first dean the late Yusif Habbi,[8] who unfortunately died in a car accident in the year 2000; it is at present run by Bishop Jacqe Ishaq. It provides a four-year course in Christian cultural, theological, philosophical and other relevant subjects. Its doors are open to all who are interested in these studies, both those preparing for the priesthood, and lay people. Christians from all denominations are accepted, and it is at present attended by about a hundred students, half of whom are preparing for the Chaldean priesthood; the other half is from the laity, and includes some preparing for the priesthood from other denominations.

3. The Institute for Religious Education, Baghdad, provides a three-year course in Christian studies intended to train catechumens. It is given at Babylon college and students awarded a diploma.

4. A two-year course in Eastern liturgy, Baghdad, at the end of which students are provided with a certificate.

5. Marriage Council Course, Baghdad, is a one-month course for those getting married. A committee of doctors contribute to it by lecturing and providing counselling. Catholics from all churches are expected to attend before getting married and present the certificate given.

6. Centres for religious instruction that give religious education for students of all levels are present in practically all parishes all over the country. Lay people are very active in teaching and instructing the students in these centres.

7. Theological centres in Mosul, Ain Kawa / Arbil and Basra, which provide courses on biblical and theological matters.

8. An inter-religious dialogue committee 'The encunter of wisdom' was established by the late dean of Babylon

College, Father Habbi, in which talks were given by speakers from the Christian and the Muslim community and in which lay people engage in dialogue.

Publications
1. *Najm al-Mashriq* (The Star of the East). Published in Baghdad.
2. *Bayn al-Nahrayn* (Between the Two Rivers), is an academic journal published in Baghdad.
3. *Rabbanoutha* (Monasticism), published in Baghdad by the monks of St Antun.
4. *Najm Bayn al-Nahrayn* (The Star Between the Two Rivers). Published in Duhok.
5. *Al Muthaqaf al-Kaldani* (The Cultured Chaldean). Arbil / Ain Kawa.
6. *Majalat al-Sawt al-Kaldani* (The Chaldean Voice).
7. *Majalat al-Ittihad* (The Magazine of Unity).
8. *Majalat Ashurbanipal* (The Magazine of Ashurbanipal).
9. Newsletter published weekly or monthly from nearly every parish.

Other activities
- A charity organization for helping the needy: 'The Chaldean charity organization'.
- Printing Press and publishing centre in Babylon College and the Patriarchate.
- Radio broadcast from Ain Kawa / Arbil.
- Websites:
  www. Chaldeanvoice.org
  www.ankawa.com

The Syrian Catholic Church

The first bishop to be consecrated for this uniate church in Iraq was Bishara al-Akhtal, who was given the name Quorillus Behnam and consecrated 'Bishop Of Mosul, Bakhdeda and Der Mar Behnam' in 1790. At present, the church is ruled by Patriarch Mar Ignatius Peter VIII, who resides in Beirut and carries the title, 'The Patriarch of

Antioch of the Syrian Catholics'. He is assisted by one bishop who resides with him in Beirut, and has fourteen other bishops under his jurisdiction. There are two bishops who reside in Rome, the first is Cardinal Mar Ignatius Musa Dawd I, who is prefect of the congregtion of Oriental Churches in Rome, and is responsible for co-ordinating relationships between the different Eastern Catholic churches and Rome. The second is Archbishop Mikhael Al Jamil, who is Patriarchal vicar to the Holy See and Apostolic visitor for Europe. In addition there are ten bishops responsible for the bishoprics of Beirut, Baghdad, Mosul, Damascus, Aleppo, Nisibis and Hasaka, Hims and Hama, Cairo, New Jersey, and Venezuela. There are also three patriarchal deputies for each of Basra, Jerusalem and Jordan, and Istanbul. In addition, there are missions represented by a priest in each of London, Paris, Amsterdam, Germany, Sweden, Greece, Detroit, Jacksonville (Florida), Los Angeles, San Diego, Toronto, Montreal and Sydney.

It is estimated that the total number of Syrian Catholic Christians in Iraq is about 75,000 with the majority being in Mosul and its surrounding villages (40,000), followed by Baghdad. In addition, there are large Syrian Catholic communities in Syria and Lebanon and an equal number in various western countries.[9]

Churches and monasteries
The Syrian Catholic Church has three functioning churches in Baghdad, six in the city of Mosul, six in Qara Qosh, one in each of the villages of Bahshiqa, Bartella, and Zäkho, and one in each of the cities of Basra, Kirkuk, and Imara.

There is one monastic order belonging to the Syrian Catholic Church for men, the Monks of Jesus the Redeemer in Mosul, and one for women, the Ephramite Nuns of Mercy, in Lebanon. There are two ancient monasteries belonging to the Syrian Catholics in Mosul: Der Mar Behnam[10] and Der Mar Qiryaqos. In addition, there are numerous religious who serve in various Catholic orders. The total number of religious as given in the website of the Syrian Catholic Church of Mosul is 130 for women and 32 for men. They are distributed among the following orders: Dominican, Franciscan, Salesian, Chaldean, Ephremites, Little Sisters of Jesus, and Jesus the Redeemer.

Activities

1. The Priests of Jesus the King. A group of dedicated Syrian Catholic priests organized themselves in 1962 as 'The Priests of Jesus the King'. They stress the importance of community life amongst the priests and dedication to evangelization and the spiritual life. Each serves as a pastor in the community assigned to him, but they have a communal life together and meet to discuss their spiritual and pastoral problems amongst themselves. It is not exclusive to the Syrian Catholic community, as it has members from the Chaldean priests. This group started to publish a progressive magazine in 1964 which they maintained for thirty-one years, after which they handed it to the Dominicans in 1995. The magazine served cultural and religious educational purposes for lay people as well as voicing progressive Christian thoughts and ideals. The Priests of Jesus the King also started a three-years' course in Sacred Scriptures in Mosul in 1989 which is still running.

2. In Baghdad, the Institute for Christian Education in the church of Mar Behnam in Hay al-Gradeer is attended by over three hundred students.

3. In Mosul a centre for Biblical studies has been established in the church of Mar Toma and the bishopric of Mosul publishes a magazine, *Shira' al-Syrian*. They also have a comprehensive website: www.syriaciraq.com.

4. In Qara Qosh, a town of 30,000 mostly Christian inhabitants, a large centre for Christian education and activities has recently been built – 'The Mar Poulis Centre'. There is also a magazine published in Qara Qosh, *Al-A'ila'* or 'The Family' and a comprehensive website: www.bakhdeda.com.

5. A charity organization for helping the poor, *'al-Gim'yya al-Khayriya'*.

In addition to the above activities, most parishes have

their own local councils, religious educational classes for various ages, a fraternity for youth, a choral group and a local newsletter.

The Armenian Churches

The presence of Armenians in Iraq can be traced back to the seventeenth century when Shah Abbas brought some Armenians with their families to be artisans in his empire. They soon became traders within the Persian and the Ottoman empires and many of them settled in Iraq. Together with the Jews they were responsible for most of the trade across the Ottoman empire, and eastwards to Iran, India and China. However, the bulk of the Armenian population in Iraq are descendants of those who survived the Armenian massacres in Turkey at the end of the nineteenth century, and at the beginning of the twentieth century, during and after World War I.

When Iraq became an independent state in 1932, the Iraqi government accepted the Armenians as Iraqi citizens, gave them Iraqi nationality and all the privileges other Christians enjoyed. Most of the Armenians belong to the Armenian Orthodox Church though about a fifth are Armenian Catholics. Both communities organized themselves, built churches in which their communities worshipped, and schools for students of all levels. In addition they had three social clubs in which they met and propagated their cultural identity. In Baghdad the Armenian Catholic community had a mixed primary school and an intermediate/ secondary school for girls. The Armenian Orthodox community had mixed schools for boys and girls at all stages, primary, intermediate and secondary. In addition, they later established a seminary, an old people's home, a charity group for women and a choral group which sings in church and on national occasions. They also have a cemetery in which there is a church where services are performed on occasions of death or special feasts.

The Armenian Orthodox community is looked after by one bishop who resides in Baghdad. One of the oldest churches in Baghdad belongs to the Armenian Orthodox community, the Church of the Virgin Mary. It is popular with Christians of all denominations as well as with Muslims, who not infrequently visit it and make offerings for specific needs. A modern basilica was also built in the centre of Baghdad, as well as a small church in the area of New Baghdad. In addition, there is one church in each of Mosul, Kirkuk and Basra. The Catholic Armenian community has one order of nuns.

It is estimated that before the onset of the first wave of emigration following the Iraqi/Iranian War, the Armenian communities numbered up to seventy thousand. Further emigrations continued following the Gulf War, and during the period of sanctions which reduced the community to less than a third of its original size. Recent estimates put the number of Armenian Orthodox in the city of Baghdad at 12,000 and Armenian Catholics 600.[11] Armenian friends tell me that they loved Iraq and were very sad to see the changes that forced them to leave in large numbers. Whether in America or in London, Armenians who used to live in Iraq continue to yearn for the country that made them feel at home.

The Protestant Churches

Protestants of all types were acknowledged as one group, independent from other Christians denominations, as a *millet* under the Ottomans in 1850 by Sultan Abdul Hamid. In *Vilayet al-Mosul* a special *firman* was sent to the pasha of Mosul in 1854, after which the Protestants appointed a representative for their community to the governing authorities. He was responsible for official matters such as records of births, deaths and marriages and of other organizational activities of the community. Since Protestants are not a single community with a centralized authority like the Catholic Church and other Eastern Churches, they all became a conglomerate organization under the title 'The National Protestant Evangelical Community' and in 1868, Iremya Shamir was made responsible for them. After the institution of the monarchy, the Protestant community continued to function in a similar way, although some of the churches put initially in the category of Protestants could no longer be accepted, such as the Lutherans and the Seventh Day Adventists.

The first Protestant house of worship was acquired in Mosul in 1840, but since the community failed to acquire a substantial number of worshippers it was closed in the middle of the 1980s and a smaller place was acquired in 1990 in a different district. In Baghdad a church was built which was inaugurated on 5 August 1954, and in Basra a church was built in 1997.

Harith Ghanima, writing in 1998, mentions that there were 350 families in Baghdad, 120 in Basra, 15–20 in Mosul, 20 in Kirkuk, ten in Bartella, and two in Bahshiqa.

The total number of the Christians belonging to the Protestant Churches in Iraq as published in the *World Church Handbook*, based on the operation of World database by Patrick Johnstone (WEC International 1993; edited by Peter Briely, London, 1997) is altogether 4692. In the same publication the estimated total number of the Iraqi Christian population is given as 573,918.[12]

The Latin Church

The Latin Church is officially represented by the Nuncio or papal representative, presently Fernando Filoni, who resides in Baghdad. In addition there is usually a resident bishop who looks after the Latin community, presently Jean Sulaiman, who also resides in Baghdad.

In addition to foreign Latin nationals who reside in Iraq temporarily for various purposes, there is a small indigenous Iraqi Latin Christian community that traces itself to earlier centuries (as early as the seventeenth or eighteenth centuries), who have emigrated from Europe, probably through trade, and came to settle in Iraq, mainly Baghdad.

Several missionary orders of the Latin Catholic Church have monasteries in which a few foreign and numerous Iraqi sisters and priests serve. For men there is one Carmelite monastery in Baghdad, one Dominican monastery for each of Baghdad and Mosul, one for Redemptorists and one for the Salesians in Baghdad. For women there are several Dominican convents in Baghdad, Mosul and some surrounding villages. In addition there is one for each of the Franciscans and Mother Teresa sisters in Baghdad.

The Greek Orthodox and Catholic Churches

The Greek Orthodox Church is the original community within the Byzantine empire which conformed with the decisions of the Council of Chalcedon. The Greek Orthodox Christians have also been called Malkites and *al-Rum al-Orthodox* (the word 'Rum' in Arabic is equivalent to Roman and Byzantine). Theologically they follow the same two-nature Christology of the Council of Chalcedon, but they separated from the Roman Catholic Church in the eleventh century since they differed on issues of leadership and the definition of the Holy Spirit. The Roman Catholic Church added that 'the Holy Spirit proceeds from the Father and the Son' to the creed in the eleventh century, while the Greeks maintained that the Holy Spirit proceeds from the Father only. Their liturgy follows the Byzantine rite.

Those members of the Greek Orthodox Church who united with the Roman Catholic Church constitute the Greek Catholic Church of *al-Rum al-Cathulik*.

Both communities have a small number of faithful in Iraq and each has a church in the capital, Baghdad.

The Anglican Church

This consists of a small community which include British subjects who reside in Iraq for work in the embassy and other British institutions. They have one church in Baghdad and one in Basrah.

The Coptic Church

The consists of a small community of Egyptian Copts who came to work in Iraq mainly during the eighties. They worship in the old Latin church in the centre of Baghdad.

II. Iraq under occupation and transitional rule

The United States and its allies mounted a military invasion on Iraq resulting in occupation of the country on 11 April 2003. Saddam's policy of confrontation and lack of co-operation with the team of inspectors of weapons of mass destruction, together with non-compliance with the United Nations resolutions, were used to justify the military assault.

One of the first actions taken by the occupying power was to disband the Iraqi army, intelligence and police services, without providing alternative measures. Consequently the borders of the country remained without any control, providing an opportunity for various factions opposed to the United States to enter the country. These include members of the well-known fundamentalist Islamic religious group, *al-Qa'ida*, and those of *al-Tawheed* and *al-Jihad*. The latter has been organized by Abu Mus'ab al-Zarqawi, a renegade Jordanian, who is as reprehensible as Bin Laden, and whose group has claimed responsibility for several destructive operations. Al-Zarqawi has since stated that his organization is closely linked to *al-Qa'ida* and is known to be stationed in Fallujah. Moreover, the absence of a police service or other power within the country to implement law and order adequately led to local violence, intimidation, kidnappings and thefts on a massive scale. Many of these incidents are attributed to ex-Saddam's men who are used to acts of terror, while others could simply be attributed to petty thieves who have been released from prison during the last few days of Saddam's rule. Recently an organization that calls itself *Ansar al-Sinna* has claimed responsibility for many acts of terrorism.

Kidnapping continues to be a daily activity and it is difficult to pinpoint a specific group. People kidnapped include individuals from most sections of the Iraqi society, though it is more common amongst the rich and the Christians. They are accused of providing services to the Americans. Kidnapped people are usually asked to pay hundreds of thousands of American dollars for their release, but some have been maimed. One example is a Muslim from a well-known family in Mosul who was involved in a cafeteria which American soldiers use. Both of his hands were cut off according to the Islamic practice, and one of his eyes was removed. The operations seem to have been performed by a surgeon since the man was anaesthetized and the wounds sutured in the proper way.[13]

A new problem has risen for the Iraqi Christians, who are now accused of being sympathizers of the Americans and the West, seen as 'the Crusaders' who have to be fought. Although this is not a new accusation, it had been effectively dealt with during the monarchy and by most of the leaders of the Republic of Iraq. The resurgence of fundamentalist Islamic movements all over the Middle East has had a major influence in reversing the good Christian-Muslim relations which had been achieved so far. Although most anti-Christian activities seem to be related to foreign fundamentalist Muslims, some seem to be exercised by Iraqi Muslims, who under normal circumstances would not voice their prejudices. One story may exemplify this point: A lady found out that rubbish was being thrown in her garden. On watching, she found out that it was done by her neighbour. One morning she asked him, 'Why are you throwing rubbish in my garden?' He answered her: 'It is because you are a Christian; you are rubbish, and unless you convert to Islam you remain rubbish.'

The problem was complicated by the arrival of evangelical missionaries with the occupying American forces, and the distribution of Bibles with food parcels. This missionary activity could only destabilize an already volatile situation and would be seen as 'the Bible following the gun' situation. The local churches have all expressed their concern that such behaviour will have severe repercussions. Not only do they see the conversion of their believers who already profess the Christian faith as a futile effort, but they also feel threatened, as these actions substantiate the false impression that the Christians are collaborators with the occupying forces. Whatever good intentions the new evangelicals may have, their actions may seriously destabilize the balance that has been achieved so far between the Christian and Muslim communities of Iraq. In the opinion of many observers, these missionaries pose a threat as reprehensible as that of any other fundamentalists.

The occupying forces have not taken measures to counteract anti-Christian sentiments amongst militant Islamic followers, and soon after the occupation specifically anti-Christian activities began. Initially, a few small unknown groups threw pamphlets in churches, asking the congregation to convert to Islam, and threatening to kill them and to destroy their churches.

In May 2003 the main door of the Syrian Catholic Bishopric in Mosul was blown out by a machine gun. Fortunately there was nobody passing in front of the door or on the stairs facing the door.

On 1 June 2003 a threatening letter reached the priest of the Chaldean Church of Mar Giwargis and Mar Yousif the Patron of Labourers, in Madinat al-Shirta. The letter begins with an Islamic greeting, then proceeds to ask the priest to pay $10,000 within ten days of receiving the letter. The money, the letter states, will be used for resistance against the American, British and Zionist presence on Iraqi soil. It goes on to threaten that if the money is not paid during a certain period, the priest and many of his followers will be torn to pieces and annihilated physically. The letter gave the name of the organization as 'The centre of faith, Jihad and martyrdom', and was signed: 'The suicide fighter Abu Karrar'. This particular threat was dealt with effectively by the authorities and local Muslim leaders who co-operated by staying with the threatened priest in order to show their solidarity with the Christians, and their denunciation of such activities. Soon after that a bomb was thrown at a convent of Chaldean nuns in

Mosul. Fortunately the bomb did not explode.

In February 2004, explosives were detonated in Mar Toma school for the Syrian Orthodox Church in Mosul, after which the school was closed for two weeks. Soon after, their church in Baghdad was threatened, and worship had to be stopped for one week.

Since the occupation, a number of Christians have been murdered, initially alcohol dealers, owners of fashion shops and beauty salons, and shopkeepers selling music recordings. However, many of those murdered were doctors, engineers and lawyers. The exact number is not known and these incidents can be blamed on the general lawlessness prevailing in the country, and on interpersonal rivalry. Many Christians were told to convert to Islam, and women were told to wear the *hijab* or the veil, including a doctor in the University of Baghdad, by the head of her unit.[14]

On Sunday, 1 August 2004, a co-ordinated attack on six churches occurred during the evening service, between half-past five and six in the evening. Since Sunday is a working day in Iraq, most of the Christians attend the evening Mass. Thus, it seems that these attacks were timed to coincide with the period when it was known that the largest numbers of faithful would be praying. Explosions ripped through five churches, four in Baghdad and one in Mosul. The first blast struck outside an Armenian Catholic church in Baghdad, to be followed by a blast near a Syrian Catholic Church, and another near SS Peter and Paul's Cathedral and its adjoining seminary in Dora, a predominantly Christian suburb of Baghdad. The fourth was near the Chaldean Church of St Elyya al-Hiri. In Mosul, the Catholic church of Mar Poulus was attacked, while one of the bombs near another Chaldean church did not explode. Eight of the faithful, and five Muslim passers-by were reported dead, and over fifty injured.[15] Windows and doors were smashed and fundamental structural damage occurred in many of the churches. Half of St Peter's Major Seminary collapsed. Soon after the attacks a group that calls itself 'The planning and follow-up organization' claimed responsibility for the bombs, saying that they were a response to the 'American crusader war'. The group called the churches 'the dens of evil, corruption and immorality and evangelization'. Furthermore they condemned Pope John Paul II for blessing the war in Iraq and said that he has the leaders of America in his hands (reported in the *Tablet*, 7 August 2004). This is rather strange, since this Pope was known to have been a strong voice against the embargo from 1990, and also made statements denouncing the war on Iraq, and any form of Western intervention.

These attacks have been strongly denounced by the local Ruling Council and were strongly condemned by Iraqi and Muslim officials as well as by Pope John Paul II and Iraqi religious leaders. The head of state, Ajeel al-Yawir, the Prime Minister, Ayad Allawi, and the assistant Prime Minister for security affairs have all issued official condemnations, and regrets for these atrocious attacks. Muslim religious leaders likewise issued official condemnations including the chief Shi'ah Muslim cleric in Iraq, Grand Ayatollah Ali al-Sistani, Imam Ahmad Abdul Gafur, Mudir al-Awqaf for the Sunnis, Abdul Aziz al-Hakim, president of the Islamic revolutionary council in Iraq, the association of Muslim Ulama', and the Sunni Islamic Party, as well as many other imams including the radical Shi'ah cleric Muqtada al-Sadr. All described the attacks as horrendous crimes, and cowardly acts of terrorism that target all Iraqis. Terrorist groups were blamed, who would benefit from creating civil disturbances in Iraq. Condemnations were also issued by al-Azhar in Egypt and by Muslim authorities in other countries. His Royal Highness Prince Hassan Bin Talal, moderator of the World Conference of Religions for peace stated: 'This is a new escalation in the extremists' efforts to incite religious war': he described the attacks as 'a particularly obscene blasphemy against the spirit of Islam and the character of Iraq, which defies the message of the Qur'an, and the example of the Prophet Muhammad'. He said the perpetrators were not believers, but called them 'the lowest dregs of irreligious power-crazed gangs'.

One week after these attacks the patriarch of the Chaldean community, Emmanuel III Deli received a chilling anonymous message saying 'We Will Kill You' and accusing the church of colluding with US-led coalition forces in Iraq. This was reported by Bishop Andrawis Aboona, one of the auxiliary bishops to the patriarch. He was on a visit to London when he was ordered to cut short his visit by the patriarch, and to return to Baghdad immediately. Bishop Andrawis spoke to 'Aid to the Church in Need', a few hours before his departure. The *Catholic Herald* reported him stating: 'Everybody is afraid, but right now the people need me. I must go back to encourage them. We want to tell them not to give up.' Jack Ishaq, the second auxiliary bishop was on a visit to Lebanon and was similarly called back to Iraq. Patriarch Deli responded with a statement that these threats would not make the Christians leave their country.

Attacks on several Christian villages have occurred sporadically, the most recent being that on the village of Baghdeda (Qara Qosh), on 10 September 2004. After celebrating the Feast of the Cross the village of 30,000 Christians came under mortar attack, and several were reported dead and injured.

Further attacks on churches in Baghdad occurred on 9 October 2004; this time it was the Syrian Orthodox Church in Battween, while on 16 October five churches of different denominations, and a hospital, were attacked over the course of an hour as Muslims were greeting Ramadan. No casualties were reported, as the attacks occurred in the small hours of the morning, but buildings were badly damaged.

All these incidents would not have happened in the presence of a strong government. As a result of all these grave incidents, most educational and cultural activities of the churches have been suspended, and attendance in the churches for Mass and prayers have declined significantly. Many have already left the country, whether after specific threats or due to the general feeling of insecurity. Christians feel that they are an easy target because they do not react with violence, and they do not see a light at the end of the tunnel. A friend coming from Mosul told me that life there has become intolerable. No woman could leave the house without wearing the *hijab*, university personnel were told to segregate males and females, and daily attacks on individual Christians have become the routine.

A mass exodus is feared imminent as the situation seems to be developing into flagrant persecution. Many journalists have in fact reported large communities of Christians from Iraq, in Jordan and Damascus, trying to reach their friends and relatives in other parts of the world. It is estimated that nearly 40,000 Christians have left the country since the war began.

It is clear that there are those with a special agenda to force their specific form of Islam on the Iraqi population, whether Christian or Muslim. Many Muslim individuals and several Muslim holy places have similarly been attacked. To mention just a few, in March 2004 Shi'ah holy places were attacked in Baghdad and Karbala on a feast day, killing more than 85 people, and in Mosul a moderate Muslim cleric who spoke against these atrocities has also been killed.

Christian leaders, in the name of the patriarchs and bishops in Iraq, made a statement as early as 29 April 2003 requesting the guarantee of civil and religious rights to the Christians. In September 2003, the Chaldean bishops made a declaration requesting that the new government should have a Chaldean representative who would speak for the community, since it is the third largest group in Iraqi society, and since prior to the formation of the Republic of Iraq the Chaldean patriarch had represented the community in the House of Senators.

Since the demise of the Ba'ath regime, several political parties have emerged amongst the Christians, as well as Christian newspapers and television. The parties vary from Christian democrats to ethnic nationalist parties. The latter belong mainly to the Assyrian and Ancient Church of the East, although some Syriac-speaking Christians from other denominations have joined. The nationalistic parties have also been campaigning for the formation of a 'safe haven' in north Iraq for the Christians. Some of their members have appealed to the Bush administration in the USA and others are lobbying MPs in London seeking the creation of such a 'safe haven' within Iraq. However, many Iraqi Christians are against the creation of such an exclusive place for the Christians: the main objection is that such a so-called 'safe haven' would be a soft target which could easily be attacked by extremists and, since it could not survive without American and other Western powers, it would only substantiate the accusation that the Christians are collaborators with foreign powers.

Most Christian Iraqi religious leaders, as well as many Iraqi Christians, think that the only way to achieve a lasting and peaceful existence for the Christians is to dialogue with our Muslim brethren and to work together towards a strong democratic government. All Iraq should become a safe haven, not only for Christians, but for all its citizens. Towards this goal the bishops of Mosul of all denominations have recently met and made the following appeal in November 2004:

> We refuse to accept the use of force, terror, kidnapping and embezzlement as a means of achieving control and we ask the occupying forces and all foreign armed people to leave our country.

Iraqi Christians have always emphasized their belonging to their country and their opposition to foreign intervention. Modern Christian thinkers have stated that to survive and develop as living churches in the Arab and Muslim world requires a spiritual vision of their relation to Islam, and serious dialogue with their Muslim brethren, rather than political or military confrontation. Many Muslims share this view. In January 2004, a call by more than 200 mainly Muslim intellectuals and political leaders from Iraq to stop attacks on Christians and cease forcing women to wear the veil, was published on the Arab website Elaph. It was directed at Muslim clerics to issue *fatwas* forbidding such atrocious crimes against humanity and the Islamic religion.

I have tried to show in this work how Christians have contributed to the emergence of civilization on Iraqi soil during Abbasid times, and to the emergence of modern Iraq in recent times. Even in the present difficult times, they continue to contribute to the depth and creative power of Iraqi society in various ways, and yearn to continue to do so as full Iraqi citizens.

It is hoped that an efficient Iraqi government would soon uproot all those dark powers with vested interests in terrorism and destabilization of a united Iraq. It is also hoped that the Western powers who have started this war will succeed in getting rid of all those who are beneficiaries of a destabilized Iraq and who endorse terrorism regardless of morals or targets. Finally, it is hoped that the Muslim world will succeed in overcoming the dark forces that are tarnishing its image, so that a tolerant and benevolent face of Islam may prevail, an Islam that was practised by generations of Muslim rulers throughout history, an Islam which maintained both considerable freedom of thought, and a tolerance of other faiths.

Addendum – Since this work went to the publishers, general lawlessness and attacks on Iraqi Christians have continued. Two major events are worth recording. On 7 December 2004, an Armenian church and the house of the Chaldean bishop in Mosul were destroyed. No one was injured by the bomb attacks. The second is the kidnapping of the bishop of the Syrian Catholic Archdiocese of Mosul, Basillios Georgis Kass Mousa on 18 January 2005. Although he was released within less than twenty-four hours of his abduction, the bishop's account of what he went through during these hours, published on the website of the Syrian Catholic Church of Mosul, is heart-rending and his courage exemplary. The identity of the kidnappers and their motives remain unclear.

Notes

1 In *The Church of the East* by Wilhelm Baum and Dietmar W. Winkler, p. 154.
2 WCC is a fellowship of churches that was formally constituted in Amsterdam on 23 August 1948. Its members confess 'the Lord Jesus Christ as God and Saviour according to the scriptures, and therefore seek to fulfil together their common calling to the glory of the one God, Father, Son and Holy Spirit'. The Council includes churches from all the main Christian confessions and denominations, including nearly all the Eastern and Oriental Orthodox Churches. At its formation the Council had 147 members; by 1993 the number had risen to 322. Although the Roman Catholic Church is not a member, since 1961 the Vatican has appointed observers: in 1964 a joint working group was formed to discuss questions of common concern and in 1968 it accepted full membership of the Faith and Order Commission and was thus involved in the 1982 report on Baptism, Eucharist and Ministry.
3 Pro Oriente was founded by Cardinal König, during the Second Vatican Council in 1964 aiming to promote better understanding between Christians of the East and West. A series of meetings between Oriental Orthodox and Catholic theologians followed. In 1971 participants were able to produce a statement on Christology which was of particular importance for subsequent dialogue, called 'The Vienna Christological formula'. Pro Oriente also organized a series of dialogues between the churches of the Syriac tradition, namely the Syrian Orthodox Church, the Maronite Church, the Church of the East, the Chaldean and the Syrian Catholic Churches.
4 Information and figures given for the Syrian Orthodox community are from *The Hidden Pearl*, pp. 98–103.
5 *Ut Unum Sint*, p. 73.
6 Bar Hebraeus's *Book of the Dove* p. 60.
7 Most of the information about the Chaldean Church in this section was obtained from the Iraqi Chaldean priest who serves the Chaldean community in London.
8 Yusif Habbi was an eminent international Syriac scholar. He was editor-in-chief of an academic journal *Bayn al-Nahryn*, head of the Babylon College of Theology and Philosophy, and professor at the Pontifical Oriental Institute in Rome.

9 Information about the Syrian Catholic Church comes partly from the priest who serves the community in London, and partly from the website of the Syrian Catholic Church.

10 The exact date of the building of this monastery is not known. The first definite evidence of the presence of an established monastery dates to the tenth or eleventh century, which is evidently based on earlier buildings. Its origins go back to the fourth century when the site of martyrdom of Mar Behnam and his sister Sarah became the place where cures began to be reported. Soon after that a small church was built called al-Jib. Hundreds of sick and mental patients arrived at the site looking for a cure and one of those cured built a house which served as a residence or a hospital. This was the nucleus for the building of a monastery in later years.

11 An Iraqi–Armenian friend, who had emigrated about twenty years ago but whose father is still alive and who is an active church member, provided me with the above rough estimates through her father.

12 From H.Y. Ghanima, *The Protestants and Evangelicals in Iraq* p. 206.

13 The man himself told his story to an ophthalmologist who saw him as a patient in London.

14 I was told the story by a horrified Muslim paediatrician visiting in the UK. Her Christian friend, who is a paediatrician in the same department, was approached by the head of her department to advise her to wear the *hijab* and follow the faith.

15 Reported in *Najm al-Mashriq* no. 39 pp. 346–598.

Glossaries

Glossary of terms

Agha: a term used by Kurdish tribes for the chief of the tribe.

Akhawiya: an Arabic word that means fraternity. It is usually used by the Christians in the Arab world for religious organizations involved in worship and prayer.

Amir al-Mu'minin: amir is prince in Arabic. al-Muminin are the faithful. The whole word means 'the commander who governs the faithful Muslim community in the name of Allah'.

Der: monastery

dhimmi: a non-Muslim individual in an officially Muslim state, usually a Christian or a Jew. Such individuals do not serve in the army and in return of their protection have to pay a special tax to the state called the *jizyah*. They are also required to follow certain rules called the *dhimmi* rules.

fatwa: an authoritative ruling on a point of Islamic law given by a mufti or Islamic leader.

firman: an official edict obtained from Ottoman authorities allowing an official mission of business to be carried within the realm of the Ottoman empire.

Hellenism: the cultural legacy of the Greeks.

hijab: the head covering or veil used by Muslim women.

jizyah: the tax paid to the Muslim state by non-Muslims in return for their protection.

malka: the Aramaic word for king.

malik: the Arabic word for king.

Malkites: the term given to the Chalcedonians of the Middle East who belong to the Greek or Byzantine Church. Since the decisions of the Council of Chalcedon were imposed by the Byzantine emperor, those who accepted them were called Malkites or the men of the king.

millet: an Ottoman word used for religious communities under their rule who enjoyed some sort of self rule by the head of their community. The system was first used by the Persians and later by the Ottomans and the Arabs.

mudir: a ruler of a local institution, like a police station or a hospital.

pasha: a term used by the Ottomans which gives the status of lordship.

Syriac: a dialect of the Aramaic language used in Edessa, which Christianity used as it developed within the Middle East.

tanzimat: a series of reforms introduced by the Ottoman government during the nineteenth century which aimed at the secularization of the State and decentralization of power.

vilayet (or *wilayat*): a Turkish term referring to an area within the Ottoman empire that is governed by a Wali or a ruler under the central sultan or king in Istanbul.

wazir: a term used by the Ottomans and the Arabs for a minister in the government.

Glossary of names
Antun: Antony
Andrawis: Andrew
Rufa'il: Rafael
Giwargis: George
Gibra'il: Gabriel
Matta: Mathew
Mikha'il: Michael
Poulis: Paul
Ya'qub: Jacob

Yuhanna: John
Yousif: Joseph
Barad'i: Baradeus

Glossary of theological terms
Christotokos: Greek for 'Bearer of Christ'.
Dyophysites: Those who believe in the two-nature Christology.
Dyophysitism: the two-nature Christology.
Hypostasis: a theological term that expresses self-existence, used by Christian theologians in Trinitarian theology as well as in Christology. Theologians used this word instead of 'person' because the latter had theatrical connotations and expressed the role being played rather than the quality of the person.
Kyana or *Kyono*: the Syriac word that is equivalent to the Greek Physis.
Miaphysitism: a theological term that expresses the one-nature Christology which can be composite as the word mia means composite one and not strictly one.
Monophysites: those who believe in the Monophysite Christology.
Monophysitism: the one-nature Christology.
Parsopa: Syriac word for 'person'.
Persona: Latin for 'person'.
Physis: A Greek word used in theology for 'nature'. It was used to ensure a descriptive functional content, meaning 'essence or substance' and is not related to the use of the word as in 'the world of nature'.
Prosopon: Greek word for 'person'.
Qnōma: Syriac word which was used in Trinitarian theology as equivalent to Hypostasis. However, in the formulation of Christology it meant the particular property of the natures of Jesus, the human and the divine, rather than hypostasis.
Theotokos: Greek for 'Bearer of God'.
Yaldat Alaha: Syriac for 'Bearer of God'.
Yaldat Mshiha: Syriac for 'Bearer of Christ'.

Glossary of alternative names for cities and countries
Antioch (Greek)/Antakya (Arabic).
Arbela/Arbil.
Bet Qatraye (Aramaic)/Qatar(Arabic).
Bactria (Greek)/Afghanistan.
Edessa (Greek)/Urhay (Aramaic)/Urfa (Modern name in southern Turkey).
Karka De-Beth Slokh/Kirkuk.
Kotchannes/Qudshani
Gundishapur (Persian), Bet Lapat (Syriac).
Ray Ardashir/Tehran.
Rew Ardashir/Elam.
Seleucia–Ctesiphon (Persian), Al-Mada'in (Arabic) also salman Pak (Site in Modern Iraq).

Bibliography

I. Publications in English

Abdullah, Thabit A.J. *A short history of Iraq: from 636 to the present*. Pearson Longman, London, 2003.

Abdul-Nour, Aziz. M. 'The Garden of Eden and its living stone. Christians in Iraq'. A review in T*he Journal of Anglican and Eastern Churches Association*, no. 47, pp. 32–7 and no. 47 pp. 50–68, 2003.

Al-Mawardi, Abu al-Hassan. *The laws of Islamic governance*. Taha Publishers Ltd., London, 1996.

Atiya, A.S. *A History of Eastern Christianity*. Methuen & Co. Ltd. and University of Notre Dame Press, 1968.

Balakian, Peter. *The burning Tigris – The Armenian genocide and America's response*. HarperCollins Publishers, New York, 2003.

Bar Hebraeus. *The Book of the Dove*. Trans. by A.J. Wesnick, Leyden, E. J.Brill, 1919.

Baum, W. and Winkler, Dietmar W. *The Church of the East: a concise history*. Routledge Curzon, 2003.

Betts, R.B. *Christians in the Arab East. A political study*. SPCK, 1979.

Bright, John. *A history of Israel*. SCM Press Ltd, London, 1981.

Brock, S. 'From Antagonism to Assimilation: Syriac attitudes to Greek learning', in *Syriac perspectives on late antiquity*. ed. S. Brock, Variorum Reprints, London, 1984.

Brock, S. 'Greek into Syriac and Syriac into Greek', in

Syriac perspectives on late antiquity. ed. By S. Brock, Variorum Reprints, London, 1984.

Brock, S. 'Syriac views of emerging Islam', in *Studies on the first century of Islamic society.* ed. G.H.A. Juynboll, Carbondale, 1982.

Brock, S. 'The Syriac Churches in ecumenical dialogue on Christology', in *Eastern Christianity – Study in modern history, religion and politics.* ed. A. O'Mahony, Milisende, London, 2004.

Brock, S. *Studies in Syriac Christianity.* Variorum, Aldershot, 1992.

Brock, S., Witakowski, E.B, Taylor, David G.K, Witakowski, W. *The Hidden Pearl.* trans World Film, Rome, 2001.

Chadwick, H. *The early church.* Penguin Books, London, 1993.

Chaillot, C. *The Syrian Orthodox Church of Antioch and all the East.* Orthdruk, Byalistok, Poland, 1998.

Coakley, J. F. *The Church of the East and the Church of England – A history of the Archbishop of Canterbury's Assyrian mission.* Clarendon Press, Oxford, 1992.

Cragg, Kenneth. *The Arab Christian: a history in the Middle East.* Mowbray, 1992.

Degen, R. *The oldest known Syriac manuscript of Hunayn B. Ishaq.* Symposium Syriacum, 1997, Orientalia Christiana Analecta no. 205.

Drijvers, Hans J. W., 'The school of Edessa: Greek learning and local culture', in *Centres of Learning*, ed. Jan Willem Drijvers and Alasdair A. MacDonald. E. J. Brill, Leiden, New York, Koln 1995.

Drower, E. *The Mandaeans of Iraq and Iran: Their cults, customs, magic legends and folklore.* Georgias Press edition, 2004.

Fakhry, M. *A history of Islamic philosophy.* Longman, London, 1983.

Fortescue, Adrian. *The lesser Eastern Churches.* Catholic Truth Society, London, 1913.

Frend, W. H. C. *The early Church, from the beginnings to 461.* SCM Press Ltd, London, 1991.

Gillman, I. and Klimkeit, H. *Christians in Asia before 1500.* Curzon, Surrey, UK, 1999.

Griffith, S. H. *After Bardaisan. The marks of the 'True Church' according to Ephrem's hymns against heresies.* Orientalia Lovaniense no. 89.

Gutas, D. *Greek thought, Arab culture: the Graeco-Arabic translation movement in Baghdad and early Abbasid society.* Routledge, London and New York, 1998.

Hitti, P.K. *History of the Arabs: From the earliest times to the present.* Macmillan Press Ltd, London and Basingstoke, 1970.

Hunter, Erica C. D. 'Syriac inscriptions from al-Hira', *Oriens Christianus,* 80. 1960.

Hunter, Erica C. D. 'The Church of the East in Central Asia'. *Bulletin John Rylands Library* 78:3, 1996.

Hunter, Erica C. D. 'The transmission of Greek Philosophy via the "School of Edessa"', *Literacy, education and manuscript transmission in Byzantium and beyond.* ed. Catherine Holmes and Judith Waring, Brill, Leiden. Boston, Koln, 2002.

Hunter, Erica C. D. 'Isaac of Nineveh the Persian Mystic', *Iqbal Review.* A special issue on Iqbal and mysticism. 1988.

Hayes, E. R. *L'École D'Edesse.* Les Press Modernes, 1930.

Joseph, John. *The Nestorians and their Muslim neighbours – A study of Western influence on their relations.* Princeton University Press, New Jersey, 1961.

Joseph, John. *Muslim Christian relations and inter-Christian rivalries in the Middle East – the case of the Jacobites in an age of transition.* State University of New York Press, Albany, 1983.

Khadduri, Majid. *Independent Iraq: a study in Iraqi politics since 1932.* Oxford University Press, 1951.

Longrigg, Stephen Hemsley. *Iraq, 1900 to 1950: a political, social, and economic history.* Oxford University Press, 1953.

Luck, Harry C. *Mosul and its minorities.* Georgias Press edition, 2004.

MacDonald J. F. *Jesuits by the Tigris – men for others in Baghdad.* Jesuit Mission Press, Boston, 1994.

Mingana, D. D. 'The early spread of Christianity in Central Asia and the Far East – A new document'. *Bulletin of the John Rylands Library*, Vol. 9, 1925.

Moffett, S. H. *A history of Christianity in Asia: the beginning to 1500*. HarperCollins Publishers, San Francisco, 1992.

Mooken, Mar Aprem. *The history of the Assyrian Church of the East in the twentieth century*. St Ephrem Ecumenical Research Institute, Kerala, India 2003.

O'Mahony, A. 'Christianity in modern Iraq' *International Journal for the study of the Christian Church*. vol 4, no. 2, July 2004.

O'Mahony, A. 'Eastern Christianity in Modern Iraq' in *Eastern Christianity – Studies in modern history, religion and politics*. Mellisende, 2004.

O'Mahony, A. 'Iraq's Christians on the edge'. *The Tablet*, 15 March 2003, pp. 6–7.

O'Mahony, A. *The Chaldean Church: Politics of the Church-State relations in Modern Iraq*, Heythrop Journal XLV, 2004, pp. 435–450.

Parry, Oswald Hutton. *Six months in a Syrian Monastery*. Horace Cox, London, 1895.

Rosenthal, F. *The classical heritage of Islam*. Routledge Kegan Paul, 1965.

Roux, G. *Ancient Iraq*. George Allen & Unwin Ltd, 1964.

Segal J. B. 'Arabs in Syriac literature before the rise of Islam'. *Jerusalem Studies of Arabic and Islam (JSAI)* 4, 1984.

Segal J. B. *Edessa the Blessed city*. Clarendon, Oxford, 1970.

Smith, M. *Studies in early mysticism in the Near and the Middle East*. Sheldon Press, 1931.

Stafford, R. S. *The tragedy of the Assyrians*. George Allen & Unwin Ltd, London, 1935.

Surma D'Bait Mar Shimon. *Assyrian Church customs and the murder of Mar Shimon*. ed. W.A.Wigram, Vehicle Edition, New York, 1983.

Vööbus, A. *The statutes of the school of Nisibis*. The Estonian Theological Society in exile, Stockholm, ETSE, 1961.

Vööbus, A. 'The origin of the Monophysite Church in Syria and Mesopotamia' in *Church History*, no. 42. American Society of Church History, 1973.

Wigram, W. A. *An introduction to the history of the Assyrian Church 100–600A.D.* SPCK, London ,1910.

The Oxford Dictionary of the Christian Church. ed. F. L. Cross and E. A. Livingstone. 1997.

The Blackwell Dictionary of Eastern Christianity, ed. K. Parry, David J. Melling, Dimitri Brady, Sidney H. Griffith and John F. Healey. Blackwell Publishers Ltd., 1999.

The Cambridge History of Iran, III, The Seleucid, Parthian and Sassanian Periods. by Yarshater, E., Cambridge University Press, Cambridge, 1983.

Ut Unum Sint. Encyclical letter of John Paul II on commitment to ecumenism. Catholic Truth Society, London, 1995.

Arabic publications and translations

Aboona, A. *The history of the Syrian Church of the East,* in three volumes: from the beginning to the nineteenth century. Dar al-Mashriq, Beirut, 1993.

Aboona, A. 'Kokhe: the first church in Iraq'. *Majalat Najm al-Mashriq,* No. 23 p. 336–52, 2000.

Al-Kaisi, abd al-Majid Hasib. *The Political and Military history of the Assyrians in Iraq.* Al-Dar al-Arabiyya for the Mawsoo'at, Beirut, 2004.

Al-Khayoon, R. *The religions in Iraq.* Camel Publications, 2003

Al-Jamil, M. *The historical chronology of the bishops of the Syrian Church from 1900 to 2003.* Beirut, 2003.

Al-Turaihi, Muhammad Sa'id. *Al-Dyarat and Christian places in Kufa and its environs.* Matba'at al-Muthanna, 1981.

Barsaum, E. *Al-Lu'lu al-Manthur – in the history of Syriac science and literature,* Dar Mardine, Alepo, 1996.

Batatu, H. *Iraq: Social classes and revolutionary movements from Ottoman times till the establishment of the Republic.* (Tr.) Afif al-Razzaz, The Establishment of Arab Research, Beirut.

Batatu, H. *The old social classes and revolutionary movements of Iraq's old landed and commercial classes and its communities.* Princeton Studies on the Near East, Al-Saqi Books, 2004.

Brock, S. 'The schools of Antioch, Edessa and Nisibis', in 'Christianity in the Middle East down the ages', pp. 143–64, [text in Arabic, trans. H. Zena and F. Abu Nasr], eds H. Badr, Suad Salim and Joseph Abu Nahta, Middle East Council of Churches, 2002.

Fiyeh, J. M. *The situation of Christians during the Abbasid Caliphate* (trans. to Arabic by H. Zena), Dar al-Mashriq, Beirut 1990.

Ghanima, H. Y. *The Protestants and the Evangelicals in Iraq.* Baghdad, 1998.

Giwargis, A. H. *The Dominican Nuns for the Presentation of the Virgin Mary* (to be published).

Goriyya, Ya'qub Yusif. *The Jews of Iraq – Their condition and emigration.* Al-Ahliya publication, Lebanon, 1998.

Habbi, Y. *The Church of the East.* Baghdad, 1989.

Kabara, H. H. 'The bloody Sunday – the hands of terrorism target the churches of Iraq'. *Najm al-Mashriq* no. 39, p. 351–8, 2004.

Khayat, N. 'Yuhanna al-Dalyathat – The sweet and calming ecstasy that mixes with those who love God when they see his glory'. *Najm al-Mashriq* no. 37, p. 41, 2004.

Qasha, S. *Tikrit-The headquarters of the Syrian Church of East.* The central Syrian library publications, Beirut, 1994.

Qanawati, G.S. *Christianity and Arab civilization.* The Arabic Institute for Studies and Publication, Beirut, 1984.

Saka, I. *My Syrian Church.* Alif Ba' Publications, al-Adib, Damascus, 1985.

Shamoon, S. *History of the Syrian archdiocese of Mosul.* Shafiq Printing Press, Baghdad, 1984.

Segal, J.B. *Edessa 'The blessed city'.* trans. Yusif Ibrahim Jabra, Alif Ba' publications, Damascus, 1988.

Christianity Through its History in the East, ed. Habib Badre, Suad Saleem and Joseph Abu Nahra. The Middle Eastern Council of Churches, Beirut, Lebanon, 2003.